MW01711068

Marvellous Melbourne and Spiritual Power

A CHRISTIAN REVIVAL AND ITS LASTING LEGACY

Marvellous Melbourne and Spiritual Power

A CHRISTIAN REVIVAL AND ITS LASTING LEGACY

Will Renshaw

Printed 2021 and as required by Lightning Source
For enquiries contact leanne.pell@gmail.com

First printed December 2014, reprinted March 2015 with Index
By Acorn Press Ltd. ABN 50 008 549 540

Office:
PO Box 258
Moreland VIC 3058
Australia
Tel/Fax: (03) 9383 1266
International Tel/Fax: 61 3 9383 1266
Website: www.acornpress.net.au

National Library of Australia Cataloguing-in-Publication entry:

Creator:	Renshaw, Will F., author.
Title:	Marvellous Melbourne and spiritual power : a Christian revival and its lasting legacy / Will F. Renshaw.
ISBN:	9780992447663 (paperback)
	9780992447670 (ebook)
Subjects:	Religious awakening – Christianity.
	Church renewal – Victoria – Melbourne.
	Revivals – Victoria – Melbourne.
Dewey Number:	269

Editor: Kristin Argall.
Cover image: Melbourne city skyline lino-cut (1996) by Evan Pell, aged 10.
Cover design: Les Colston.
Text design and layout: Graeme Cogdell.
Printed by: Openbook Howden Design & Print.

Contents

Acknowledgements

Although this book relies heavily on primary sources, I am deeply indebted to the influence of a special group of people, now in glory, who were colleagues in Melbourne's interdenominational evangelical ministries, with whom it was a privilege to have had fellowship.

This group led by example and influenced those younger in years to understand the blessings that had been received from the labours of those who had gone before. Amongst many others, the group referred to includes such leaders as Alfred Coombe, Leonard Buck, Bill Clack, Charles Sandland, Ralph Davis, Harold McCracken, Murray Clarke, Arthur Pocklington and Oswald Sanders.

While I was too young to know H.P. Smith during most of the years of his remarkable ministry, this book could not have been written without his use of the many gifts that had been bestowed upon him and which were used to the fullest extent in his Spirit-filled life. These included a gift in journalism which he exemplified when editing *The Keswick Quarterly and Upwey Convention News*, which, in the almost 90 issues he edited, proved to be autobiographical in nature.

The spiritual influence of my father, Ernest Renshaw, is also deeply acknowledged. As a young man, in 1904 he travelled from country Victoria to attend the Geelong Convention where he first met members of the Smith family and was later to become one of the six men who comprised the founding Council of the Melbourne Gospel Crusade, of which Mr Smith was leader. Words cannot express my gratitude for the encouragement of my father and mother, who showed by example how the Spirit-filled life was daily lived. This was particularly exemplified through family worship, in adversity by always exclaiming 'Praise the Lord' and in their spiritually encouraging 'Birthday letters' written to each of their five children until their early 20s.

The encouragement, assistance and unfailing support received from a number of special people in compiling this book are also most sincerely acknowledged.

It was Professor Stuart Piggin, Director of the Centre for the History of Christian Thought and Experience at Macquarie University, who first brought to my notice the uniqueness of Melbourne's lay-led interdenominational evangelicalism through his research, writing and lectures in the 1980s and 1990s. He strongly urged further research into this subject before all of those earlier generations of leaders had been called to be with the Lord. I am also greatly indebted to him for agreeing to write the Preface to this book. His contribution in fact went well beyond this, as being an experienced author, he generously advised and guided me in the process that led onwards to the publication of the book.

I am particularly indebted to Dr John Leach for painstakingly reading through the drafts of chapters as they were written and for his encouragement, informed advice and many helpful corrections and suggestions. This was a time-consuming and very practical contribution in the completion of the book, for which I am most grateful.

The encouragement of Dr David Price is most warmly acknowledged. His long-time involvement and gifted leadership of the Belgrave Heights Convention, the Christian Leaders' Training College of Papua New Guinea, the Melbourne School of Theology and Pioneers of Australia, all strategic ministries that derived from Melbourne's spiritual initiatives, has set a standard in godly leadership and vision for later generations to follow.

Special thanks are expressed to Dr Kristin Argall for her meticulous and helpful editing, her friendly encouragement and her work particularly in compiling the footnotes and other valuable references.

The project would not have been possible without the assistance, loving support and cheerful and practical help of my wife, Joan. She was a true partner during the years of my business life while I was involved in Christian work for much of the time. Throughout these years she complemented her cheerfulness and love of people with her gift of hospitality that has been a blessing to so many. She has proven to be of particular help during the writing of this book, when I was beset with increasingly low vision. Joan has indeed been God's special gift in providing all the support and assistance that could be desired in the publishing of this book.

List of Abbreviations

ADEB	*Australian Dictionary of Evangelical Biography*
BCV	Bible College of Victoria (formerly MBI, then later MST)
BEM	Borneo Evangelical Mission (later incorporated with OMF)
CIM	China Inland Mission
CLTC of PNG	Christian Leaders' Training College of Papua New Guinea (originally known as New Guinea Christian Leaders' Training College)
CMS	Church Missionary Society
CSSM	Children's Special Service Mission
ESA	Evangelisation Society of Australasia (formerly the ESV) (also referred to as the 'Evangelisation Society')
ESV	Evangelisation Society of Victoria (also referred to as the 'Evangelisation Society')
ISCF	Inter-School Christian Fellowship
IMF (Vic.)	Interdenominational Missionary Fellowship of Victoria
KQ	*The Keswick Quarterly and Upwey Convention News* (also referred to as *The Quarterly*)
MAF	Missionary Aviation Fellowship (now known as Mission Aviation Fellowship)
MBI	Melbourne Bible Institute (later BCV, then MST)
MGC	Melbourne Gospel Crusade
MST	Melbourne School of Theology (formerly MBI, then BCV)
OAC	Open Air Campaigners (now OAC Ministries)
OMF	Overseas Missionary Fellowship (formerly CIM)

SIM	Sudan Interior Mission (now SIM Australia)
UK	United Kingdom
US	United States of America
WEC	Worldwide Evangelisation Crusade
YMCA	Young Mens' Christian Association
YWCA	Young Women's Christian Association

Preface

Will Renshaw is both a student of history and a maker of it. It is his commitment to the gospel which has made him both. Vital Christianity has been far more formative of Australian history in general and Melbourne history in particular than our secular historians have told us. Will Renshaw understands the dynamic way in which Christian enterprise works within human history. It has indeed contributed to making Melbourne 'marvellous' and Australia one of the most stable and prosperous nations on earth.

As a successful businessman who has fellowshipped with other outstanding leaders at the heart of Melbourne commerce (see the second half of Chapter 16 for Australia's own 'Clapham Sect' as I have previously called them), Will Renshaw has himself contributed to Melbourne's rich reserves of financial and spiritual capital. He understands the motivation (the inclinations of the soul and the convictions of the mind) of those who gave Christian leadership in church and society. Over many years he has shared his insights, based on deep research, in a circular entitled 'Some Melbourne Notes and Comments'. The 'Notes' were on subjects which enlightened the mind of those interested in the role of the church in society. The 'Comments' encapsulated the considered wisdom and unique perspective of one who had long reflected on all that the Lord was doing in our midst. Now the essentials of that research are gathered in one place, and, like all good history, are summed up in one key insight – the role of spiritual power in human history, secular as well as divine.

We have here the story of how revived Christianity's spiritual energy was translated into determined, innovative evangelism and sustained nation building based on godly policy and honest dealing. Here is a record of wide-ranging evangelistic ministries and missionary endeavours at home and abroad and of the conventions for the deepening of the spiritual life which so often nurtured them. And, since all such enterprises are the work of anointed leaders, the spiritual power is personified in the Christian leaders who populate its pages. We begin with the remarkable Henry Reed of Tasmania, grandfather of the founder of Qantas. We meet amazingly effective evangelists such as John MacNeil, who was so Spirit-filled he was a walking conflagration. In C.H. Nash, the founder of the Melbourne Bible Institute (now the Melbourne School of Theology), young men were mentored for lives of service in the ministry, on the mission field, in the professions, and in the business world. As with all readable histories, this one has a surprising hero, Hervey Perceval Smith, manager of the Federal Hotel, a temperance hotel also known as a coffee palace. It is not as an individual that he shines, but in fellowship with, and as complementary to, other like-minded warriors such as C.H. Nash. We meet H.P. Smith first in the Introduction, and by the time we meet him again in Chapter 7, Will Renshaw's own powers of writing on spiritual subjects have reached full momentum! The pace is sustained to the end. The reader is left with a longing both to be involved in work of similar effectiveness and to be instrumental in the revival of the faith to which Australia owes so much.

Stuart Piggin
Centre for the History of Christian Thought and Experience,
Macquarie University

Introduction

Following the discovery of gold and the development of sheep-grazing areas, a rapid population explosion within just a few decades brought untold wealth to Victoria and its capital, Melbourne.

Railway lines were built which networked the state. These enabled the quick transportation of people and goods, enhancing the state's wealth and opening up the settlement of vast new areas. Impressive public buildings were built, many of which enhance the city to this day.

Within a mere 50 years, the population of Melbourne had grown to nearly half a million. Melbourne had become the biggest city on the continent and displayed its pride by holding an international exposition in the newly built Royal Exhibition Building less than 60 years after first settlement. In 1901 this impressive building was to become the venue for the inauguration of the Commonwealth of Australia. In 1902 it was the main location for meetings of the Torrey-Alexander Mission.

About this time the city was touted as 'Marvellous Melbourne'. However, although the city's rapid economic growth and development testified to human ingenuity, there was also ample evidence of humanity's fallenness: greed, unscrupulous land and company speculation, corruption and scandals not infrequently involving immorality. Nevertheless, 'where sin abounded, grace did much more abound.'

Over the centuries, the Divine hand had clearly been revealed in the history of the English-speaking peoples. Immigrants to Victoria at this early time mainly came from Britain, bringing with them the spiritual energy of the Wesleyan revival. As the colony was a British possession, laws and infrastructure based on the Judeo-Christian tradition were woven into the fabric of its public morality and regulations.

Christian clergy and laymen were active in meeting the challenges of the hour. Churches were forthright in proclaiming the gospel. In 1873, the Evangelisation Society of Victoria (ESV) was founded, an interdenominational organisation of laymen that was to impact Melbourne and beyond in a far greater way than its members could ever have anticipated. Another of these initiatives occurred in the early 1890s, when evangelical ministers of the major denominations formed a Prayer Band, meeting to pray for revival in their own lives and in the lives of members of their congregations.

The Torrey-Alexander Mission in 1902 came as an answer to those prayers. The impact on the Christian church in Melbourne, in Australia and then in Britain and other countries as diverse as India and Korea, with influences spreading to the revival in Wales in 1905, was extensive and profound.

In Melbourne, the manager of the opulent Federal Hotel, Hervey Perceval Smith, surrendered his life to the will of God. His conversion led to one of the most remarkable stories of spiritual power that came out of 'Marvellous Melbourne'.

H.P. Smith initiated regular meetings for Christians at the Federal Hotel, from which the ministry of the Melbourne Gospel Crusade (MGC) commenced. His early Christian experience was influenced by the message of the Keswick Convention in England, where large meetings 'of spiritual power' were followed by smaller meetings expounding deeper life teaching from the Keswick Convention. In Melbourne, the first Keswick-style convention was held at Upwey a few weeks after the end of World War I.

In the next decades, the twin effects of the growing convention ministry and the establishment of the Melbourne Bible Institute (MBI) under the Keswick-influenced founding principal, Rev. Clifford Harris Nash, precipitated an unprecedented lay-led movement for the advance of evangelical endeavour. It raised up a generation of consecrated Christian business professionals who became leaders in this movement, a fellowship of gospel-focused men and women who believed the whole Bible. They applied the Bible's teaching in open-air work, in an extensive visitation ministry – particularly to the needy in the Great Depression-hit working-class suburbs of Melbourne – and in an extensive motor van evangelistic ministry that brought the gospel to a myriad of farms and small towns. Together, these efforts led to further development of the Upwey/Belgrave Heights Convention and the MBI (later the Bible College of Victoria [BCV] and now the Melbourne School of Theology [MST]).

All of this activity undergirded an extensive interest in world mission that led to new enterprises set up in Melbourne for world mission and resulted in missionaries being sent to every corner of the globe. These missionaries were men and women whose lives were consecrated to the service of God, who lived the Spirit-filled life that they had experienced after hearing the message of Keswick.

Those involved undertook united, believing and persevering prayer, which God answered powerfully through the advance of the gospel. The transformation of lives in Melbourne and Victoria spread throughout Australia and profoundly contributed to the spiritual fabric of the nation.

Now, more than two hundred years since its founding, Australia has a standard of living that non-Christian nations surrounding this island continent, even with thousands of years of civilisation, have not attained. Australia is looked upon as a stable and favoured country amongst the nations of the world. Today, however, many in Australia have turned away from the country's Judeo-Christian heritage of Old Testament law and the New Testament's 'do unto others as you would have them do unto you' – a scriptural balance of mercy and judgment. There is now an urgent need in Australia for spiritual revival.

The life of Hervey Perceval Smith was a life lived to the glory of God. My prayer is that this account of his remarkable conversion and the Spirit-filled life that followed will result in the fulfilment of words found in Ecclesiastes 11:1, 'Cast your bread upon the waters, for you will find it after many days.'

Will F. Renshaw

CHAPTER 1 Founding Days

The first preaching of the gospel in Melbourne

The first recorded preaching of the gospel on the site that was to become Melbourne was within three to four months of the city's first settlement.[1]

John Batman was the first to settle on the site when he arrived in May 1835 via the Yarra River on the schooner *Rebecca*. His diary entry for 8 June 1835 records, 'This will be the place for a village.'[2]

Henry Reed, a 28-year-old merchant and an evangelical Methodist local preacher in Van Diemen's Land (later Tasmania), wrote:

> having the welfare of the native population in view, went over to Port Phillip in the spring [probably September or October] of 1835 and in one of the only two or three huts that had then been extemporised for shelter, read and expounded a portion of sacred Scripture, and offered prayer to Almighty God.
>
> The congregation had in it William Buckley, the escaped convict who had been living in a state of wildness and barbarism with the natives for over thirty years, the brother of Mr. John Batman, and three natives from Sydney who but imperfectly understood the English language.
>
> I had prayers in the hut with these five men every day, read the Scriptures, expounding to them the Word of Life, and telling them of the love of God for poor sinners ... I went over to devise some means for preserving

> the natives from destruction ... The Yarra Yarra tribe '*corrobberied*' to me, and alone I accompanied them up the river, and lived with them. Having gained all the information I required, I returned to Launceston, the Lord having mercifully preserved me whilst living with them in the wilderness.[3]

This was the earliest attempt to bring the city's inhabitants 'to the feet of King Jesus', and it was the first recorded preaching of the gospel on the site that within 50 years was to become known as 'Marvellous Melbourne'. Reed was still a young Christian – it was less than five years after he had committed his life to Christ.

Henry Reed's conversion at sea

Reed had emigrated to Tasmania from England in 1827 and soon grew prosperous. He had a great aptitude for business: he was involved in founding a bank and had interests in bridge building and shipping, as well as other commercial enterprises. Point Henry in Port Phillip Bay was named after his vessel, *The Henry*, during a trip to Geelong in May 1836.

During a tumultuous storm at sea off Cape Horn when returning to England for a short time in 1831, he experienced a sudden conversion.

> I saw all the mercies and deliverances of God; and when I saw them how astonished I was at the ingratitude of the wretch who had been watched over by that loving God, and not even thanked Him! ... When I saw it, I wept bitterly ... I was conscious that I had hold of God, and that God had hold of me.[4]

Shortly afterwards Reed returned to Tasmania, where he became a Wesleyan Methodist lay preacher. It was then that he first travelled across to the Port Phillip settlement to preach the gospel.

In 1875, in response to requests from 'the Churches of every name', Reed again visited Melbourne. It was no wonder that after his first experience of the city he would feel such a deep interest in the place. How changed were the surroundings! After a 40-year absence, he now found a large and beautiful city. He held two open-air services, one as nearly as he could decide on the spot where he had lived with the natives so many years before. He was invited to preach in several of the churches and did good work in the short time he was able to spend there.[5]

Until his life's end, Reed was engaged in constant preaching, his supreme passion being the spread of the gospel. He was a keen and successful evangelist whose sympathies lay especially with the poor and the friendless, and he was also a strong supporter of William Booth in the development of the Salvation Army.[6]

He was as zealous for overseas missions as he was to evangelise at home, and he made extensive contributions to them. This included purchasing a steam launch in 1875 for Rev. George Brown to pioneer Wesleyan Methodist missions in New Britain. In the 1880s, when living in Launceston, his eldest daughter Mary went to China as a missionary with the China Inland Mission (CIM, later OMF International) until ill health required her to return home.[7]

The call to lay gospel initiatives

In the preface to a biography of Reed's life, William Booth wrote, 'Oh that a larger number of its wealthy sons and daughters would consecrate themselves in the same bold and daring fashion to the glorious Christlike work of extending the Kingdom of God, as did Henry Reed!'[8]

Henry Reed was a Christian businessman who had a passion for evangelism. He was a forerunner of lay leadership, for which Melbourne was to become known. Among the lay leaders were those whom God had prospered in business and who, in the decades of Marvellous Melbourne's unique spiritual power, gave generously to promote the kingdom of God at home and overseas.

Included among these leaders was John Pascoe Fawkner, who arrived from Launceston in the *Enterprize* on 17 October 1835 and settled in Melbourne. The day after his arrival, he held a service to 'Praise his Maker' for bringing him, his wife and his party safely to the new country. According to his notes at the time, 'only our own people and Mr Buckley attended'. By the middle of the next year, Fawkner, with other members of that early settlement, witnessed the building of 'a mere wooden shell, shingled and incapable of keeping out the cold' on the western side of what is now William Street, to function as a church and a school. It was known as the 'Pioneer Church'.[9]

In 1837, the Governor of New South Wales, Sir Richard Bourke, visited the Port Phillip settlement and named it Melbourne in honour of the British Prime Minister, Lord Melbourne, who at the time was a close adviser of the young Queen Victoria. Melbourne was officially declared a city by the Queen in 1847.[10]

The early settlers were for the most part God-fearing people who were genuine in their faith. They sought to establish the settlement at Port Phillip on the basis of it becoming a Christian civilisation such as they had experienced in the country from which they had come.

CHAPTER 2

The Influence of Melbourne's Judeo-Christian Heritage

Victoria in the 1850s

The 1850s saw the founding of the Melbourne City Mission, an evangelistic ministry given to social work, by Dr John Singleton, a Christian philanthropist, evangelist and social reformer who visited prisoners and was instrumental in the creation of the Royal Children's Hospital. Singleton had arrived in Melbourne just before the gold rush began in 1851.[1]

In 1851 Port Phillip became a separate colony and was named Victoria in honour of the queen. The gold rush of the 1850s and 1860s significantly increased its population and wealth, and by the time of Federation in 1901, this sudden wealth had transformed the relatively small port town of Melbourne into Australasia's financial centre.

It is said that immigrants leaving Britain in 1852 bought more tickets to Melbourne than any other destination in the world. Generally the new arrivals chased a single dream – gold, although some women emigrated to marry as there was a shortage of women in the colony. Thousands arrived every week. In 1853, for example, 94,000 immigrants entered Victoria. Lodging houses and hotels were packed to capacity. Makeshift houses of iron, timber and canvas were springing up on the city's edge and throughout the colony.[2]

Although gold brought progress, it also brought problems. Before the end of 1851, ten tons of the precious metal had been found in Victoria. The lure of the diggings drew men from their businesses and sailors from their ships. No licences were issued for the sale of liquor and drunkenness was rife. It was difficult to stand against the stream of gold, and the community was slowly submerging under soaring prices and wharves jammed with cargo and disembarking migrants. Society seemed to have been turned upside down.

The Judeo-Christian heritage

The colony's British immigrants were still bound to the country from which they had come by the ties of language, kinship, literature, queen and faith in an Almighty God.

Many of these new arrivals had been greatly influenced by the revival in Britain following the preaching of the Wesley brothers and George Whitefield.[3] In the midst of so much upheaval, the lifestyle of these immigrants brought a counterbalance of honesty and integrity into the life of the community.

These influences, which were based on a Judeo-Christian heritage, were succinctly summed up by the famed London Baptist preacher, Dr F.B. Meyer, when addressing the National Council of Evangelical Free Churches in England in 1904:

> Every great Revival of religion has issued in social and political reconstruction. In no history has the effect of the one upon the other been more carefully traced than in Green's 'History of the English People'. Take, for example, his account of the Revival of the twelfth century. 'At the close of Henry's reign,' he says, 'and throughout that of Stephen, England was stirred by the first of those great religious movements which it was afterwards to experience in the preaching of the Friars, the Lollardism of Wycliffe, the Reformation, the Puritan enthusiasm, and the mission and work of the Wesleys' ... We assert that the movement which led to the abolition of the Slave Trade originated in the evangelistic efforts of Wesley and Whitefield. Society can only be saved through a great Revival of Religion.[4]

Of the events in England in the 17th century, J.R. Green wrote, 'There was one thing dearer in England than free speech in Parliament, than security for property, or even personal liberty, and that one thing was, in the phrase of the day, "the Gospel".'[5]

History attests to how much England has been influenced by its Judeo-Christian heritage – the bringing together of the Old Testament laws and the New Testament precept of 'Doing unto others as you would have them do unto you' in its parliamentary and civil laws. Furthermore, in the British monarchy, as distinct from a republic where power is derived from the people, the crown derives power from Almighty God and acknowledges that Jesus Christ holds dominion over all the earth. These profound influences were foundational in the lives of many immigrants who streamed into Victoria.

An immigrant's testimony

By 1861, Melbourne was a city of 125,000 people. Gas street-lighting, regular piped water and solid buildings gave the city a more permanent appearance. New civic buildings – the Customs House, Post Office, Treasury Building and Parliament House – all publicly displayed power and affluence. The instant city was maturing.[6]

One of the city's female immigrants who came out from England in 1864 to marry was Mary Anne Bedford, whose faith typified that of many newcomers. As it happened, Mary and her fiancé had both been baptised as infants at St Thomas' Church of England at Stockport in Cheshire. As a 23-year-old, she travelled unaccompanied from Liverpool on the sailing ship *Champion of the Seas*. She kept a diary, which commenced on 7 August 1864:

> We are still out on the [Mersey]. We had service this morning on deck. The text was from the 4th Chapter of Philippians and the 19th verse, 'But my God shall supply all your need according to His riches in glory by Christ Jesus'. We sang the hymn beginning, 'Rock of Ages' and the one, 'Guide Me O Thou Great Jehovah.'[7]

A week later, she wrote:

> It is fearfully rough this morning with seas mountains high ... Just now there was such a crash we all thought the ship had been hit by a big boat. No one at home could think how bad it is when it is rough at sea. We have passed the Bay of Biscay and are now in the Atlantic Ocean.[8]

In the calmer equatorial waters, she wrote:

> I proposed to some that it would be better to hold a short prayer meeting while others were dancing on deck, as I thought it would do us all more good and I asked a few and they agreed it would be better for all of us. So they wanted to know when we should begin. So I told them I thought we had better begin them that night and about twenty of us went down then. I read two Psalms. We sang many hymns that we had sung so often at home – among them 'Rock of Ages' and 'I'm bound for the land of the pure and holy'. The last one was the evening hymn and we had two beautiful prayers. They were all very well pleased and we agreed we would have one every night.[9]

After a voyage lasting over 100 days, on 15 November 1864 she recorded her first sighting of Victoria:

> A beautiful, fine morning. It is just like a summer's day. We had Cape Otway in sight all day ... A nice breeze sprang up this afternoon and tonight about 9 o'clock we were at the Heads of Melbourne ... They fired a number of rockets up and soon the pilot was on board and we anchored down. They do not let them pass here until the doctor has been on board.[10]

As the vessel sailed up Port Phillip Bay, Mary Anne Bedford wrote:

> 1. We'll praise our God for all that passed,
> And offer faithful prayers;
> That He may safely waft us on
> With wind both strong and fair.

2. And when at Melbourne we arrive,
   Our praises shall ascend
   For all our comforts on the deep
   We'll praise Him to the end.

3. All incidents of note I've pen'd,
   Since first I've come to sea;
   Our voyage is almost at an end,
   We are in Port Phillip Bay.

4. So let us all unite and praise
   Our Saviour and our Friend;
   Who brought us safe across the seas,
   So now my log doth end.[11]

From Sandridge (Port Melbourne), she travelled by train to Kangaroo Flat, near Bendigo, where she was met by her husband-to-be, David Renshaw. They were married on 21 November 1864, four days after her arrival in Melbourne, by Rev. Edward King, Wesleyan Methodist minister at Tarnagulla, a gold-mining town about 48 kilometres from Bendigo. His daughter, Caroline King, whom the bride had not previously met, was the bridesmaid. Edward King had previously been minister of the Brighton Wesleyan Methodist Church when an extensive revival commenced there in 1859 and then spread throughout Australia.

One of the children of David and Mary Anne Renshaw, David Ernest Renshaw, was to become one of the six men who comprised the MGC. Before there was a permanent Upwey Convention Council, the meetings at Upwey, the first of which was held at Christmas-New Year 1918–19, were organised by the Crusade.

These spiritual influences in the colony were not in any way unique, but rather indicative of the Christian background that thousands of immigrants brought with them from Britain.

Revival in Victoria and the influence of the Methodists

Professor J. Edwin Orr wrote:

> In the mid-nineteenth century, gold was discovered in Australia, chiefly in Victoria. A gold rush set in ... church attendance in Victoria increased 50% in 1852, but membership in South Australia and Tasmania showed corresponding losses, all-Australia membership remaining the same ...
>
> Fifty thousand people were busy wresting gold from the earth.[12]

Many observers deplored moral conditions.

> There was considerable pessimism in Victoria about the prospects of churches in the midst of population movement ...
>
> A conference of ministers meeting in mid-1857 resolved to pray for general revival and themselves, seeking a richer baptism of the Holy Spirit, promising to pray for each other and to promote Saturday evening meetings of prayer.[13]

Professor Orr continued:

> Prayer meetings were held in Melbourne, Ballarat, Bendigo and Geelong in 1859, interdenominational in character, but with the goodwill and occasional leadership of the Anglican Bishop of Melbourne ... It was not long before the rising tide of prayer produced a flooding of revivals throughout the Australian Colonies. The Victorian revivals began at Brighton on 22 May 1859.[14]

The revival at Brighton in 1859

In *The Early Story of the Wesleyan Methodist Church in Victoria*, by Rev. W.L. Blamires and a colleague, Rev. J.B. Smith, the authors describe a revival at Brighton:

The tide of revival mercy in 1858 ... carried spiritual health and salvation over the Churches of the land. The Wesleyan [Methodist] Church was largely blessed by it. She is the child of revivals, and has a strong liking and affinity for sound and Scriptural ones ... The revival at Brighton may be placed in the front of our notice, as it was one of the earliest in order of time ...

The sorrow for sin shown by numbers expressed itself in tears and prayers for mercy. Nine persons professed that night to have their mourning turned into joy ... others went to their homes 'sorrowing after a godly sort', and seeking the salvation of Christ. Then special services were held daily, and private devotions increased in intensity and spiritual power, so that soon there was 'a sound of abundance of rain'. The work went on amazingly, affecting all classes, the tender child and the aged sire, the educated man and the unlettered peasant. Answers to prayer were swift or immediate in a wife's conversion, a husband's decision and prayerfulness, and in whole families brought to love and serve God ...

The results of this religious revival were peace and goodwill where brethren had been at strife; the greatly quickened piety of professed disciples of Christ; the spirit of praise, prayer, love, self-denial, benevolence, triumphant in them; scores of careless, hardened sinners brought to seek the everlasting welfare of their own souls and those of their families and acquaintances; many trained in godly families taking the important steps of religious decision and surrender to Christ; between one and two hundred new members added to the Churches; and the fruits of good living thereafter manifesting the genuineness and power of the work.[15]

Blessing spreads

Blamires and Smith continue:

> In the revivals in the Victorian goldfields, miners from Cornwall and Yorkshire remembered the revivals of earlier years and joined with the preachers in earnestly beseeching the divine outpouring.
>
> The Melbourne Circuits shared in the blessing. In Wesley Church (in Melbourne) many conversions took place; at the Brunswick Street Church, a great ingathering of converts was reported, and scenes of Pentecostal power were witnessed. The Castlemaine and Sandhurst (Bendigo) Circuits were the scenes of like revival movements and power ... In Ballarat, there were 'deep searchings before God and a revival of God's work occurred in 1859; in 1860 'glorious revivals' were reported at Bendigo ... In the Castlemaine district the power of the Lord was reported as present ... 'to wound and to heal'. At the end of the year 1859, Drysdale was visited with a similar work of grace. This revival and others that have succeeded it, have made Methodism the strongest religious denomination in the Drysdale and Bellarine District – about 42 per cent of the population returning themselves at the last census (1881) as Wesleyans.

The growth in the number of Wesleyan Methodists in Victoria in the middle of the 19th century as a percentage of the total population is reflected in the government census returns taken at 20-year intervals (see Table 1).

Table 1: Population of Wesleyan Methodists, 1841–1881[16]

	1841	**1851**	**1861**	**1881**
Number of Wesleyan Methodists	650	4,988	40,799	97,115
Total population of Victoria	11,738	77,345	540,322	862,346
Proportion of Wesleyan Methodists to population	5.5%	6.5%	7.6%	11.3%

The first census in the colony was taken in 1841; the census in 1851 was just after the discovery of gold; 1861 was shortly after the revival movement had commenced; and 1881 was the year of the last census before Blamires and Smith's book was published.

Professor Brian Dickey has commented:

> The Methodists were the evangelicals par excellence through the nineteenth century: they carried revival and their Bibles all over Australia and beyond to proclaim the Cross as the way of salvation, to call men and women to repentance and conversion, and on to an active life of service. They were the Protestant light cavalry of Australia.[17]

CHAPTER 3 Marvellous Melbourne in the 1880s

Melbourne: a world city

By 1881, the population of the State of Victoria had grown to 862,000. In the following decade, 'Marvellous Melbourne' became the popular way to describe the town as it grew and developed into a major world city. Its population reached almost 500,000 by 1890,[1] making Melbourne the second-largest city in the British Empire after London. Visitors to Melbourne at that time were amazed. Here in the Southern Hemisphere was a city larger than most European capitals.

While Sydney was seen as slow and steady, Melbourne was fast and reckless. Ornate office buildings up to 12 storeys high rivalled those of New York, London and Chicago. Money was poured into lavishly decorated banks, hotels and coffee palaces.[2] The Exhibition Building and Carlton Gardens were completed in 1880 for Melbourne's first international exhibition, a product of the optimism, enthusiasm and energy of its people. After many years of gold fever, a group of men decided in 1885 to form a company to build the elegantly furnished Federal Coffee Palace to further the cause of temperance. It was completed in time for the opening of the Centennial Exhibition in 1888 and boasted the largest dining room in Australia at the time.[3]

Following the limited use of horse-drawn trams, Melbourne's tram system expanded its operations in 1885 with the introduction of the first cable tram line. Melbourne was on its way to becoming the city with the largest urban tramway network in the world. The system was world-class and operated successfully for 55 years. After bridges were built over the Yarra River, Melbourne began expanding out into residential suburbs with leafy streets rather than up into high-density apartment blocks like those seen in European cities. This expansion fuelled a massive land boom. Huge fortunes were made from speculation, and business and politics were open to manipulation and corruption.[4]

The Christian armoury

Fired with the energy of Methodist evangelism, churches of all denominations were rapidly being built throughout the colony. This expansion included the gold-mining areas. Up until now, church services had frequently been held for miners in the open air. Many miners heartily sang their doctrine in the hymns of Charles Wesley, particularly hymns focusing on Christ's Atonement such as '*And can it be, that I should gain an interest in the Saviour's blood?*'[5] The miners, along with their fellow pioneering immigrants, were a hardy and adventurous people. With a hopeful theology, Christian zeal, missionary vision and a Divine charity, they settled into developing their new surroundings and bringing many to trust in Jesus Christ as Saviour and Lord. The impact of evangelical Protestantism in particular on church, community and political life was profound, and it was a transforming power in society.

As mentioned briefly in the previous chapter, periodical revivals of religion have been a phenomenon in the history of England and particularly among English-speaking peoples. There have been times of corruption, luxury, indolence and vice, during which nations seemed to have forgotten God and given themselves up to drunkenness, gambling, greed and immorality. At such times, love for God has grown cold. Without any presumption for the future, history attests that God in his great goodness has blessed this people by bringing forth a spirit of repentance and revival at times of great need.

Against this backdrop, Melbourne was developing an evangelistic endeavour that had its own integrity and character, with a spiritual unity in prayer that resulted in great blessing as it developed. In practical terms it was bringing many to know Christ and cleaning up broken lives and relationships. It brought assistance to those in poverty and deep need, gladdening the hearts of many across every strata of the community with the grand message of repentance, forgiveness and eternal life.

The Evangelisation Society of Victoria

In 1878–79, Rev. H.B. Macartney Jr visited the United Kingdom (UK), where he attended the Keswick, Dublin and Mildmay Conventions. Macartney was the Vicar of St Mary's Church of England, Caulfield, a suburb of Melbourne, and the son of the first Dean of Melbourne. Inspired by his experiences, on his return he held deeper-life meetings at St Mary's. He promoted interest in the Church Missionary Society (CMS) and CIM and helped form the United Evangelisation Association. In 1883 this became the Evangelisation Society of Victoria (ESV).[6]

Both the *Wesleyan Methodist Spectator* and the Baptist *Victorian Freeman* carried advertisements in their July 1883 issues announcing that the ESV had been formed, 'With the view of reaching the non-church-going population of Victoria' and stating that 'The work is conducted on strictly undenominational grounds, the Evangelists going out, not as members of any particular Church, but to preach Jesus to the unconverted.'[7]

The Executive Committee comprised the Hon. James Balfour, MLC, R. Gillespie and the secretary, Theo Kitchen. Amongst the 28 Committee members named were H.B. Macartney Jr, the English evangelist Rev. A.J. Clarke, Rev. Dr Thomas Porter, James Griffiths, Philip Kitchen and Dr William Warren.[8]

It was also during the 1880s that the Salvation Army commenced its work in Victoria, as did the Christian Endeavour movement, the Children's Special Service Mission (CSSM) and Scripture Union, all of which were to make an incalculable contribution to evangelical life. Following the influence of Methodist evangelism with its holiness emphasis, together with the Ministers' Prayer Band, these movements had an immense impact on the development of Melbourne's influential and unique lay-led missionary, evangelistic, convention and Bible college ministries for the decades to follow.

The 1888 centennial mission in Victoria

In 1887, the ESV called a meeting of clergy and laymen of all Protestant denominations to plan a Centennial evangelistic mission for the following year, to coincide with the International Centennial Exhibition planned for 1888 to mark the centenary of European settlement in Australia in 1788.[9] The ESV wanted every man and woman in the state to hear the gospel. After receiving the general approval of all the main denominations, two ESV committee men, businessman David Beath and medical doctor William Warren, travelled to England to invite George Clarke, a well-known lay Anglican evangelist in London, to lead the mission.

The evangelist accepted, and from June 1888 he commenced a well-planned six-month mission in numerous suburban and country centres, speaking in churches of all the major denominations as well as in the Melbourne Town Hall and other key locations.

The results of the mission greatly encouraged the clergy and laymen of churches throughout the state, as well as the members of the ESV. Importantly, it came about through a unified evangelical activity and purpose, for which Melbourne and Victoria were becoming so well known nationally and internationally.

The Ministers' Prayer Band

'The source of the Australasian Awakening of the early twentieth century,' wrote Professor Orr, 'was traced back to

1889 when the evangelist, the Rev. John MacNeil, enlisted a band of ministers to pray for revival throughout Australia. The decade that followed proved to be one of accelerating evangelism, and it culminated in a notable awakening in the early twentieth century.'[10] The Band grew to more than 30, ministers not just meeting together but fervently praying for power in preaching to meet the needs of their people, planning evangelistic meetings and conventions, always on fire for the Lord!

John MacNeil

John MacNeil emigrated to Australia from Scotland in his teenage years and lived in Ballarat. After graduating with a BA from Melbourne University, he undertook theological studies in Scotland. In 1881 he was ordained to the Presbyterian ministry and returned to Australia, where, through a Methodist colleague, he was introduced to the Keswick movement. About the same time, he also experienced the anointing of the Holy Spirit for service.

MacNeil began preaching in the open air in Victoria. After his first effort, it was said that 'two thousand people were spellbound by the Holy Spirit'. Released from his pastoral work, he travelled widely as an evangelist. In Melbourne, MacNeil met John Mott, an American missionary statesman and chairman of the Student Volunteer Movement, who later shared the Nobel Peace Prize. Mott asked MacNeil what had led him to desire the fullness of the Holy Spirit. MacNeil replied that it was the American evangelist A.B. Earle's little book describing his work, *Bringing in the Sheaves*. The narrative made MacNeil so dissatisfied with the comparative barrenness of his own life and work that he shut himself up alone with God until 'he was baptised with the Holy Ghost in power'. 'A flame of fire,' said Mott.[11]

An understanding of his passion for the Christian to live the Spirit-filled life, and the simplicity required for it to be received, can be gained from a short excerpt from MacNeil's book *The Spirit-filled Life*, based on John 7:38–39:

> He that believes in Me, as the Scripture has said, out of his heart will flow rivers of living water. But this He spoke concerning the Spirit, whom those believing in Him would receive; for the Holy Spirit was not yet given; because Jesus was not yet glorified.

'One may ask,' MacNeil wrote,

> What is it to be 'filled with the Spirit'? The Teacher Himself makes answer. It is to have 'rivers of living water flowing' from one's soul. See the universality of the promise, 'He that believes on Me'; *no* believer, even the weakest, obscurest, is outside its magnificent sweep, unless by its unbelief it puts him there ... note more closely its hugeness, its Godlike vastness, '*Rivers*!', not a trickle or a babbling brook, or a stream, or a river, but rivers! What Divine prodigality! It is the Brisbane, the Clarence, the Hawkesbury, the Murray, the Murrumbidgee, the Tamar and the Derwent all rolled into one – Rivers! ... See the freshness, the freedom, and the spontaneity of the service ... none of the hard labour of the 'soul in prison' (Psalm 142:7). When the 'Rivers' begin to flow the worker may sell his force-pump; his prayer has been answered, 'Bring my soul out of prison.'[12]
>
> ...
>
> If you want to fill a corked bottle with water, and take it to a running tap but neglect to remove the cork, how long will you have to wait holding it under the tap before it is filled? Remove the cork, and the bottle is running over in a few seconds! Many a one has cried and waited, and waited and cried for the Fullness of the Spirit, but the stopper of unbelief has been in their empty hearts, and so no wonder that they did not get what they wanted! Of what avail will all God's giving be if a man does not 'receive'?[13]

MacNeil went on,

> In driving between Melbourne and my home [at Sandringham, a bayside suburb], I often stop at a wayside trough to give the horse a drink. I notice that the trough is quite full of water and that there is a box in one end of it. As the horse drinks, the water is lowering, and presently I hear the sound of a running tap ... Within the box is a tap connected by pipes with the Yan Yean Reservoir up in the Plenty Ranges. Attached by a lever to the tap is a metal ball, which rests on the surface of the water ... The lowering of the ball opens the tap and the Yan Yean begins to pour in ... The trough is being filled so that it is always full. Thus it may be with the soul of the believer. The outflow depends directly on the inflow; one can only give as he gets. It is ours to see to the connection between us and the infinite Reservoir away up among the hills of God being kept open, to see that the tap is kept in proper working order by faith and prayer and meditation. Then, one might almost say, automatically, the heart will be kept full, 'filled with all the Fullness of God', no matter what the spiritual drain upon us may be; for now it is not a question of our capacity to contain, but a question of God's infinite supply for all our needs.[14]

The Scriptures do not change in their application for today. The Reservoir is full.

Where there is no vision

Those Christians in early Melbourne knew that without the vision that the churches stood for, nations shrivelled like weeds. Here was an opportunity to build a solid Christian foundation into an emerging nation. They knew that what was needed was salt in the soul, moral stamina, a sense of the unseen, for where there is no vision the people perish. There could be no national stability without a reverent recognition of God.

In the words of John Anderson, Deputy Prime Minister of Australia from 1999 to 2005:

> I believe that society is only the sum and total of the individuals that make it up. If change is to occur it will take place only because people are transformed by the renewing of their minds. It was the transformation of sufficient European minds particularly in Great Britain through the Reformation and the subsequent great revivals that so civilised our society. What a tragedy if we were to throw it away forever.[15]

According to Proverbs 29:18, 'Where there is no vision, the people perish,' which can be translated as, 'Where there is no revelation, the people cast off restraint.' Israel found itself in this situation, when 'every man did what was right in his own eyes' (Judges 21:25) and 'The Word of the Lord was scarce in those days; there was no open vision' (1 Samuel 3:1). The settlers in Melbourne were determined to avoid such a situation. They had a burden for their new homeland and for those around them who were living godless lives amid the excitement of newfound wealth and unprecedented development. They were fired with the words of the Great Commission to 'go and tell'. Hence, the churches set to work to evangelise with the gospel of Christ.

They knew that this was such a moment for God to work, a situation where a prophet's word was needed. The Prayer Band prayed for the church congregations to know the empowering of the Holy Spirit for service, and ESV members proclaimed the exceeding sinfulness of sin, seeking to reveal its nature as high treason against God and teaching its sure coming judgement. They preached, in the language of that day, 'That there was a hell to be shunned and a heaven to be won', and as a result men and women feared to go far into sin.

They had seen that when people cast off restraint, the law of the land could only do so much, and the best that politicians could do was to make a few more laws. It was the law of God and the word of the gospel that was the answer.

The result was that Christians had a fresh vision and declared God's truth. The way was being paved for a great work of God that was shortly to follow.

The big crash of 1891

In 1891, as an aftermath of excess speculation and corruption, Victoria experienced a spectacular economic crash, with banks and businesses failing in large numbers. Many thousands lost their jobs, homes and savings. Some escaped unscathed, but many were plunged into hardship.[16]

Meanwhile, Melbourne's ministers – particularly those who were impacted in some way by the Prayer Band – felt a burden for a deepening of their own spiritual lives and the lives of those in their congregations, as well as for power in their witnessing for Christ.

By the start of the 1890s, there was evidence that the prayers of God's people were being heard.

CHAPTER 4

The 1891 Geelong Convention

Regarding the commencement of the convention movement, Dr F.B. Meyer writes:

> It is difficult to discover the precise moment when the term 'Convention' came into general currency; but the thing itself seems to have originated in the desire of a number of university men who had been greatly blessed at Cambridge during some special gatherings held at Cambridge during term time in the early part of 1874. They caught a glimpse there of the possibilities of the Christian life, of unbroken communion with our Lord, and victory over known sin; and what they had realised, so far from satisfying them, only led them to desire further opportunities for conference and prayer.[1]

§

'Apostolic Christianity – is it ours?' 'Do you know the Holy Spirit?' The Minister's Prayer Band, who had been giving themselves to prayer and had overseen the proliferation of praying circles, came to believe that many of their contemporaries were living on the wrong side of Pentecost. Together with their colleagues, the Band's convenor, Rev. Samuel Chapman, Minister of Melbourne's Collins Street Baptist Church, and co-secretary, John MacNeil, called a convention to be held at Geelong in September 1891. At the time the organisers considered Geelong to be most central and accessible from all parts of Victoria.

The visit of George Grubb

Rev. George Grubb, a Keswick missioner from the UK, readily consented to preside at the Convention, and in 1891 he visited the southern states of Australia. Grubb and his Australian friends, including John MacNeil and Rev. John Watsford, the son of a convict, the first Australian-born Methodist minister and a veteran missionary to Fiji, pooled their time and talents to hold regular conventions throughout Australia focusing on the deepening of the spiritual life.[2]

In a circular promoting the Convention, it was claimed to be 'the first of its kind held in Australia'. It mentioned that conventions of this character had become established in Great Britain, the United States of America (US) and other countries, where they had been the means of great blessing, and that many Christians had been asking whether similar gatherings could take place in Australia.

With such clear indications of spiritual hunger, all Christian people who were seeking a deepening of the spiritual life and the revival of the church were invited to attend these non-denominational meetings, 'in the Name of our Coming Lord'.

The overall theme of the meetings was 'Apostolic Christianity', which went back to the early days of the Christian Church. The first day's subject was 'Apostolic Christianity: Is It Ours?'; the second day, 'Apostolic Christianity: How It May Become Ours'; and the third and final day, 'Apostolic Christianity: Its Source and Its Effects'.

Samuel Chapman's opening message

In a message on the opening morning of the Convention in his role as chairman of the promoting committee, Samuel Chapman remarked:

> A few years ago there were some Christian men who met for prayer. They were frequently asking counsel of one another and talking about their work ... They felt that they were overwhelmed by the difficulties of their

position. They believed that the Lord had called them to preach for Him, but sinners were not being converted; true, here was one, and there one, but where were the nine? They felt that the Lord had called them to battle with the vice with which they were surrounded, but they were able to make scarcely any impression upon the great mass of sin and misery about them. The devil remained uncast out ...

I need not say that difficulties like this had led to a great deal of prayer, and so they were led to believe that Christ intended them to cast out the devil and they were not doing it.

As they read the New Testament, the position was forced upon them more and more deeply that if they were in the position in which God intended them to be, they could look to Him for power to do His will; that with an Omnipotent God they ought not be impotent. They did not set themselves up to judge the Church; they left the Christianity of the nineteenth century alone, all they considered was their own Christianity. They did not say, 'Why cannot the Church cast him out?' but 'Why cannot *we* cast him out?' They began to read about Apostolic Christianity. 'Oh, but,' you say, 'the Apostles were remarkable men, and their experiences can never be repeated' ...

The brethren of whom I have spoken read about this Apostolic Christianity, and said, 'Is it ours?' Shall I tell you what they answered? They said: 'I don't exactly know, but I think we are the Apostolic Church.'

Apostolic Christianity – is it ours, brethren and sisters? If you begin to ask that question, you will find that it is the Lord that is asking it. Apostolic Christianity – is it ours? We do not think things are as bad as when Wesley and Whitefield began their mission, and the Lord brought a glorious revival of Apostolic Christianity.

Apostolic Christianity – is it ours? You respectable Christians, you model Churchmen – you are the people to whom the question should come. Is yours this fellowship of believers? Is yours this spirit of liberality? Is yours this bounding gladness of heart? Is yours this joy in the Holy Ghost? Is yours this power for service?

This little Band had to answer, 'No'. But the next thing they said was: 'We are bound to get it; we will continue seeking till we get it, if we do not find it till we are a hundred years old.' They came back to a word – the key-word of all I have said, the word spoken by Jesus for all centuries. Jesus looked round on His disciples and said these words – I want Him to say them to you today.

He said: 'I will send you the Spirit of Truth, whom the world cannot receive, because it neither sees Him nor knows Him.' The world can only take what it sees. Now comes the pinch. 'But you know Him.' But how do we know Him? Not, says Jesus, because I have told you of Him, or because there are professors in Jerusalem or Geelong, but because 'He dwells in you and shall be in you.'

Do you know the Holy Spirit? That word came upon that little company of men, and it searched them through and through. Jesus says if you are one of His disciples you know Him, not because of the testimony of others, but because of your own personal reception of His gift.

Then this Band of men came to see they were living on the wrong side of Pentecost. So they called this Convention.[3]

The opening address by George Grubb

This message is as relevant, or even more so, to the Christian church in the 21st century as it was to the church near the close of the 19th century. Can the Lord do a work of grace today? In his opening address, Grubb said,

> Since the days of our childhood, we have been singing,
>
> Were the whole realm of nature mine,
> That were an offering far too small;
> Love so amazing, so Divine,
> Demands my soul, my life, my all.
>
> When I survey the wondrous cross,
> On which the Prince of Glory died,
> My richest gain I count but loss,
> And pour contempt on all my pride.
>
> Well then, how is it that so much of your pride remains? The object of this Convention is to give you an opportunity of pouring contempt on all your pride. The one thing that prevents you from living in the fullness of the blessing is that you are unwilling to give up pride.
>
> It is no use saying, 'I don't understand the teaching; there are rival theories about these doctrines.' You will understand everything about it pretty soon, if you are only willing to pour contempt on all your pride. If not, you had better go out of the meeting, it will do you no good unless you are ready to confess that you are all wrong. It is a terrible thing for a clergyman to confess that he has been wrong all along; it was a terrible thing for me before three thousand people to confess this ... The life and death of my Lord and Saviour is a standing rebuke to all my pride. There is not a single species of pride that is not minutely analysed in the New Testament, and it is pride that stands between us and the blessing ...

Have we pride of birth? The King of Glory was born in a stable ... more like a foundling than anything.

Are you proud of having amassed a certain amount of money? ... 'but the Son of man has nowhere to lay His head.'

Are you proud of your personal appearance? 'His visage was so marred more than any man' ... It was your sins ...

Are you proud of your reputation? 'Can any good thing come out of Nazareth?' ... 'a friend of publicans and sinners.'

Are you proud of your independence? The Lord Jesus had to accept food from those who ministered to Him.

Are you proud of your learning? 'How knows this man letters having never learned? He has not been to any of our schools.'

Are you proud of superiority in any way? Jesus said, 'I am among you as one who serves.'

Are you proud of success in your ministry? 'He came unto His own, and His own received Him not.'

Are you proud of your popularity? We are told ... 'many of His disciples went back and walked no more with Him'. And you?

Are you proud of self-reliance? Jesus says, 'I can do nothing of Myself.' 'He came to do the will of Him that sent Him.'

Are you proud of your own bigotry? 'Master, we saw one casting out devils in Your name ... Forbid him not ...'

> Have we the pride of resentment against those who have wronged us? How gently He answered Judas, 'Judas, betrayest the Son of Man with a kiss?'
>
> Have you the pride of reserve? We think it is weak and foolish to let others know what our joys and sorrows are, but our Lord spoke out in His distress, 'Don't leave me alone now ... my soul is exceeding sorrowful, even unto death.'
>
> Have you pride of sanctity? Are you fancying yourself better than anybody else? "This man receives sinners and eats with them.' Be careful, there is a pride that can ape humility.
>
> In all its forms our Lord can pour contempt on all our pride. Of Him Paul says, 'Being found in fashion as a man, He humbled himself.'
>
> Oh, we bless Thy name, Lord Jesus, Thou conqueror of pride in all its hydra-headed forms. Destroy it utterly in us, we beseech Thee. Curse this barren fig-tree in us. Lord, Lord, deliver me from my pride. Show me what it is to be freed from this monster. Oh, gracious Saviour, pour contempt on all my pride.[4]

The Missionary Meeting

At the Missionary Meeting, which was the final meeting of the Convention, John Watsford commented:

> I will put before you one or two facts that may help to encourage you in labour for the Master in the missionary field. Forty-seven years ago I went out to poor cannibal Fiji. Its inhabitants were considered the most ferocious people on the face of the earth. We did not go asking: 'Can these bones live?' for we knew they could. We had God's word for it. Now there is not a heathen to be found in the whole group of islands.[5]

The South Australian *Christian Colonist* gave the following account of this meeting:

> There was nothing in the addresses to excite, and no persuasion used to influence those present to offer themselves for mission work. They were rather told to go and confess and live Christ in their homes and among their friends.
>
> Yet when the chairman asked those who felt led to do mission work for the Lord, there was a very spontaneous movement in the hall, and after the meeting forty young men and women testified to go wherever the Lord wished them to go.
>
> Then came the question of money. There was no pressure brought to bear on the people at all. The Holy Spirit opened hearts and pockets. One person sent up two pounds. A man and his wife promised 120 pounds a year; another 50 pounds and another 100 pounds. Amounts of 5 pounds and one pound were freely promised. Notes were handed up from all parts of the room and read aloud. Here are some of them – 'I have given my son', 'I have given my daughter'. 'Savings of seven years, 4 pounds.' 'Savings of three years, 7 pounds.' 'If my husband goes, I am willing to go with him.'... Gentlemen took off their watches and chains, and rings, and ladies divested themselves of rings, earrings and bracelets, and gave them to the Lord.
>
> There was no excitement, no hysterics, no rushing from seats and clapping of hands. The Holy Spirit just laid on the people's hearts an intense yearning for the heathen, and gave the world a practical illustration of 'Apostolic Christianity'. It was estimated that the value of the offerings was 1,000 pounds.[6]

The Prayer Band and the Convention's promoters

The following list of members of the Prayer Band shows the unity of purpose in prayer across the Protestant denominations – ministers who had been praying that God would do a new work in reviving his church in Melbourne and throughout Victoria and Australia.

- Rev. Alfred Bird, Baptist minister, Hawthorn; speaker at the Convention
- Rev. A.R. Blacket, vicar of St Matthew's Church of England, Prahran; member of the Convention committee and also a speaker
- Rev. W.C. Bunning, Baptist minister at West Melbourne; member of the Convention committee and also a speaker
- Rev. Samuel Chapman, minister of Collins Street Baptist Church (for 22 years); chairman of the Baptist Association of Victoria on three occasions; key instigator in the establishment of Whitley College in 1891; leading supporter of the CIM; convenor of the Convention committee
- Rev. E.H. Ellis, Baptist minister, East Melbourne; a speaker at the Convention
- Rev. Edward Harris, Baptist minister, Fitzroy; a member of the Convention committee and also a speaker
- Rev. J. East Harrison, Congregational minister, Ballarat; a speaker at the Convention
- Rev. Matthew Hart, Presbyterian minister, Footscray; a member of the Convention committee and also a speaker
- Rev. Samuel Kent, formerly leading Congregational minister from Sydney, later an Anglican clergyman, vicar of St Silas', South Melbourne; a participant in Christian Endeavour and CMS
- Rev. H.B. Macartney Jr, vicar of St Mary's, Caulfield; gave addresses at early-morning prayer meetings at UK Keswick in 1878; active worker for the Bible Society,

YMCA, YWCA, CIM, and missions to Jews, Aborigines and Chinese; key instigator in the founding of CMS Victoria
- Dr D. Stewart MacColl, Melbourne physician; life member of Collins Street Baptist Church; council member of CIM; speaker at the first Upwey Convention; chairman of conventions at Upwey; member of Upwey and MBI Councils; speaker at UK Keswick in 1934
- Rev. John MacNeil, Presbyterian minister/evangelist; co-secretary of the Convention committee, speaker at the Convention and author of the *The Spirit-filled Life*
- Rev. David O'Donnell, Methodist (Wesleyan) minister/ evangelist in New Zealand and Australia; conference evangelist for South Australia and Victoria in 1895
- Rev. Dr Thomas Porter, pastor of Baptist Church, Ballarat; speaker at the Convention and also at the first Upwey Convention in 1918–19
- Rev. John Watsford, Methodist (Wesleyan) minister; missionary to Fiji; evangelist; speaker at the Convention
- Rev. Allan W. Webb, Baptist minister in NSW, NZ and later pastor of Albert Street Baptist Church, East Melbourne, then at Aberdeen Street Baptist Church, Geelong; co-secretary of the Convention committee and also a speaker
- Rev. Dr William Williams, Methodist (Wesleyan) minister; involved in movements for the promotion of holiness and the deepening of the spiritual life; president of Victoria and Tasmania Conference.

Other members of the first Geelong Convention committee were Samuel Knight, Joseph Ross, George Soltau and W.H. Hosken. The Prayer Band also included W.Y. Blackwell, William H. George, Edward Isaac, Charles Lancaster, George Sproul and E.S. Sumner.

Professor Orr has traced the spiritual awakening evident in early 20th-century Australia back to 1889 when John

MacNeil brought together a band of ministers to pray for revival throughout Australia.[7] It was truly remarkable what happened when this group of ministers from across denominations regularly met together, united in purpose, to seek God's help in returning to Apostolic Christianity. In this group of ministers there appeared to have been just one layman, Dr Stewart MacColl, a Melbourne medical specialist whose wisdom and experience was warmly accepted in a wide range of evangelical ministries. Yet the prayers of this almost exclusively clergy Prayer Band were to lead to a lay-led work of God of profound and extensive proportions in Melbourne. The effect, like ripples when a stone is thrown into a pool of still water, has continued for decades and is still seen in the 21st century – albeit, and sadly, with diminishing effect. It is time for another stone to be thrown!

John MacNeil and 'the Spirit-filled life'

Before preparing for the Presbyterian ministry, John MacNeil had worked as a steam engine driver out of Ballarat. Following his death, his colleague, the Church of England minister H.B. Macartney Jr, recollected:

> He could drive an engine, for he once said to me with great emphasis, when talking about 'More of the Spirit', 'Brother, it's not so much more of the Spirit that's wanted; it's more room for the Spirit. If I want to drive a long line of loaded trucks up an incline, I don't need more steam for the steam-chest, but more of the steam-chest for the steam!'[8]

During the years of his work with the Prayer Band, John MacNeil was writing a book that received worldwide attention and acclaim. *The Spirit-filled Life* was first published by the London, Edinburgh and New York publishers, Marshall Brothers Ltd, circa 1894. It had a preface by the well-known holiness preacher and author Rev. Andrew Murray, with an introduction by Macartney, a member of the Prayer Band.

The first edition sold out within three or four months.

Numerous editions followed with translations into many languages. It caught the attention of D.L. Moody and other evangelists, including those who were to be involved in the large Torrey-Alexander missions in the early 20th century. John Mott, who had met John MacNeil, took copies with him on a visit to China to give to every missionary he met.

John MacNeil was in Brisbane at the Baptist Tabernacle in 1896 for a convention he was conducting on 'The Return of Christ' at the time of his unexpected death at age 41. The pre-millennial return of the Lord was a subject he promoted, and he had just completed the manuscript for a book, *Some One Is Coming*. The introduction was again written after his death by H.B. Macartney Jr.

'Once when wanting an audience,' recalled Macartney,

> John MacNeil stood at a street corner, and with that rich, glorious shout of his, which could be heard a mile away, rang out, 'Fire! Fire!' 'It hasn't descended yet my friends,' he said when the crowd gathered, 'but it's on the way. Oh, flee from the wrath to come!' That was John MacNeil exactly![9]

A century later, a fellow Presbyterian minister, Rev. David J. Innes (who followed John MacNeil from Scotland to Melbourne), came across the biography *John MacNeil: Author of 'The Spirit-filled Life'* written by MacNeil's widow, Hannah.[10] In 2002 he wrote:

> How tragic that this well-written and well-documented biography of such a faithful and fearless evangelist is not better known today! I commend it most warmly to Australians of the twenty-first century, and pray that the Lord will raise up men of this calibre today, to stir up our decadent church, and spread the glorious Gospel in this vast and sin-sick land.[11]

Church growth in Australia

The ESV men, who often met in the office of Melbourne parliamentarian the Hon. James Balfour, and the members of the Prayer Band would have prayed for, but could scarcely have envisaged, the thousands, even tens of thousands of men and women around the globe who were to be converted to Christ as a result of those prayers. With an expanded vision, the ESV changed its name to the Evangelisation Society of Australasia (ESA) in 1897. Two members, William Warren and G.P. Barber, were to act as emissaries from the ESA to seek out 'a Spirit-filled evangelist', inviting Dr Reuben A. Torrey to come to Melbourne with Charles Alexander for their first international mission in 1902 (see Chapter 5).

Methodists and evangelism

During the years leading to Federation in 1901, the Methodists had been at the forefront of church growth. Spiritually, revivals within Australian Methodism probably explain the growth of that particular denomination from 7.6 % of the Australian population in 1861 to 10.2% in 1901. The impact of Methodism was most evident in Victoria, the state with the highest population growth in the second half of the 19th century.[12]

Evangelism in the Protestant churches undergirded the interdenominational work of evangelical organisations. The development of strong networks between ministers and their congregations, and between churches, led to a unified effort among evangelicals to reach the community for Christ and encourage each other in their efforts. In the home it was a normal activity for Christian parents to encourage their children, for husbands and wives to encourage their spouses, and for Christians to witness to their friends through caring and committed relationships. And so the church grew.

Commenting on the age grouping of those who have biographical entries in the *ADEB*, Brian Dickey writes:

> Why the dominance of entries from the 1870s? Some might be the children of gold rush migrants. But does the dominance of those born in the 1870s also reflect

> a climactic effectiveness of evangelicalism in Australia, say 1890–1914? As *ADEB* itself reveals, these were the years of the great new missionary efforts which drew on Australia – most notably the China Inland Mission, and of the great new missionary training institutions which nurtured them. The call of faith missions, and especially the China Inland Mission was notable in Australia.[13]

Christians in Melbourne were at the vanguard of these great evangelical and missionary initiatives.

Visitors to Melbourne

George Muller, whose experiences of God's great faithfulness in supplying the needs of his orphanages were known around the world, visited Melbourne in the late 1880s. He never made requests for financial support, nor did he go into debt, even though his five homes cost thousands of pounds to build. On one well-documented occasion, thanks were given for breakfast when all the children were sitting at the table, even though there was nothing to eat in the house. As they finished praying, a baker knocked on the door with sufficient fresh bread to feed everyone, and the milkman gave them plenty of fresh milk because his cart broke down in front of the orphanage. During his visit, Muller exhorted Christians to walk by faith and not by sight.

Another evangelist known around the world, Henry Varley, whose life had significantly impacted both D.L. Moody and C.H. Spurgeon, moved to Melbourne with his family. He conducted evangelistic missions and urged abstinence from alcohol and gambling, the causes of much social evil.

In August 1890, the founder of CIM, Hudson Taylor, visited Melbourne and spoke in the Melbourne Town Hall to 3000 people. This resulted in H.B. Macartney Jr forming an Australian council for this mission and increased interest in missionary endeavour, particularly for China.[14] Phillip Kitchen was the council's first treasurer and was succeeded on his death in 1898 by Dr John James Kitchen, who gave up his medical practice to devote himself fully to the work of CIM.[15]

By 1892, there was a great need for a place where missionary candidates could be trained, and William Warren and his wife opened the Missionary Training Institute in Kew. It was the first missionary training college in Australia.

'For what Melbourne was about to receive ...'

Awaiting the arrival of Dr Reuben Torrey and Charles Alexander, at the invitation of the ESA, Melbourne was on the eve of one of the most significant evangelistic missions in Australia – one that had extensive global ramifications.

The pioneer Presbyterian and Methodist missionaries, from the time of their entry into Korea in 1884, had concentrated on teaching the Bible and fostering local leadership. In 1907, a great revival occurred there (see Chapter 6). Professor Orr, when speaking at the 1984 Easter Belgrave Heights Convention, said:

> The revival in Korea was in the wake of the Welsh Revival and it was in the wake of the Prayer Movement that began with John MacNeil in Geelong.
>
> I would like to ask you bluntly, 'Did you repent when you believed', or are you one of those who just made a profession and your life hasn't changed? ... Oh that we could have an outpouring of the Holy Spirit to convince Christians of their shortcomings, and at the same time, to convince the ungodly of their great need. How can we have it? It is a simple secret. We can pray. We can pray. We can pray.
>
> It was when men like John MacNeil decided to pray for Australia, that Australia had a twenty-five year run of blessing with all the whole world looking on and saying, 'What's going on in Australia?' With people sending observers to Melbourne to see how the prayer meetings worked. We ought to pray. Let us pray.[16]

CHAPTER 5 Torrey-Alexander: Revival Comes to Melbourne

Reuben A. Torrey

In 1899, an invitation with 15,381 signatures had been sent to Dwight L. Moody asking him to come with Ira D. Sankey to conduct a mission in Melbourne. However, because of existing commitments it was not possible for him to accept. As it happened, Moody died in the last few days of 1899.[1]

After hearing of the inability of Moody and Sankey to come to Melbourne, the leaders of the ESA sent William Warren and G.P. Barber to Great Britain and Ireland in the hope of securing a 'Spirit-filled evangelist'.

The two men failed to find an evangelist they cared to invite and started on their homeward journey through the US. A son of Barber's was studying at the Moody Bible Institute in Chicago, which was under Dr Reuben A. Torrey's leadership. Torrey had been invited by Moody in 1889 to head up the Bible Institute of the Chicago Evangelization Society, renamed the Moody Bible Institute after his death. He had also become pastor of the Chicago Avenue Church, later renamed the Moody Church.

Torrey was a man particularly needed at this period of religious history, not only in the US but also in Australia. As a young man he had studied in Germany, where his faith had been deeply challenged through doubts expressed in teaching about the inspiration of the Bible, the miracles and the Virgin birth. He had 'passed through a bitter spiritual experience, becoming a thorough sceptic, but found his way out of the barrenness of doubt into a [more] definite and exultant faith than he had previously known'.[2]

The teaching he had experienced was generally known as 'German Higher Criticism', and it was taking forms such as 'the Down-Grade Controversy' in Charles Spurgeon's England and 'Modernism' as it generally became known in Australia and elsewhere. While this erroneous teaching has come in different forms and titles, it goes back to the earliest simple yet profound question in Genesis 3:1, 'Has God said ...?'

The invitation to Melbourne

Hearing Torrey preach, the visitors were at once impressed that here was the man for whom they were looking, and they laid their concern and invitation before him. Unbeknown to them, while they had been travelling across the Atlantic to the US, Torrey had been led to pray about his availability for a wider ministry and now, believing it was of God, he accepted the invitation to Melbourne.

Arrangements were made for him to leave for Melbourne in December 1901, visiting students in Japan and China on the way. Torrey had been asked to take a singer to complement the spoken word, just as Moody had ministered with Sankey. Before leaving Chicago he got in touch with his former student, Charles Alexander, and arranged to meet him in Melbourne.[3] It was a partnership that was to mean much to both of them in their future ministries for the kingdom of God.

The Melbourne Simultaneous Mission

In April 1902, Torrey and Alexander met in Melbourne and began their month's mission. It was known as the Simultaneous Mission because, apart from the main meetings in Melbourne, there would be meetings held at 50 other suburban locations conducted by local evangelists from Methodist, Baptist, Anglican, Presbyterian and Congregational Churches, the Brethren and the Salvation Army. The arrival of Torrey and Alexander heralded the greatest evangelistic campaign in

Australia's history, possibly apart from the Billy Graham Crusades nearly 60 years later.[4] Spiritually, and measuring the proportion of responses to the total population, the 1902 mission has probably not been exceeded.

The main Torrey-Alexander meetings were held in the Exhibition Building, with special meetings – such as those for men – held in the Melbourne Town Hall, and other meetings in several city theatres. Meetings then went out into regional centres. Attendances totalled a quarter of a million each week, when Victoria's population was about one million and Melbourne's half of that.[5] There were about 10,000 attending each night in the Exhibition Building. Up to 15,000 tried to get in nightly. Some 8,600 converts were recorded and the news of the awakening stirred all of Christendom.

The preacher and the song leader

Reuben Torrey was described as having a fiery eloquence, a clear-cut face, white hair and a trim white beard, while Charles Alexander was relaxed, genial and equipped with a mingled charm and ability that seemed to draw pure melody from the lips of those who followed his beat in songs as old as Zion and as new as the century. It was said that he and Torrey were like a combination of 'thunder and dew'.

The singing

There were 2,500 choir members in the Exhibition Building. *The Glory Song* ('O that will be glory for me') seemed to set the city on fire. Just a few days after the conclusion of the mission, the chairman of the mission, Baptist minister Rev. S. Pearce Carey remarked that one of his happiest memories was the Alexander choir and commented, 'What an unspeakable mercy it would be if our churches should determine to make their choirs and their singing throb with power after the fashion of the beloved Alexander.'[6]

Rev. Dr W.H. Fitchett, founding principal of the Methodist

Ladies' College in Melbourne and editor of *The Southern Cross* (then Melbourne's Christian newspaper), wrote in describing the singing:

> With its ease, its fire and exultation, and the note of triumphant faith which runs through it all, [it] melts the audience [like] a fire would melt wax ... Music, as the servant and vehicle of religion, has fulfilled its true and highest office. It has set human souls vibrating in gladness. No one need doubt that the Gospel can be sung as effectively as it can be spoken. And what other creed can be set to music in this fashion?[7]

On the first night *The Glory Song* was sung by the choir and the vast audience, Fitchett wrote:

> With a thrill of recognition, the chorus is sung by the choir, then by one gallery after another, and then by the people on the floor of the building. And then with one word by Alexander, 'Everybody', it was sung by such a volume of melody that the roof rings to the shout:
>
> > Oh, that will be glory for me,
> > Glory for me, glory for me,
> > When, by His grace, I shall look on His face,
> > That will be glory, be glory for me.
>
> Then there arises a mighty, humming melody. The words are indistinguishable, but the air is one everyone knows. Thousands of people are singing, 'Nearer my God to Thee', and up in the organ loft the effect is even greater than when the 'Glory Song' rang out. Another pause, and then, 'There is Power in the Blood' declare the voices. One of the visiting team members shouts, 'Well done! I never heard such singing.'[8]

'Alexander's Hymn Book'

Almost immediately the first Australian *Alexander's Hymn Book* appeared, with messages of gospel songs that were quite new to Australia. It was everywhere hailed as a potent agent in the cause of aggressive evangelism. Alexander's publisher was T. Shaw Fitchett, son of W.H. Fitchett.

Alexander had drawn what he called a 'cut' (i.e. clipping) from his pocket and asked Shaw Fitchett whether he could print a few thousand leaflets from it. It was *The Glory Song*. T.S. Fitchett asked him whether he could have all the 'cuts' of all the hymn prints that he had brought with him for which he had the rights. Within a few days, the first hymn book was on the market, supplying Alexander with the means to set ten thousand people singing.[9]

It was the forerunner of *Alexander's No.3 Hymn Book*, used in the later Chapman-Alexander missions, which included many melodies written by pianist Robert Harkness of Bendigo. The hymn book is still well known to many older-generation Christians. However, it is not so generally known that the two hymn books which preceded *No.3*, as well as *Alexander's Male Choir Hymn Book*, originated in Melbourne.

W.H. Fitchett also published a special 96-page broadsheet souvenir edition of *The Southern Cross* in September 1902, following the close of the Torrey-Alexander missions in Australia. It was said that this edition was responsible for the main London newspapers endorsing the mission in Great Britain. On seeing the 'splendid photographs, numbering thousands (of people)', one said, 'There must be something in these men.' Such were the results of the mission that W.H. Fitchett's work was referred to as 'One of the greatest accomplishments in using the power of print.'[10]

Reviewing the mission

The Melbourne mission was supported by 214 local churches, 700 local committees and approximately 2,000 personal workers. It has been estimated that no fewer than 117,000 people attended one or other of the 16,000 home prayer meetings. In addition, up to 2,000 Prayer Bands were conducted in various sections of the country, praying continuously for revival.

Thus, the Melbourne mission had been preceded by prayer, work and unity at a staggering level. The evangelical churches across denominations drew together in support of the committee of 70, which organised for every house in Melbourne to be visited twice, and divided the suburbs into 50 mission centres with 50 local evangelists preaching in local halls and 30 large tents.[11]

The main mission in Melbourne lasted four weeks and ended on 11 May 1902. Missions then followed in Warrnambool, Geelong, Ballarat, Bendigo and Maryborough. It was in Bendigo that Charles Alexander met and led Robert Harkness to Christ. Harkness was a brilliant young musical genius who became Alexander's pianist and soon joined the team for the rest of their tour.[12]

Charles Alexander returned to Melbourne in 1907 on a brief, private and evangelistic gospel-music visit. He visited again in 1909 with Dr J. Wilbur Chapman, and the four months of meetings were characterised as a 'time of Pentecost' for the whole of Australia. Again, in 1912, Alexander returned with Chapman and held another campaign. All missions, with overflowing crowds attending, were reminiscent of the original Torrey-Alexander mission.

Further reflections on the Torrey-Alexander mission

In March 1903, William Warren, who with G.P. Barber had issued the invitation to Reuben Torrey in Chicago, wrote:

> Within a few weeks, the Spirit of God laid hold of the Christians, and there was a conscious assurance that the city and its suburbs of nearly five hundred thousand population was going to be moved as never before ... Whole families were brought to Christ, as well as infidels, publicans, and actresses ... A policeman averred that since the mission opened in his district,

> he and his fellow constables had practically nothing to do. Theatrical managers declared that if the mission continued they would have to close their establishments ... Do you wonder? God's people were in earnest, the Holy Spirit was given His way, and believers greeted each other with, 'The big revival has begun. Glory to God'.[13]

Behind Warren's reference to 'the big revival' is the story of one of the most concerted prayer efforts in Australian evangelical history. Torrey himself explained:

> When Mr. Alexander and I reached Australia we found that there was a group of about 10 or 12 men who had been praying for years for a great revival in Australia. They had banded together to pray for 'the big revival' as they called it in their prayers, to pray for revival no matter how long it took. The group was led by the Rev. John MacNeil, the author of 'The Spirit-Filled Life', but he had died before we reached Australia. A second member of the group, the Rev. Allan Webb, died in the first week of our meetings in Melbourne. He had come to Melbourne to assist in the meetings, and died on his knees in prayer. A third member of the group, even before we had been invited to Australia, had been given a vision of great crowds flocking to the Exhibition Hall, people hanging on to the loaded street cars wherever they could, and when that vision was fulfilled he came a long distance to Melbourne just to see with his own eyes what God had revealed to him before.
>
> We also found that a lady in Melbourne had read a book on prayer and had been deeply impressed by one short sentence in the book, 'Pray through', and that she had organised prayer meetings all over the city before we reached the place, indeed, we found when we reached Melbourne that there were 1,700 neighbourhood prayer meetings being held every week in Melbourne.

> In the four weeks, 8,642 persons had made a definite profession of having accepted the Lord Jesus Christ as their Saviour ... The report of what God had done in Melbourne spread not only all over Australia, but to India, and England and Scotland and Ireland, and resulted in a wonderful work of God ... the outcome of prayer meetings in Chicago, and of the little group of men in Australia.[14]

When the Billy Graham team came to Melbourne in 1959, pasted into the Crusade book in the section devoted to Prayer was a pamphlet which was a united prayer program. It opened with 'A sure way to have a revival' by Dr R.A. Torrey, indicating that Graham endorsed this aspect of Torrey's tradition.

CHAPTER 6 Melbourne's Influence Spreads

News of revival reaches Keswick, England

London newspaper man William T. Stead, in his book *The Revival of 1905*, wrote:

> From Australia the news of the Revival was brought to the Convention at Keswick in 1902. The Rev. F. Paynter, late Rector of Stoke-next-Guildford, read a paper calling attention to the part which the Prayer Circle had played in Melbourne, where ten thousand conversions were reported as the result of the Torrey-Alexander Mission.
>
> Mr. Paynter suggested that Prayer Circles should be formed all over the world, to pray for the outpouring of the Holy Spirit upon all flesh. A Central Circle of Prayer for World-wide Revival was formed, with its headquarters at Keswick House in London. These Prayer Circles have now spread throughout the whole world. It is computed that there are some 300,000 pious souls who have bound themselves to pray daily for a world-wide Revival. In the opinion of the missioners, it is these unseen praying folk to whom the success of the movement must be attributed.[1]

Stead continued:

> As some of my readers may not know anything of these Prayer Circles, I venture to reprint the following particulars from the leaflet, 'How to Start a Prayer Circle'.

This was made available from Keswick House in London and included the following:

Among the suggestions offered to those who wish to form Prayer Circles are the following:

1. Dedicate yourself to God for this service of intercession.

2. Ask Him for the anointing of the Holy Spirit.

3. Ask that you may be guided as to whom you should invite to join the Circle.

4. Seek for guidance as to details, such as time of meeting, subjects of prayer, &c.

5. In a book reserved for the purpose, keep a list of all subjects for prayer laid upon your heart. Refer to this list constantly, and when any petition is graciously answered, make a record of the fact.

6. Watch for answers, and any indications of answers to the prayers offered, but do not be discouraged if definite answers be delayed. Intercessory prayer often requires the exercise of much faith and patience.

7. If a definite answer be vouchsafed, mention it at the next Circle meeting. Be on the look-out for these tokens of encouragement, and expect them and mingle praise with prayer.

Meantime all should continue instant in prayer, remembering Carey's great sayings, '*Ask great things of God*' and '*Expect great things from God*'.[2]

News reaches India

Once news of the success of the Simultaneous Mission in Melbourne quickly spread, calls came for Torrey and Alexander not only to come to England but to visit India en route. They stayed in India for six weeks, holding campaigns in several cities.

When speaking at the Belgrave Heights 1976 Easter Convention, Professor Orr commented:

> What was the start of the movement at Nellore and Dohnavur in India? Pandita Ramabai of Mukti [Mission] heard of the prayer meetings in Melbourne where 10,000 people were praying simultaneously [for the Torrey-Alexander Mission in 1902]. She sent her daughter to Melbourne to study the movement and to find out what was happening. She went back and that was the start of revival in India.[3]

The records from Mukti in India indicate that:

> The news of the Revival in Australia aroused Ramabai to send her daughter Manoramabai, and Miss Minnie Abrams to Melbourne, in order that they might catch the inspiration of the Revival fire, and form Praying Bands ... The burden that Ramabai sent by their hands to the newly-revived Australian Churches was, 'Brethren, pray for us.' About that time she organised a system of prayer circles.[4]

After early news of the revival in Wales was received, Pandita Ramabai said:

> I was led by the Lord to start a special prayer-circle in January 1905. There were about 70 of us who met together each morning, and prayed for the true conversion of all the Christians including ourselves, and for a special outpouring of the Holy Spirit on all Christians of every land.[5]

On 29 June 1905,

> the Mukti community experienced the start of a special outpouring of the Holy Spirit which lit a flame that spread across India ... The outcome was that revival fires swept vast areas of India during 1905–1906.
>
> It is amazing to see how one woman, whose life overflowed with love, compassion and dedication,

> was used by God for the cause of the orphans and the widows. As a simple instrument in the hands of the Master Potter, the Lord used her marvellously to shape broken lives and make them whole again.[6]

When Pandita Ramabai died on 5 April 1922, *The Times of India* remembered her as one of the 'makers of modern India'. At the turn of the 21st century, the government of India named her 'Woman of the Millennium'.[7] (The Misses Rosa and Alice Smith, sisters of H.P. Smith, went from Melbourne as missionaries to the Pandita Ramabai Mukti Mission in India. Rosa died at Mukti in 1927 after nearly 23 years of service there for Christ. At the time, H.P. Smith was president of the Auxiliary Council of the Ramabai Mukti Mission in Melbourne. For more about Smith, see Chapter 7 onwards.)

News reaches Korea

As already mentioned in Chapter 4, Professor Orr has argued that 'revival in Korea was in the wake of the Welsh Revival and it was in the wake of the Prayer Movement that began with John MacNeil in Geelong.'

The Korea miracle is an amazing story of a great revival which came to full fruition in 1907 after the first stirrings were felt in 1903. It is recorded in the *Journal of the General Conference of the Methodist Church* that the year after the revival, a Methodist missionary, Bishop M.C. Harris, wrote:

> The effects of the movement are wholly good; the church has been raised to a higher spiritual level. Scores have been called to the ministry, larger congregations are searching the Word. Drunkards, gamblers, thieves, adulterers ... and thousands of devil-worshippers have been made new men in Christ, the old things gone forever.[8]

Lord William Cecil wrote in *The Times* in London:

> The Koreans who were at the original meetings have gone forth, like Wesley's converts, their preaching has

> been wonderfully successful – so much so that there are not a few who say that it is through Korea that the light of Christianity will shine to the Far Eastern world.[9]

As we witness the growing influence of the Korean church over 100 years later, perhaps these words were written in 1908 with prophetic insight.

The Simultaneous Mission in the United Kingdom and Ireland

The Simultaneous Mission planned for the UK and Ireland was on a scale previously unknown there. Like the mission in Melbourne, it was preceded by a period of united prayer. There were numerous missioners, including Henry Varley, who had arrived from Melbourne, and who preached over 20 times in ten days. He wrote, 'Many have received Christ, the Lord's people have been built up and established in their most holy faith.' Varley was missioner in his native county of Lincolnshire where, at the conclusion of the mission there, a minister wrote to the local paper, 'I can testify that my own mind has been illuminated, my soul refreshed, my hope brightened, my zeal animated anew and the spiritual earnestness of my Church quickened.'[10]

At the reception given by the London Evangelical Council to Torrey and Alexander on their arrival in Britain in January 1903, Torrey told his hosts:

> I believe that you and I – I was going to say are at the dawn – but we are beyond that, we have crossed the threshold to one of the greatest epochs of the Church of Christ on earth – I believe you and I are to see one of the great Revivals of all time, one of the greatest Revivals in all the world's history. A Revival in earlier days meant something more or less circumscribed. A Revival in any day of this age of post, telegraph, newspapers, and all the ease of modern communication, a Revival in Australia, means a Revival all round the globe ...[11]

Torrey and Alexander undertook meetings in the main cities of England, Scotland, Ireland and Wales. Included in those mentioned by William Stead where hundreds made public confessions to follow Christ were Edinburgh, Glasgow, Liverpool, Dundee, Manchester, Birmingham and Bristol, as well as Dublin in Ireland and Bolton and Cardiff in Wales. The London Mission itself was planned for 1905.

Birmingham: Helen Cadbury and Charles Alexander

It was during the meetings at Birmingham in 1904, where Helen Cadbury and her widowed mother offered themselves as counsellors, that Helen, a daughter of Richard and Emma Cadbury, founders of Cadbury's Chocolates, met Charles Alexander. The Cadburys were devout Christians. They had been Quakers for generations although Emma was an Anglican before her marriage. They lived prayerful, godly lives, helping many needy people through charitable and philanthropic work. They were passionately concerned that others should put their faith in Jesus Christ as their Saviour and were energetically involved in evangelism. As a young teenager at school, Helen, with one or two other girls, commenced a ministry that became known around the world as 'The Pocket Testament League'. Following visits by Charles Alexander to the Cadbury home during the meetings in Birmingham, a deep friendship developed between them which led to their marriage.[12]

Meetings in Wales, the Welsh Revival and Evan Roberts

In September 1904, the team held a meeting in Bolton, Wales where 3,600 made a decision to follow Christ. They then moved on to Cardiff, holding meetings in a 7,000-seat auditorium which witnessed 3,700 decisions for Christ. Among those attending was Evan Roberts, who became the leader of the revival in Wales that started in early November, just a month or so after the Cardiff meetings. The Cardiff Torrey-Alexander meetings were believed to be one of the sparks in a spiritual fabric which lit the fire for the revival that led the nation of Wales to God in 1905.

William Stead wrote:

> At Cardiff at least ten of the songs that had been introduced to Britain by Charles Alexander were adopted by the Revival in Wales. They had been translated into Welsh and sung with Welsh enthusiasm. The chorus of one of them, 'Never lose sight of Jesus', with the tune composed by Robert Harkness, following his conversion [at Bendigo] during the Australian mission, was said to have been sung 200 times over at one Revival meeting, at which Mr. Evan Roberts, under whose ministry the Welsh revival had started, was present.[13]

Speaking about the revival in Wales at the 1976 Easter Belgrave Heights Convention, Professor Orr recalled:

> I knew Evan Roberts. Of course, he was an old man then. He had only been at Bible School for two months. He was invited to speak after the Prayer Meeting on Monday night. Seventeen people waited behind. He said, 'I have a message for you from God. You must confess any known sin to God, put away any doubtful habits out of your life, obey the Spirit promptly and confess your faith in Christ publicly.'
>
> This created such an impression that he was asked to speak at the next meeting. The second week the break came. Great crowds of people were drawn to South Wales. Shopkeepers were closing early. Steelworkers and miners were coming straight from work. The reporter from the local newspaper wrote, 'I felt this was no ordinary gathering!' The revival packed every church in Wales for 18 months. David Lloyd George, later Prime Minister of Great Britain, said that the total revenue from drink on a Saturday night in his town in

> North Wales was four pence ha'penny. The illegitimate birth rate after 12 months dropped 44%. Crime was cut in half. In county after county, there were no charges to be heard in the courts. Stories were given of police forming quartets to sing at meetings and juries singing hymns.[14]

The great Welsh revival: its beginnings

There is an extensive fabric in the movement of the Spirit of God preceding any revival. In a personal testimony given by Rev. Dr G. Campbell Morgan to his Westminster Chapel congregation in London in the early days of the Welsh Revival, he spoke of the beginnings of the revival:

> Let us all cease trying to find it! At least let us to cease trying to trace it to any one man or convention. You cannot trace it. And yet I will trace it to-night. Whence has it come? All over Wales – I am giving you roughly the result of the questioning of fifty or more persons at random in the week – a praying remnant has been agonising before God about the state of the beloved land, and it is through prayer the answer of fire has come. You can tell me that the revival originates with Evan Roberts. I tell you that Roberts is a product of the revival. You tell me that it began in the [Christian] Endeavour meeting where a young girl bore testimony. I tell you that was the result of a revival breaking out everywhere ... Within five weeks, 20,000 have joined the Churches.[15]

Furthermore, there was

> No advertising. The whole thing advertises itself. You tell me the Press is advertising it. I tell you they did not begin advertising it until the thing caught fire and spread. And let me say to you, one of the most remarkable things is the attitude of the Welsh Press. Many were converted by reading the accounts in the newspapers.[16]

The singing

Morgan continued:

> Let me speak of some of the incidental peculiarities of the Revival as I saw it ... There were the organs, but silent; the ministers, but among the people, rejoicing and prophesying with the rest, only there was no preaching ... No order, yet it moves from day to day, week to week, county to county, with matchless precision, with the order of an attacking force. No song books, but ah, me, I nearly wept to-night over the singing of the last hymn! When the Welsh sing they abandon themselves to their singing. We sing as though we thought it would not be respectable to be heard by the one next to us. No choir, did I say? It was all choir.
>
> And hymns! I stood and listened in wonder and amazement as the congregation sang hymn after hymn, without hymn-books. Oh, don't you see it? The Sunday School is having its harvest now. The family is having its harvest now. The teaching of hymns and the Bible among those Welsh hills and valleys is having its harvest now.[17]

From Cardiff, the evangelists travelled to Liverpool to conduct a nine-week campaign. The hall chosen for the meetings seated 12,500, yet at times it proved inadequate. It was estimated that 35,000 were turned away on the last day of the campaign. An old resident commented that it had surpassed the Moody-Sankey revival some years previously. The choir numbered over 3,500, which was the largest evangelistic chorus that had ever been organised.

The 1905 London Mission

From February to June in 1905, the London Mission was held. Meetings took place at the Royal Albert Hall for the first two months; then in a building seating 5,500 in South London for the next two months; and later in another seating over 5,000 in the heart of London on the Strand for the last month. A 1,000-voice choir helped nightly. It was said that it seemed as though all of London began singing revival hymns. *The Glory Song* captured the city. It was sung at every service.

Some 6,500 made decisions at the Royal Albert Hall with special meetings for men and children also packing out the hall. Meetings held in the South London location produced 5,000 converts and then in the final month another 2,500. A closing service at the Royal Albert Hall announced the totals: 202 meetings, 1,114,650 attended (average 5,500 per service) with over 17,000 converts.

Wrote Stead, 'Wherever they had gone the halls were unable to hold the crowds. Not since the days of Moody and Sankey had Great Britain been so stirred. A total of 70,000 came to the Lord during these three years of ministry in Great Britain.'[18]

Torrey's public invitations

Reuben Torrey was strongly in favour of insisting on public confession. In an interview with William Stead, he said,

> I don't want to make it too easy. The more difficult it is, the greater the struggle, the more definite and decisive is the break with the past. To make public confession of your wish to serve Christ as Saviour may cost a great effort at first, but it is a test of your willingness to do something for Him, and do it at once. We would probably get more immediate apparent results if we were less strict, but we should not reap such permanent results.[19]

The Revival of 1905: The Revival in the West

Stead wrote several pamphlets that were brought together in his publication *The Revival of 1905: The Revival in the West.* In identifying 'the West', Stead was referring to the culture with which Anglo-Saxon nations identify. The purpose of the publication was to attest 'to the widespread interest awakened by the Revival throughout the land'. He was realistic and noted that 'interest was by no means always sympathetic'. He hoped the publication 'might serve a useful purpose in rousing public attention to the immense importance of making the most of the present opportunity'.

Stead linked three significant movements of the Spirit of God at the time. The first was the interest created in London by the Torrey-Alexander Mission that was on the eve of commencing in the Royal Albert Hall. The second was the 1904 National Free Church Missions that had conducted meetings in Britain 'by an extraordinary evangelist with a remarkable testimony', Gipsy Smith, who a few years later made his first visit to Melbourne with the Chapman-Alexander Mission team. The third was the revival in Wales that began in November 1904.

In commenting on Evan Roberts and Gipsy Smith, two of the leaders of these missions, Stead wrote:

> Here is a Welsh collier who has not completed his first year in college and a gipsy boy, born in a tent, who has never been to school in his life. It is one of the hallmarks of the Christian faith. For as Mary sang in the beginning, '*He hath regarded the lowliness of His handmaiden*'.[20]

The following information is mostly a 'narrative of facts' written by Stead in February 1905.[21]

It started in Melbourne – with prayer

> It began at the uttermost ends of the earth. It was in response to a call from Australia that Dr. Torrey and Mr. Alexander began the Mission, the end of which no one can as yet foresee.
>
> That the Albert Hall in London has been secured in order that religious services may be held in it twice every day for two months on end is primarily due to the fact that some years before the close of the nineteenth

century, while Dwight L. Moody still lived, it entered into the hearts of the members of the Victorian Evangelization Society to get up a requisition, which was signed by thousands of Christian men and women in all parts of the Colonies, begging Mr. Moody and Mr. Sankey to come over to the Antipodes and help them.

At that time the famous American evangelists were in London, and it was thought they might be induced to extend their tour to Australia. Mr. Moody found it impossible to accept the invitation. There the matter remained for some years. But the extraordinary success of the Simultaneous Mission at the beginning of 1901, which was conducted under the direction of the National Free Church Council in England, revived the hopes and quickened the resolution of the Australians.

After obtaining full information as to how the Simultaneous Mission had worked, they organized themselves on the same basis and decided to seek missioners from Britain or America to replace Moody and Sankey.

In 1901 two well-known Melbourne men, Dr. Warren and Mr. G. P. Barber, both of the Evangelization Society, were deputed to visit Great Britain and to hear the various great preachers of the day, with a view to obtaining the services of one or more of them for a lengthened series of missions in Australia. They heard many of the prominent men in England and Scotland, but did not come across anyone who they thought would meet their demand.

Meantime, before they had even started in their search for the man they wanted, the hearts of the members of what had been Mr. Moody's old Church in Chicago, but which was then Dr. Torrey's, had been deeply stirred within them as to the need of a world-wide Revival.

Torrey's remarkable prayer ...

For three years before the call came, a prayer meeting was held at 10 pm each Saturday evening in Dr. Torrey's church; but after the general prayer meeting had ended, several men of faith were accustomed to go into a small room and keep on praying until the small hours of the morning for a world-wide awakening. Dr. Torrey was one of this little band, and one night he was led to utter a strange prayer. He describes the occurrence thus:

'It was a prayer that I had not dreamed of offering when we entered that hallowed place that night. The prayer was this, that God would send me round the world preaching the Gospel; and when I had ceased praying I knew I was going around the world to preach the Gospel. How, I did not know. With a large Church, with an increasing membership to be pastored, I did not see how I could leave them. With the Bible Institute to be guided and instructed, I did not see how I could leave it. But I knew the call had come from God, and that God would open the way.'

... and God's remarkable answer

Even while he was praying, the machinery which had been set in motion years before the prayer meeting was started was ready to work out an immediate answer to his petition. For the two Australian emissaries, despairing of finding the man they wanted in Great Britain, were even then on their way across the Atlantic, heading straight for Chicago. As soon as they reached that city they attended some lectures at the Moody Institute and some services in the Chicago Avenue Church. In both these places they heard Dr. Torrey, and immediately their minds were made up that he was the man they needed.

The invitation to Torrey

Within a week after Dr. Torrey's prayer was uttered the two men stepped up to him after a Church prayer meeting, and in the name of the united Churches of Melbourne, Australia, gave him an invitation to come there and conduct a Simultaneous Revival campaign. It seemed impossible to accept the invitation. But it was so manifestly an immediate and direct answer to prayer that the members of Dr. Torrey's Church felt that they would be opposing Divine Providence if it did not release their pastor and bid him obey the call. He summoned Mr. Alexander to his assistance, and they started before Christmas.

Prayer is the key

The origin of the Mission therefore was in the prayer meeting, and what appears to have been absolutely the original germ was a prayer meeting attended by about a dozen Christians in Victoria, which for eleven years had kept up a persistent pleading for an outpouring of the Holy Spirit.

...

Dr. Torrey has always ascribed the whole success which has attended the Mission solely to prayer. As he said at a welcome when he first arrived in London, '*You have heard a great deal about the preaching, but, friends, it was not the preaching; it was not the singing; it was the prayer. And God hears prayer.*'

Before the evangelists started out, about five thousand letters were issued from the office in Chicago to five thousand Christian people, asking them to pray for the work and the workers, and as many replies came back saying, 'We will pray every day.' There we have the secret of the wonderful work which has been accomplished. It is all summed up in one word – prayer.

> Both Mr Torrey and Mr Alexander are believers in prayer, as George Muller was and Dr Barnardo is. They plant their feet firmly upon the text, 'In everything by prayer and supplication with thanksgiving, let your requests be made unto God.' It is their responsibility to send in their petitions.

Pray! Pray! Pray!

We have recalled how Melbourne had its faithful Praying Band that preceded spiritual blessing around the world for decades to come.

At the conclusion of his testimony, Campbell Morgan said that there was nothing so important as the saving of men, women and children, and when the church says that, and is ready, God will come. The need then is to wait upon him in earnest, constant prayer. He said:

> Oh, brothers, sisters, Pray, PRAY. PRAY. Pray alone! Pray in secret! Pray together! And pray out of [a] sense of the world's sin and sorrow ... Oh, the sin and sorrow of the whole world! May God lay it upon our hearts as a burden. And out of that agony let us begin to pray and go forward the moment He opens the door, and indicates the way. Are we ready for God?[22]

Return to America

Torrey returned to America where he continued with his work at Moody Bible Institute. Until 1906 he was also the minister of the Moody Church in Chicago. He continued on for some years with his evangelistic meetings. One who was converted in a crusade in Toronto was Oswald J. Smith, who became the founder of The Peoples Church in Toronto, one of the world's great missionary-minded churches.

Several years later, in 1912, William Stead was to lose his life in the sinking of the *Titanic*.

Charles Alexander left Torrey in 1907–8 and joined up with J. Wilbur Chapman. 'When they had left Belfast,' recalled Robert Harkness,

> there were literally miles of people lining the wharves and docks, singing many of the Gospel hymns as the steamer slowly moved from its moorings into Belfast Lough. It was evening, and the darkness was gradually creeping over the city when from thousands of lips there rose in one mighty wave the words of that beautiful time-honoured hymn:
>
> 'Abide with me, fast falls the eventide,
> The darkness deepens, Lord, with me abide;
> When other helpers fail and comforts flee,
> Help of the helpless, oh, abide with me!'[23]

The secret of great revival

In writing on the Wesleyan revival in words that have scarcely been surpassed, W.H. Fitchett describes how

> The secret [of revival] belongs to the spiritual realm. It is idle to seek for it in the personal qualities of the men who were its agents, in the overwhelming oratory of [George] Whitefield, the hymns of Charles Wesley, the ordered and matchless industry, the genius for organisation, of John Wesley ...
>
> In its last analysis the secret of the great religious movement ... is to be found in the rich outpouring of the living Spirit of God on the nation ... in a particular group of men, fit instruments, with fit measure of devotion and faith, for a work so great. Flowing through the channel of true doctrine, and using the agency of fit human instruments, the grace of the Holy Spirit wrought this great work.[24]

'But what are evangelical doctrines?' asked Dr Fitchett:

A chain of mountain peaks, that pierce to the crown of the heavens, and on whose summits brood perpetual sunshine! They constitute a close-knitted succession of truths that break out of eternity and have its scale. Truths that relate to sin, and proclaim its measureless guilt, its hurrying and inevitable doom; but which also reveal an immediate and personal deliverance from sin – a deliverance which comes as an act of divine grace, and on the simplest terms of penitential acceptance ...

A divine redemption; a realised pardon; a restored relationship with God through faith ... And all this made intelligible and credible by the redeeming work and offices of Jesus Christ – and by the saving energies of the Holy Spirit in the human soul! This is the evangelical version of Christianity! ...

These are the doctrines that send out missionaries, that inspire martyrs, that regenerate slums! They awaken deeper vibrations in the human soul than all other truths put together. They are the doctrines in which dying men find comfort. All the great hymns of Christian worship reflect them; all the great prayers of human need give them speech. They formed exactly the message which the dying Christianity of the England of the day needed. 'Men,' the message ran, 'are in utmost and instant peril; they need ... a divine deliverance accomplished through redeeming grace. And this salvation is possible. A Saviour walks amongst men, touching them with hands of tenderness. Hope is born! All men may be saved here and now.'[25]

CHAPTER 7

The Conversion of Hervey Perceval Smith

A life transformed

Through the conversion of Hervey Perceval Smith, the Torrey-Alexander Mission had a profound and significant effect on Melbourne's interdenominational evangelicalism and missionary enterprises for many decades.

H.P. Smith had been heading for a career in journalism when in February 1890, at about 20 years of age, he emigrated with his widowed father and nine brothers and sisters from Worcester in England to Australia. After arriving in Melbourne, his father was appointed to be secretary and manager of the recently built prestigious Federal Coffee Palace.

The Federal Coffee Palace

A particular feature of Marvellous Melbourne's boom years had been the opening of two of the most extravagant temperance hotels – the Grand in Spring Street, later known as the Windsor Hotel, and the Federal at 555 Collins Street on the corner with King Street, strategically placed close to shipping and rail transport terminals. The construction of the Federal coincided with the holding of the 1888 Melbourne Centennial Exhibition.

These temperance hotels – 'coffee palaces' – sprang up encouraged by an influential temperance movement and built during a time of economic boom. The Federal was said to be the grandest of all coffee palaces, and it superseded the Grand in its luxuriance.

The Federal had seven floors crowned by an iron-domed

tower. Able to accommodate about 650 guests, it had nearly 500 rooms including 370 bedrooms which were on the top five floors, while the ornate ground and first floors contained 'majestic dining, lounge, sitting, smoking, writing and billiard rooms', as well as a cafe and shops. It was entered through a magnificent arcaded lobby with a glass roof and an ornately balustraded white and red marble staircase.[1] It was described in *The Age* as

> The greatest, the most exotic hotel Australia had seen. It has six accident-proof lifts, its own ice plant in the basement to keep kitchen supplies fresh, gas light on all floors and even electric service bells.[2]

For many years it was the focal point of Melbourne society gatherings and business conventions. In 1897 it was renamed the Federal Palace Hotel, and in 1924, just before it obtained a liquor licence, its name was changed to the Federal Hotel.

Enter H.P. Smith

On the unexpected death of his father in 1893, H.P. Smith, at age 23, was invited to succeed him as secretary of the Federal Coffee Palace. He was appointed into a world of opulence, extravagance and executive responsibility. Within a very short time, he had also become its general manager, responsible and accountable for the Federal 24 hours a day, seven days a week – a position that would have severely taxed the energies of most people. His accommodation was provided at the hotel, and he merged three rooms into one large area for card and smoke nights for the private entertainment of his guests and friends. However, as he neared 30 years of age, a desire to seek after truth was born in him, and he began attending the Collins Street Independent Church (now known as St Michael's Uniting Church) and showed interest in a branch mission at North Melbourne.

In 1902, the Torrey-Alexander Mission team stayed at the Federal. H.P. Smith had been appointed a prayer-meeting convenor and put his organisational and business skills to good use in this role. However, he became increasingly conscious of his spiritual ineptitude.

Conversion

Almost ten years after he began work at the Federal, at age 32, H.P. Smith had the life-transforming experience of conversion during the Torrey-Alexander Mission. After his death, his widow, Sarah Ann, wrote that one evening during the Torrey-Alexander Mission, when her husband had attended the Exhibition Building, Melbourne, he heard Torrey declare: 'The basis of judgement, above everything else, is what we do with Jesus Christ.' As he walked back to the hotel after having heard Torrey refer to John 3:18, 'He who believes in Him is not condemned, but he who does not believe is condemned already, because he has not believed in the name of the only begotten Son of God,' Smith decided he would now definitely trust in Christ. Then quickly into his mind followed the words of Jesus in John 5:24: 'Most assuredly I say to you, he that hears My word and believes in Him who sent Me has everlasting life, and shall not come into judgement, but has passed from death into life.' He prayed, 'Lord, I will hear, I do believe, and so I have everlasting life,' and immediately had the assurance that he was indeed a new creature in Jesus Christ.[3]

H.P. Smith's mother, who had died when he was fourteen years of age, was a sister of Rev. Walter Searle of the South African General Mission. Smith believed that it was his mother's prayers for her children that had been the means of winning them for Christ after her death.

Service for Christ begins

After his conversion, H.P. Smith, or 'H.P.' as he was often familiarly known, as a master of detail did not take long to get to work for the Lord. He was a fine businessman, a master of detail, prompt, unhurried, approachable and always in control of the situation.[4] Gifted with leadership and administrative skills and having at his disposal the facilities of the Federal Coffee Palace, strategically located as it was in the city of Melbourne, he was uniquely placed and motivated to foster meetings and programs arranged independently of denominational control. Full use was made of the entertaining room at the Federal, formerly used for card and smoke nights. Christians now met there weekly for fellowship. Given the constraints of a six-and-a-half-day working week, Saturday afternoons and evenings were popular choices for these meetings. Older Christians were used by God to guide those who met there into the deeper truths of the living reality of Christ and the indwelling power of the Holy Spirit.[5] One who attended, Ernest Renshaw, who was closely associated with H.P. Smith, wrote, 'I cannot forget the atmosphere, the spiritual power manifested in these meetings.'[6] A more detailed discussion of these Saturday meetings can be found in Chapter 10.

The depth of the outworking of Smith's conversion was seen when he was walking along Bourke Street on a Saturday afternoon handing out invitations to gospel meetings and preaching the gospel in the open air on the Yarra Bank on Sunday afternoons, where crowds of hecklers and others gathered, while he was manager of one of the most exotic hotels Australia had seen. These were indications of a Spirit-filled life.

CHAPTER 8 A Life of Service

The following is a personal reminiscence by H.P. Smith, written 26 years after his conversion, following Dr Torrey's death on 26 October 1928:[1]

> The homecall of Dr. Torrey has removed one of the most faithful and outstanding servants of God that Australians have been privileged to hear in their own land. Many of the Lord's people in Australia thank God for the visit of Dr. Torrey in 1902. Melbourne had planned a great simultaneous mission, no fewer than fifty centres around Melbourne having evangelistic missions in tents, town halls, or similar buildings at the same time. The writer was an enthusiastic worker at the Erskine Street, North Melbourne tent, where the Revs. F.E. Harry and G.S. Mackay were alternately the missioners, and later at the Exhibition Buildings, in the great meetings there. He well remembers how, during this North Melbourne Mission, he heard the Gospel preached for the first time, although two years previously he had turned from the world and its politics, and partly also its amusements, and had joined the Church. He was impelled by a sense of duty in this, and became an enthusiastic slum mission worker in North Melbourne, whilst retaining his business position in the city. It was as a representative of the Boundary Road Mission that he became a worker at the Erskine Street tent, and as a new and enthusiastic member of the Collins Street Independent Church he was appointed to organise the preparatory prayer meetings in the homes of members. His enthusiasm knew no bounds, and he

gladly gave time and labour to the work of preparation for the coming great Simultaneous Mission.

'All have sinned and come short'

But he knew not himself to be a sinner needing a Saviour; and it was not until the Erskine Street tent meetings were well advanced, he having attended every meeting, including early morning prayer meetings and committee meetings galore, that he one night was convicted of the fact that he, even he, was amongst the 'all' that had 'sinned and come short of the glory of God.' But no sooner had the Spirit of God wrought this mighty conviction in his soul as he walked home alone in the moonlight after 11 p.m. from the Gospel meeting than the same Holy Spirit brought to his remembrance the words, 'He that believeth on the Son hath everlasting life.' There was an immediate response – 'But I do believe on the Son,' and quick as lightning came an overpowering assurance – 'hath everlasting life', and the walk home was continued with great joy in the heart and a song of praise on the lips.

It was now that, in the gracious purposes of God, Dr. Torrey came into the life. After the fortnight of suburban missions came the great meetings – attended nightly by seven or eight thousand people – in the Exhibition Building. During the suburban meetings Dr. Torrey conducted the mission in the Hawthorn Town Hall, and here Mrs. Smith – then Miss Nettie Greenwood – was an active worker. It was then she arranged her first children's meeting – the real forerunner of the present quarterly evangelistic children's meetings, carried on now for many years by the Melbourne Gospel Crusade at the Protestant Hall in Exhibition Street.

'I preach Hell'

Standing night after night by the side of the platform in the Exhibition Building – there was never a seat left – God spoke to the writer and used Dr. Torrey as His mouthpiece. The first message he remembers was Dr. Torrey's sermon on 'Hell.' Up to this time he had definitely disbelieved in Hell, thinking it inconsistent that a God of love could send a man to Hell. But Dr. Torrey believed all the Scriptures taught about Hell, and he preached Hell. 'I preach "Hell",' he shouted down the great building, with a strong American accent, and a voice that thundered, and the echo of that shout rings to-day. Dr. Torrey preached from the Scriptures the fact of Hell, and also gave his reasons for his belief in Hell. 'Despite most of the preaching of the times in which we live,' said Dr. Torrey, 'I believe in Hell.' And before he had finished, the hearer standing by the platform believed also, and since has had no doubt whatever as to the awful reality of Hell, as revealed in the Scriptures.

The Bible – the infallible word of God

The second great message by Dr. Torrey, used mightily of God in the same way, was his sermon on the Bible as the infallible Word of God. During his two years of church membership, and the previous year, when he had been making diligent inquiry concerning spiritual things (attending churches of all denominations), the writer had not once, to his recollection, heard anyone say he believed the Bible from cover to cover. But he had heard very much preaching tending to produce in the hearer the very opposite of faith in the Bible as the very Word of God. He was, therefore, not only surprised, but almost staggered when he heard Dr. Torrey declare not only his belief in the Bible as the infallible Word of God, but that he believed the Bible from the first verse of Genesis to the last in Revelation.

Furthermore, that there was not a verse too many nor too few to convey God's message of salvation to man. The statement, we say, was a staggering one, and the newly born-again soul had to face here a crisis of the greatest magnitude. For his belief was that the Bible was merely a collection of old literature however excellent some parts of it might be. He thought the four Gospels were just as four varying newspaper accounts of an event, all partly true but also all partly erroneous. And now to be told that all the books of the Bible formed one complete whole, and that every one was written by the Spirit of God – through men – having only one purpose, the salvation of man, was something new indeed and required very earnest thought.

Up to the present he had taken no step hastily in his journey from the City of Destruction, where unbelief and worldliness reigned, to Christ. Every step, such as acceptance of the resurrection or the Deity of Christ, had been taken very deliberately. But here was something tremendous. He was asked to believe something he could not understand; in short, a real step of faith was called for. Could he, should he, believe what he did not understand? His attitude had been, so he supposed, that he would believe only what he understood. Could he now take a stand and say, 'I'll believe what I don't understand'? Instead of saying, 'I'll believe every part of the Bible I prove to be true,' could he say, 'I'll believe every part of the Bible until I prove it to be false'?

Before that meeting was over he had taken what he then declared to be a great 'leap in the dark'; in future he would believe absolutely whatever he read in the Bible until he had proved it to be false. Needless to say, this made the Bible a new book to him, and from that night he has had no difficulty in accepting the written Word as verily the Word of God, forever 'settled in heaven,' and 'a lamp unto the feet and a light unto the path.'

Drinking and smoking

It was in a meeting of ministers, held on Dr. Torrey's return from New Zealand, in the old Collins Street

Baptist lecture hall, to which he had been invited by the late G.P. Barber, who was largely responsible for Dr. Torrey coming to Australia, that the writer came to a very important decision. From a boy he had taken alcoholic liquors in moderation, and from the age of sixteen had been a heavy smoker. But in a heart to heart talk with the crowd of ministers present, Dr. Torrey declared that, whilst in using these things men of God might not be actually sinning, yet they were indulging in an unclean habit, the doubtful thing, something that certainly would not help their influence for Christ in the community, especially among the young. The writer knew this to be true for he had felt obliged, some time previously, to discontinue smoking in the neighbourhood of the Boundary Road Mission – or how could he discourage the boys there in the pernicious cigarette habit?

Dr. Torrey urged those present to give God the benefit of the doubt wherever any doubt existed, and discontinue the doubtful thing. The writer went home from that meeting resolved never to touch these doubtful things again. He emptied out the whisky demijohn and quietly put aside the pipe and cigars, and they have not once been taken up since.

Dr. Torrey's book on the Holy Spirit, and later the study of doctrinal truths, with the aid of his 'What the Bible Teaches', were the next great factors in the new life in Christ Jesus, and it is with a heart full of thankfulness to God that a witness for the truth such as R.A. Torrey was permitted to come into the life that these lines are penned.

The study Bible and the Bible student

An address by Torrey on the Bible and its inspiration had made a deep impression on H.P. Smith, who had listened in amazement to the great voice booming out, 'I believe the Bible from cover to cover; things I don't understand, yes, but is that going to make me disbelieve God's Word? I believe it from cover to cover.' From then on Smith decided to read Scripture with an open mind.

His extraordinarily gifted mind soaked up Scripture. Shortly after his conversion, Smith purchased his first study Bible, a *Bagster's Polyglot Study Bible*, in which is inscribed 'Hervey Perceval Smith, Federal Palace Hotel, Melbourne'. Handwritten on the flyleaf are the words, 'Apply thyself wholly to the Word. Apply the Word wholly to thyself.' The verses 'Draw nigh to God, and He will draw nigh to you' (James 4:8) and 'Call unto Me, and I will answer thee, and shew thee great and mighty things, which thou knowest not' (Jeremiah 33:3) are pasted on the front pages. Also included are Henry Drummond's notes on 'How to learn God's will', as well as a handwritten definition of repentance, perhaps reflecting his own experience: 'A change of mental and spiritual habit respecting sin, involving a hatred of, and sorrow of it, and a hearty and genuine abandonment of it in conduct of life.'[2]

The number of handwritten annotations in this study Bible reflects the many hours of regular study and absorbing of Scripture as H.P. Smith surrendered his life to the will of God and sought to do God's will. They express the owner's character, his deep spirituality and the commitment to Christ that his life reflected throughout his many years of Christian service. His last two Bibles, it is said, were wide-margin editions, allowing plenty of room for notes, study and meditation. He also made use of a number of hymn books, which he studied and used in private and public meetings.

This heart and head commitment found practical expression in an active life of service for Christ. Out of the meetings Smith commenced at the Federal on a Saturday night developed the MGC with its multi-faceted evangelistic, Bible teaching and missionary ministries.

The Melbourne Gospel Crusade

Aided by the helpful influence of other like-minded Christians including 'the beloved physician', Dr D. Stewart MacColl, H.P. Smith went on to promote a number of other activities. As these grew in number, extent and diversity, with his administrative vision he realised the need to establish an umbrella organisation to organise, support and coordinate these developing ministries. The resulting organisation was the MGC.

It is not entirely clear how or when the MGC Council first came together. There are references in the Crusade's 1918–19 and later Annual Reports, although the Council was not officially formalised until 10 February 1920.

The first minutes of the formalised Council in 1920, handwritten by Smith, record:

> After a season of prayer, Mr Smith explained that he had invited the brethren to gather to discuss the affairs of the Melbourne Gospel Crusade with a view to the formation of a Council or advisory body. That whilst he did not wish to retire from his responsibilities as Secretary-Treasurer of the Crusade, he yet felt it to be of the Lord that brethren in full sympathy with the work should act in co-operation for its furtherance as the Lord may lead.[3]

This document indicates Smith's leadership role and the spiritual qualities of the men he chose to support the work.

The MGC emerged as a significant entity in the spiritual life of Melbourne, with Frank Varley, son of evangelist Henry Varley, as its first chairman and H.P. Smith as its secretary. The Council promoted and encouraged a diversity of initiatives and continued to do so with far-reaching consequences from that early period and through the years of World War II. From the outset, the term 'Melbourne Gospel Crusade' referred not to the Council, but to a range of Christian ministries and meetings operating under the Council's aegis, each deriving its support, direction, character and legitimacy from the name, and where appropriate, from the Council itself. The aim of the MGC was to declare the truth of God summed up in the three R's: 'Ruin by the fall, Redemption by the blood of Christ and Regeneration by the Holy Spirit.'

The MGC planned and undertook evangelism in Melbourne streets, a venture referred to as the 'Bourke Street Stunt'; it sent out teams into country locations using vans with students from the MBI as missioners; and it held quarterly Saturday afternoon evangelistic meetings for children and promoted Scripture instruction in schools.

Perhaps the most significant of the activities overseen by the MGC, and ones that were always covered with prayer, were the weekly Saturday night 'meetings of spiritual power' held at the Federal, which focused on deeper life teaching and overseas missions (see Chapter 10). Eventually the numbers attending the Federal for these gatherings under the direction of H.P. Smith became too great for the accommodation available, so meetings spread to other halls within the city until they settled at the Protestant Hall in Exhibition Street. This hall accommodated about 600 people and on many occasions overflowed.

The meetings were a constant source of spiritual power and blessing. Many missionaries were heard to say, 'I got my call at the Saturday night meeting.' These gatherings led to an impetus of missionary interest and endeavour that resulted in the call of many to go into service in Australia and elsewhere. The call of faith missions, especially CIM, was significant in Australia. It came to fruition not long after the end of World War I when C.H. Nash became the founding Principal of the MBI following J.J. Kitchen's vision to establish the Institute to train missionaries (see Chapter 9). In the first half of the 20th century, denominationally linked training colleges took on an important role in the deployment of missionaries for work among Aboriginal people and in other parts of the world.

Other ministries followed that worked closely with C.H. Nash and H.P. Smith, focusing particularly on evangelistic outreach, Bible study and exposition, and overseas missions. Vibrant organisations were founded, including the Bible Union of Victoria, Borneo Evangelical Mission (BEM), Unevangelised Fields Mission (now Pioneers), Missionary Aviation Fellowship (MAF), Melbourne City Men's Bible Class and Campaigners for Christ. There were also the MGC's country van ministry, open-air preaching, children's evangelistic work, home visitation, Scripture instruction in schools, and tract distribution that included placing texts in trams in Melbourne and then later in the provincial cities.

Meetings of the MGC also led to what some might consider to have been one of the most important and longest-continuing results of the Torrey-Alexander Mission – namely, the Upwey (now Belgrave Heights) Convention for the deepening of the spiritual life, discussed in greater detail in Chapter 9.

Eric J. Daley, editor of the Christian newspaper *New Life*, in an article on the MGC at the time of H.P. Smith's death, wrote:

> The story of the Melbourne Gospel Crusade alone would make thrilling reading. From the small beginnings at 'The Federal', the Saturday evening meetings continued to grow.
>
> Mr. Smith was Secretary of the Crusade Council and leader of the meetings. They proved a source of constant blessing; missionaries on furlough and evangelists and Bible teachers were welcomed, and many of Melbourne's ablest expositors of the Word spoke from the platform. Evangelistic meetings for children were held quarterly [later monthly] and were the means of winning many children for Christ. Meetings for prayer were a regular feature of the work.[4]

Resignation from the Federal

When the issue of the Federal obtaining a liquor licence was raised, H.P. Smith told the directors that if it was acquired, he would be obliged to resign. The chief director and largest shareholder, living in London at the time, sent his son to Melbourne to persuade Smith to change his mind. However, his instructions were that if that was not possible, the idea of the licence would need to be abandoned. Smith was told that if it was him or a liquor licence, then the liquor licence had to go.

After the death of the influential chief director, the young directors determined to acquire the licence. Smith therefore tendered his resignation when the licence was granted in 1923, exactly 30 years to the day after he had commenced work there. He left behind all living accommodation and a substantial salary, and went out not knowing what the Lord had for him to do.

Keswick Tea Rooms and Book Depot

Some Christian businessmen, identifying a need for sound Christian literature, suggested that Smith should open a Christian bookshop. He considered that this might not be commercially viable; however, he thought that with his knowledge of the catering industry, a bookshop could be successful if linked with a cafe/restaurant. In conjunction with his brother, Alex, he opened the Keswick Tea Rooms and Book Depot in 1924 in the basement of 315 Collins Street, Melbourne, 'five doors west of Elizabeth Street, downstairs', where 'Light Refreshments, Hot Luncheons, Dinner, Grills and Afternoon Teas could be obtained'. The name 'Keswick' was chosen by Smith, acknowledging the influence of the Keswick Convention that had been held in England since 1875.[5]

The Keswick Book Depot ministry began in a very small way, but it quickly became known throughout Australia for its wide range of sound evangelical literature. It was not long before it became an influential centre for evangelical activities in Victoria, where meetings formerly held at the Federal were now held. It gained a reputation as the missionary and convention centre of Melbourne, and its influence spread worldwide. The cafe section was closed in the late 1930s.

After Smith's death, the Keswick Book Depot continued in the main city area of Melbourne. Eventually it became a not-for-profit organisation, with all of its trading surpluses distributed for missionary, evangelistic, convention and Bible college ministries. When the Keswick Bookshops were disposed of in 2004, there were branches in Ballarat, Bendigo, Dandenong, Frankston, Geelong and Wodonga, as well as the outlet that operated at Belgrave Heights during conventions.

It is recounted that H.P. Smith often said that the Upwey Convention and the Keswick Book Depot were his children, so deeply were they woven into his heart.

The Keswick Quarterly and Upwey Convention News

Even before his conversion, H.P. Smith's background prepared him for what was to follow. He had been heading for a career in journalism, having been on the staff of *The Worcester Journal* when the family had emigrated to Australia. He then worked for a time at the oldest newspaper in Victoria, the *Geelong Advertiser*, first published in 1840. This background gave him the experience he needed for the editing and publishing of *The Keswick Quarterly and Upwey Convention News.*

The MGC minutes dated 19 January 1926 recorded that 'Mr. Smith had brought up the question of the advisability of now going ahead with the oft suggested regular publication to convey news of our work, prayer requests and the like, to our many friends scattered over town and country.'

The publication would include reports of the MGC Van Ministry and Country Missions, and similar reports would be invited from evangelists such as Norman Lumsden and

George Hall, who were working for the Evangelisation Society. It was envisaged that these reports would be helpful for the prayerful interest of their many friends. Also, there were women involved in Scripture instruction in schools and as visiting sisters of the City Mission, who would be helped by having their reports published. Many friends had a common interest in overseas missions and reports from missionaries would be channels for prayer and blessing.

In February 1926, shortly after he left the Federal, H.P. Smith published the first issue of *The Quarterly.* His editorial mentioned that it would be published in the months of February, May, August and November, without charge to subscribers, and that donations would be invited to cover the cost.

Contents of The Quarterly

The Quarterly regularly published the details and locations of forthcoming missionary prayer meetings that were to be held in Melbourne and its suburbs. Often there were more than 100 prayer meetings listed for the next quarter.

H.P. Smith used the front cover and the editorial to publicise matters of current relevance and issues that were of special interest. It was not surprising, therefore, that more than half of the editorials and covers publicised forthcoming Upwey Conventions and reviewed past Conventions. In this way, *The Quarterly* kept Upwey Convention friends in touch with one another during the year and publicised arrangements for future conventions – 'should the Lord tarry', as Smith so often interpolated. The importance of the Keswick message was emphasised by the convention motto, 'All One in Christ Jesus.' Short contributions on the cover by Keswick leaders regularly reminded readers of the Keswick message, while articles on 'The Keswick Message and Its Meaning' were often published. One heading in 1946 read, 'The Message of Keswick: It is also the Upwey Message.' [6] The challenge confronting wartime conventions and the need for repentance were given prominence in the early 1940s.

Articles by trustworthy Bible teachers, many being addresses given at Keswick England, were regularly included, for 'we are not unmindful of the word of the Apostle "to feed the Church of God which He has purchased with His own blood."'[7] Discerning book reviews also appeared regularly. In addition to MBI reports, *The Quarterly* occasionally published reports from Bible colleges in Sydney, New Zealand and other locations.

One only has to leaf through an issue of *The Quarterly*, of which nearly 90 issues had been published at the time of his death, to understand where H.P. Smith's sympathies and prayers were directed. From its inception, *The Quarterly* continued to be an unexcelled reference for convention matters, as well as missionary and evangelistic reports and information. Smith edited every issue until November 1947, the last being just before his unexpected death. Altogether he edited 88 issues, many in the 1930s exceeding 80 pages and some reaching print runs of 10,000 copies.

To enable an understanding of the comprehensive nature of *The Quarterly*, some of the evangelists and workers named in the publication during the 1930s and 1940s included:

- G.L. Aitken
- Rev. W.F. Betts
- Bruce Bryson (Campaigners for Christ)
- George R. Brown (ESA)
- Brooking Hannah
- Leonard Buck
- Rev. A. Cyril Cato
- Rev. Adam Clarke
- Eric Clarkson
- Alfred Coombe
- Russell Costello
- Spencer Colliver

- Stan Drew
- Miss Una Dodds
- Pastor Laurie Dyer
- Colin Ferguson
- Ken Finger
- G.H. Fuhrmeister
- Miss A. Giddings
- Alex Gilchrist
- T. Grogan (The Pocket Testament League)
- Dr Howard Guinness
- George Hall
- Fred Levett
- Norman C. Lumsden
- H.H. Janetski
- A.T. Kerr
- Philip Knight
- Harry Lang
- Harold McCracken
- Miss F. McHutchinson
- Malcolm McOmish (OAC)
- W. Merriweather
- Trevor Morris
- Bruce Morton (ISCF/CSSM)
- Stewart Morton
- Jack Neilsen
- Rev. W.P. Nicholson
- Alex Oliver
- Rev. Ray Outhred
- Arthur Pocklington
- Robert Pocklington
- Frank Prescott
- Rev. Dr John Renshaw
- Rev. John Ridley
- Les Roberts
- J.A. Robinson

- J.H. Robinson
- C.G. Sandland
- Stella Sandland
- Bishop Alfred Stanway
- John Thompson
- Bruce Townsend (Campaigners for Christ)
- S.P. Waddingham
- J.B. White
- Rev. G.W. Wilson
- Reg Wright.

Visits were reported of Dr J. Edwin Orr, Dr Oswald J. Smith, the Maréchale (Mrs Booth-Clibborn), Rev. Lionel B. Fletcher and Lieut. General Sir Wm. Dobbie, while deaths were reported of Edwin Lee Neil (1934), John (Jack) Neilsen (1936), Dr D.S. MacColl, H.B. Denniston and F.C. Crosby (1938), C.A. Sandland and Thomas Graham (1939), Frank Varley (1942), J.M. Griffiths (1943) and N.C. Lumsden and R.S. Tregaskis (1944).

Included amongst missionary society reports were those from:

- Australian Aborigines Mission (later United Aborigines Mission)
- Aborigines' Friends Mission
- Aborigines Inland Mission
- Argentine River Mission, South America
- Australian Nepalese Mission
- BCH Mission, Orai, India
- Bethesda Aborigines Mission
- Bolivian Indian Mission
- Borneo Evangelical Mission
- British Syrian Mission
- Central Japan Pioneer Mission
- Ceylon and India General Mission
- China Inland Mission
- Christian and Missionary Alliance

- Church Missionary Society
- Door of Hope, Shanghai
- Dutch West Borneo Mission
- Egypt General Mission
- India and Nepali Children's Home
- Evangelical Union of South America
- Japan Rescue Mission
- Kurku and Central Indian Hill Mission
- Methodist Mission, The, Davuilevu, Fiji
- Mildmay Movement (World Wide Witness Fellowship)
- Mission to Lepers, The
- Oriental Missionary Society
- Poona and Indian Village Mission
- Ramabai Mukti Mission, India
- Regions Beyond Missionary Union
- Roodeport Compound Mission, South Africa
- Russian Missionary Society
- South Sea(s) Evangelical Mission
- Sudan Interior Mission
- Sudan United Mission
- Telugh Village Mission, South India
- Unevangelised Fields Mission
- Worldwide Evangelisation Crusade
- Yotsuya Mission, Japan
- Zenana Bible and Medical Mission.

Over a similar period, some of the home organisations whose reports were published were:

- 3GL Geelong Upwey Fellowship
- 3KZ Campaigners
- Australian Christian Colportage Association (later reverting its name to ESA)
- Australian Institute of Archaeology
- Australian Nurses' Christian Movement
- Bible Union of Victoria
- Biblical Research Society

- Brien Hall Gospel Mission
- Campaigners for Christ
- Children's Mission Work
- City Girls' Bible Class
- CMS League of Youth
- Collingwood Free Breakfast Mission
- Conventions
- Children's Special Service Mission
- Eaglehawk Gospel Mission
- Evangelical Fellowship
- Evangelical Mission to Seamen
- Everyman's Huts
- Gospel in the Universities, The
- Interdenominational Missionary Fellowship (Victoria)
- Inter-School Christian Fellowship
- Inter-Varsity Fellowship Conference
- Melbourne City Men's Bible Class
- Melbourne City Mission
- Melbourne Men's Mission
- Methodist Local Preachers' Holiness Convention
- Methodist Motor Church
- Noone Street Mission Clifton Hill
- Open-air Sunday Schools
- Pocket Testament League, The
- Postal Sunday School Movement
- Prayer Union for Israel
- Radio broadcasts on 3AK Melbourne
- Queensberry Street Mission, Carlton
- Scripture Gift Mission
- Scripture Instruction in State Schools
- Scripture Union
- Second Coming of Christ Convention
- Spring Street Mission
- Sunday School Union of Victoria
- United Prayer for Revival

- Victorian Christian Endeavour Conventions
- Victorian Mission to the Jews, The
- White & Warn Mission Work
- Williamstown Gospel Mission
- Women's World Day of Prayer
- Mr & Mrs L. Roberts Visual Evangelism.

H.P. Smith's editorials

While always endeavouring to maintain the unity of the Spirit, H.P. Smith was alert to the danger of false teaching infiltrating the church. In the words of Jude 3, he endeavoured to 'contend earnestly for the faith which was once for all delivered to the saints'. Consequently, in 1927 he wrote about a candidate who was rejected for the British Methodist ministry because he was not open to modernist teaching.[8] In the 1930s, he warned of the teaching of evolution, and later an editorial was written on the difficulty of holding to the Christian faith in the modern world, sometimes because good organisations were 'sub-evangelical'. He then followed up with the article 'The apostasy is here: Preaching of the Christian faith that is a travesty and a sham', and in November 1944, 'The state of the church: The great need for the definite preaching of the gospel of salvation.' As the war in Europe was approaching its end he wrote an editorial on 'The great need for gospel preaching: No new order without new man.'

There was always a graciousness in his relationships and attitudes. Smith 'endeavoured to speak the truth in love' (Ephesians 4:13), yet in denouncing error, the trumpet did not give an uncertain sound.

Smith's editorials supported the visits of evangelists to Melbourne such as Gipsy Smith and Rev. W.P. Nicholson. In 1942, he appeared to be the first to promote the evangelistic ministry of a converted Jew, Dr Hyman Appleman, resulting in an invitation for him to visit Australia. After the war finished in 1945, a committee was formed which resulted in the successful visit in 1948 of Dr Appleman to Australia, although Smith had died just a few months previously and did not see the result of his efforts.

He consistently included articles to build up Christians in their faith such as 'A scholar's profession of faith' by J. Gresham Machen. Then there were those that helped in the practical outworking of the message of Keswick, including 'Victory through our Lord Jesus Christ' by Rev. A.B. Simpson, 'The experience of Pentecost' by Rev. Dr W. Graham Scroggie and 'A Keswick message' by Lieut. General Sir William Dobbie.

Other articles included warnings in the 1930s of widespread slavery, including 'The Aboriginal question in Western Australia: New regulations "absolutely iniquitous"', and the threat of Islam. In May 1940, an article appeared on the need for aeroplanes for missions in New Guinea as being the most efficient means of transportation. During the years of World War II, reports were included from those taking the gospel into military camps, including Campaigners for Christ and the YMCA.

The editors of **The Quarterly**

After the death of H.P. Smith there were several editors, some acting in a joint capacity. They included W.L. Wright, Arthur Pocklington, J. Howard Kitchen and J. Oswald Sanders. Reflecting the change in location of the Upwey Convention to Belgrave Heights, the name was changed to *Keswick Quarterly and Belgrave Heights Convention News* in October 1954, although the first meeting at the new location had been held on 23 December 1950.

It appears that the last issue was November 1969, when the publication was known as the *Keswick Record and Belgrave Heights Convention News*. However, following H.P. Smith's death, the publication lost much of its news value, one reason being that the Christian newspaper *New Life* was filling that need (see Chapter 14).

Taking the gospel to the travelling public

H.P. Smith had a mind that constantly explored new ways of bringing the gospel to as many people as possible. In the November 1926 issue of *The Quarterly*, he wrote:

> In comparing the mass of the people in the city of Melbourne and suburbs with the few who attended any place where the gospel is preached, one is faced with the problem of how to effectively present the gospel to fellow citizens. By open-air preaching on a sufficiently extensive scale it could be done, but at present the supply of workers is insufficient. An alternative is reaching the masses through the eyegate. Practically every man, woman and child travels in or about the city in train or tram. By placing suitable scripture texts in the advertisement spaces of train and tram cars the issues of life and death could be brought before the people who are too indifferent to the claims of Christ to attend a service or read a tract.[9]

In the May 1927 issue of *The Quarterly*, Smith recollected: 'In Melbourne some years ago, the Melbourne Gospel Crusade for a period of a year or two had Gospel texts in all the city trams, and on many suburban railway stations, which were a constant public declaration of the Gospel truth.'[10]

One of the texts used on railway stations referred people to the open-air meeting on a Sunday evening over Princes Bridge and read:

GET RIGHT WITH GOD

MELBOURNE GOSPEL CRUSADE

Over Princes Bridge – SUNDAYS 7.30 p.m.[11]

With this passion to reach the unconverted with the gospel, Smith commenced a 'Texts in Trams' ministry that he personally conducted and to which he invited friends to contribute.

He often reminded his readers that 'the texts are the Word of God, and in His Word, God says, "My Word ... shall not return unto Me void, but it shall accomplish that which I please, and it shall prosper in the thing whereto I sent it" (Isaiah 55:11)'.[12] Other verses about God's word that were quoted included 'The Word of God which liveth', 'quick and powerful, and ... sharper than any two-edged sword, piercing even to the dividing asunder of soul and spirit', and able to make 'wise unto salvation'.

During the 1930s, texts were being displayed in 100 Melbourne electric trams, the cable trams of the Clifton Hill depot, and in every one of 27 trams in Geelong. Later, a report in *The Quarterly* in 1941 mentioned that 'The display was on trams working from the Malvern, Hawthorn and Essendon depots; they are now showing on 50 trams operating from the Kew, Coburg and Brunswick depots.'[13] The tram routes where the texts were used were regularly changed, other depots such as Camberwell, Glenhuntly, Footscray and South Melbourne being used. Texts were also displayed in buses running between Frankston and Ferntree Gully.

Reports of help and blessing were regularly received. Some of the texts used were:

- 'I know that my redeemer liveth.'
- 'Redeemed with the precious blood of Christ.'
- 'Christ Jesus came into the world to save sinners.'
- 'Believe on the Lord Jesus Christ and thou shalt be saved.'
- 'Come unto me all ye that labour and are heavy laden and I will give you rest.'
- 'The gift of God is eternal life through Jesus Christ our Lord.'
- 'The Son of God who loved me and gave himself for me.'
- 'A faithful saying, Christ Jesus came into the world to save sinners.'
- 'Except a man be born again, he cannot see the kingdom of God.'

- 'The Lord is good, a stronghold in the day of trouble: and he knoweth them that trust in him.'

This ministry extended for over 20 years. After Smith's death, the ministry was not continued in Melbourne trams and the cards were transferred to trams in Geelong, Ballarat and Bendigo as a ministry undertaken by other Christian friends.

Mission societies and other involvements

In addition to his leadership of the Upwey Convention and the MGC, H.P. Smith was also a founding member of the MBI Council and active in the Bible Union of Australia. The latter took an uncompromising stand against modernism, a theology that was beginning to infiltrate and decimate the spiritual life of many churches.

It was said that you could leave a donation with H.P. Smith for any one of about 50 mission societies and the gift would always get to the right place. He was an office-holder or member of the councils of numerous mission and evangelical organisations. These included MBI, the Bible Union, Worldwide Evangelisation Crusade (WEC) (president), the Unevangelised Fields Mission (treasurer, Australian Council), SIM, India & Nepali Children's Home, Ramabai Mukti Mission and Central Japan Pioneer Mission.

The 'home call' of Miss Rosa Smith

While Smith was president of the council of the Ramabai Mukti Mission in Australia, he received the sad news that his sister Rosa, who had worked for the Mukti Mission in India for nearly 23 years, had unexpectedly been 'called home'. Mention was made that another sister, Alice, was also serving in India at the time, but she 'was three days journey away'. The Smith family were overtly involved in the cause of Christ. H.P. Smith carried the burden of having a family member exposed to the uncertainties associated with missionary service.

CHAPTER 9

Conventions: Upwey and Elsewhere

The Keswick message

In *Rivers of His Grace: The Jubilee Story of Belgrave Heights*, Irene Cleverdon wrote:

> Origins are always fascinating to the enquiring mind, and the early springs from which the now mighty Keswick Convention flows, is no exception. Canon T.D. Harford-Battersby, Vicar of St. John's Keswick, made the following entry in his diary on September 15, 1873:
>
> 'At this moment I am feeling much inward struggle and questioning about this "higher Christian life" which is so much talked of and written about ... I feel that I am dishonouring God, and am wretched myself by living as I do: and that I must either go backwards or forwards, reaching out towards the light and the glory which my blessed Saviour holds out to me, or falling back more and more into worldliness and sin ... a great prize is before me; shall I not seek after it? Is it not worth every possible effort to attain to? God reveal to me the secret of this "more excellent way", and enable me to walk in it now and always. Amen.'
>
> The following year his prayer was answered as he discerned the difference between 'seeking' and 'resting' faith. He said to himself – 'I WILL rest in Him ...'
>
> Two years later in 1875 the first convention was held at Keswick. Canon Harford-Battersby subsequently stated his early experience of the victorious life of faith in the following terms:

> 'I got a revelation of Christ to my soul, so extraordinary, glorious and precious from that day it illuminated my life. I found He was all I wanted. I shall never forget it; the day and hour are present with me. How it humbled me yet what peace it brought.'[1]

In the 1870s, Frances Ridley Havergal, daughter of a Church of England clergyman and famous for her hymns and devotional verses, had a similar experience. She 'saw clearly the blessedness of true consecration. I saw it as a flash of electric light ... so I just utterly yielded myself to Him, and utterly trusted Him to keep me.'[2] Thus she was able, before her early death, to write hymns identified with Keswick including *Lord, speak to me*; *Like a river, glorious is God's perfect peace*; and *Take my life and let it be consecrated, Lord, to Thee.*

Melbourne and the message of Keswick

Among the many positive outcomes and effects of the simultaneous missions in Melbourne were the informal grassroots expressions of the need for Christian fellowship. There was a desire, particularly among evangelicals, to maintain and even extend the interdenominational unity and fellowship experienced during the activities of the missions. In their aftermath, many were conscious of a hunger for Bible study, and there was a heightened concern for the lost and for a closer, deeper walk with the Lord.

Within this context, there developed an embryonic convention movement, which was built on the visit to Keswick in the late 1870s by H.B. Macartney Jr, the ministries of the ESV in the 1880s, the Geelong Convention of 1891 and the Prayer Band, resulting from the conversion of H.P. Smith. This fledgling movement evolved over time into the regular Saturday evening meeting at The Federal led by Smith. The message preached at Keswick had come to Melbourne.

Early conventions

In the second edition of *The Quarterly* in May 1926, Smith, as editor, had 'a glance backwards' to the commencement of Upwey and the published reports of each of the early conventions that had been held there. These had been taken from the yearly reports of the MGC, which he had originally compiled:

> In the beginning, there was no thought whatever of forming an Upwey Convention Council. It had been the custom for several friends of the Melbourne Gospel Crusade to meet for fellowship and prayer during the holiday season. Several of such seasons had been spent at Eltham [1909 to 1912], then for the sake of the young folk the seaside was chosen – Black Rock for two years [1913 and 1914] and Beaumaris [1915]. After this, smaller and more private gatherings were at Vermont for two years [1916 and 1917], and then at Christmas [1918] came Upwey.

The first convention at Upwey 1918–19

In December/January 1918–19, just after the end of World War I, the first Upwey Convention, later to be transferred to Belgrave Heights, was held under the auspices of the MGC in the Upwey Union Church. In later meetings, a marquee was used, followed by a structure, now enlarged, which is still the basis of the main auditorium at Belgrave Heights.

Irene Cleverdon describes a meeting that took place between J.H. Robinson and H.P. Smith that led to Upwey being chosen as the convention venue:

> Mr. J.H. Robinson recalls being in homes under the leadership of such men as Rev. C.H. Nash, Dr. Stewart MacColl and others. He goes on, 'Whilst Norman Baker and I were unable to proceed to China owing to the war, we were conducting evangelistic meetings with the Melbourne City Mission. On the final night

> of the mission at Richmond, we were kept busy with enquirers until the last tram left. My colleague decided to walk home while I went into the City to the Federal Hotel where Mr. H.P. Smith was the manager.
>
> 'Since I had no luggage, the night-porter eyed me suspiciously but when he learned I had no money to pay and knew Mr. Smith, he agreed to give me a bed and check with the manager in the morning about the mysterious late-comer.
>
> 'Very early next morning, Mr. Smith came to my room and then invited me to join him and Mrs. Smith at morning tea. This gave me the opportunity I had been waiting for, to tell him of a proposal to hold a Convention at Upwey and of the need for a leader. Many friends had been urging me to go ahead with this.
>
> 'Imagine my joy when Mr. Smith said, "What can we do to help?" They were uncertain at first about Upwey, but in view of the restful surroundings, nearness to Melbourne, the sympathetic attitude of local Christians, and the practical interest of Mr. John Griffiths, one of Melbourne's leading Merchants and a prominent Anglican, they decided to go up to investigate. They were favourably impressed, and a month later, some houses were booked for what was to be the First Upwey Convention.'[3]

The publicity material for the first Upwey Convention, held in the Upwey Union Church Hall, explained its purpose:

> The meetings will be evangelistic, and the Second Coming of Christ will be proclaimed. Definite Missionary Messages will be given by those who know the need and the opportunities of the heathen world, and Christians will be shown the necessity for a closer walk with God ... Early morning Prayer Meetings and Open Air Gospel Meetings will also be arranged.

The speakers included Rev. C.N. and Mrs Lack of the CIM, D. Stewart MacColl, Thomas Porter, Frank Varley and W.J. Foster.

The MGC Report of the Convention continued:

> For Christmas and New Year [1918/19, just a few weeks after the finish of World War I] – in conjunction with Mr. J.H. Robinson, who sails for China this month – we organised the Upwey Convention. This proved to be a season of great blessing, and many, we believe, will look back with hearts full of praise to God. The Convention meetings in the Upwey Union Church, the Bible readings in the houses, the early morning prayer meetings, open-air preaching at Upwey and Belgrave, were all features that were manifestations of spiritual power. We were specially thankful for the visit of Rev. C. and Mrs. Lack, of the China Inland Mission, whose presence, as well as their many messages, was a token of God's blessing. Many have asked if the Upwey Convention is to be an annual one. We dare not say it is, for the cloud may move in another direction, or may not move at all. In this we ask the prayers of the Lord's people, that we may know and do the will of the Lord.[4]

The number attending the first convention was given at 'about 100 to 150'.

Upwey 1919–20: influence spreads to the country

In its second issue, *The Quarterly* continued with extracts from the MGC reports of the early conventions:

> The Upwey Convention was a season of marked blessing, of which brief mention must be made. The Victorian Open Air Mission joined with us by arranging for their missioner, Mr. Norman Lumsden, to spend a month at Upwey over the period of the Convention. This resulted in two bands of country converts from Mr. Lumsden's mission at Yandoit and Tyabb coming for part of the time. The Convention was a great blessing to these, and indeed to all who were able to attend.

> A special feature was the daily Bible reading meetings of Rev. C.H. Nash, who was the guest of Mr. John Griffiths [of Griffith Bros. Teas] at Forest Park, for the period of the Convention. Many talked of the Convention next Christmas as if it were a settled matter. If this being so in the counsels of Him – Whom we love and Whom we serve – then let us pray that we may know and do His will in this, as in all other things lying before us in the strenuous times that are ahead – 'till He come'.[5]

J.H. Robinson recalled 'the stirring open-air meetings each evening at the railway station led by Evangelist Norman Lumsden assisted by Mr. Jack Neilsen; the vigorous early morning prayer meetings, and the contribution of those who conducted house-parties'.[6]

Upwey 1920–21: deeply spiritual and increasing numbers

A local newspaper, *The Mountaineer*, in its January 1921 issue wrote about 'The Gospel Convention' and commented in particular on the wonderful singing:

> The songs of the party as they rang out on the evening air, told of a desire to lead the thoughts of mankind into high and lofty realms. As the toy trains glided their way along, the eager passengers listened to the Gospel message as its music floated on the eventide: and, listening, more rejoiced.

The report on the 1920–21 Convention continued:

> The Christmas and New Year Convention at Upwey was again a season of very real blessing, and in some respects in advance of previous years. The numbers were rather greater and the meetings from the first of a deeply spiritual character. There must have been nearly 200 friends – who stayed at Upwey or Belgrave for the Convention, for a longer or shorter period – not

all at one time – and nearly all testify to a season of glorious refreshing in the presence of the Lord. Mr. Lumsden and other friends of the V.O.A.M. [Open-air Mission] united with us most heartily, and the success of the Convention was largely contributed to by their presence and efforts.

Special features were the ... Bible readings by Rev. C.H. Nash at 10 o'clock – much used of God in revealing new truths from the Scriptures to many who attended, and the evening open-air meetings at Upwey and Belgrave when the Gospel rang out clearly to large and attentive audiences. The testimony of young believers to their new-found joy in Christ was at some of these meetings most helpful. Other features were Dr. MacColl's message on Boxing Day – powerful and searching; Rev. Edgar Miller's testimony to God's personal dealings with himself of late, and the revival in his church at Pinaroo, S.A.; Rev. Carment Urquhart's answers to questions on the Second Coming of Christ; and last, but not least, an all-important meeting, when the new Melbourne Bible Institute was discussed.[7]

The beginnings of the Melbourne Bible Institute

It was later said of the MBI that it was 'suggested in Melbourne and started at Upwey'. The relationship between the MGC and the Institute was a profound one. Within two years of the first Upwey Convention, MBI began under the scholarly, Cambridge-educated C.H. Nash, who spoke and taught from 'a full heart the message of the Word as it is written. MBI provided scores, even hundreds, who responded to the Convention message, with a good knowledge of the Bible and training to equip them for service at home and abroad.'[8] H.P. Smith was a founding member of the MBI Council.

The following is an excerpt from the Christmas 1920 MBI Report:

> At this meeting the [recently appointed founding] Principal of the Institute, the Rev. C.H. Nash, outlined the progress made to date, and many present expressed their determination to enrol at the opening for the new year on the 15th February [1921]. Several of these will need to be wage-earners (to pay for their board) as well as students, and ways and means by which they might work part-time were discussed. All present felt that the Melbourne Bible Institute had been inaugurated under the hand of God, to supply a great need of the Church in this land.

For over 50 years, MBI held an annual meeting at the Convention, usually on the morning of Missionary Day. Students present and past, some on furlough, spoke. The meeting would often be handed over to the Principal, C.H. Nash, who before the meeting closed would call 'for those now yielding themselves to the Lord for service at home or abroad, to stand as an indication of their surrender'.

In an address at Upwey several years later, Nash told how he himself had come to Christ:

> Look here, young fellows, I am going to tell you who led me to Jesus Christ. He is a man who had no brains to speak of. He is dead now, and just smiling in glory. He was a man who had no particular intellectual power, and he used to come and talk to me, and I would knock him out every time. But he gave up arguing, and he got me one night on my knees with another man. Both these men ultimately did a mighty work for God; one is alive still. And he, and this non-intellectual and I knelt in that room, and we started kneeling at nine o'clock in the evening, and we finished at three in the morning, and nobody spoke a word. They didn't argue. Not much in argument. Any personal worker will tell you that. It isn't argument the other fellow wants. It is the power of Christ coming into his life and beating him to the ground.[9]

In 1888 Nash encountered the two elements of evangelicalism that were to shape his permanent contribution to Melbourne evangelicalism – the Ridley Hall of H.C.G. Moule and Keswick evangelical piety. Moule by then had already become a convert to Keswick teaching. Although Nash was at Ridley for a year, it was long enough for him to be greatly influenced by Moule. Quietly influential amongst those of the next generation of leaders in Melbourne was Charles George Sandland, who would comment, 'When I read Moule, I heard C.H. Nash speaking.'[10]

A close fellowship existed over the years between the Convention and MBI councils. Amongst those who had been or who would become members of both councils were John M. Griffiths, H.P. Smith, John James (J.J.) Kitchen, D.S. MacColl, W.L. Wright, A. Kenny, Samuel Howell, Alex S. Eggleston, Alfred E. Coombe, J. Oswald Sanders, Leonard E. Buck, Charles G. Sandland, J. Harold McCracken, Ralph C. Davis, Arthur Pocklington, Dr A. Murray Clarke, Eric J. Daley, Graeme G. Smith, Will F. Renshaw, Howard Barclay, Peter E. Rowse, Rev. Dr David J. Price, Rev. J. Beatty, Rev. R.V. Merritt, Rev. J.G. Miller and Rev. H.H.E. Knight. Others, such as Rev. Alex Stevens, were faculty members of MBI and also members of the Convention Council.

At the time of the retirement of the 'honoured and loved founding Principal of MBI, the Rev. C.H. Nash' in 1942, *The Quarterly* reported that more than one-half of all students had entered full-time service. The figures given were: China 86, Australian Aborigines 72, Pacific Islands 62, India 58, Africa 46, South America 19, Japan and Korea 5, other Muslim lands 3, Home Service 182, a total of 533.[11] Over the following years, MBI (BCV/MST) provided workers for numerous denominational and interdenominational missions, evangelistic endeavours, religious instruction in schools, service organisations and the pastoral ministry (ordained and non-ordained).

Upwey 1921–22: increasing missionary interest

The MGC report on the 1921–22 Upwey Convention stated:

> Upwey Convention – This year's Convention at Christmas and New Year at Upwey – the fourth to be held here – was a time of very great blessing. A large increase in the number of friends availing themselves of the opportunity of spending their holidays on the edge of the Dandenongs in fellowship with the Lord's people was an outstanding feature, the number of furnished houses taken being nearly half as many again as in previous years. The presence of the Lord in meeting after meeting was most manifest. There was again early morning prayer daily in the Church Hall, and the Bible readings conducted by Rev. C.H. Nash, Principal of the Melbourne Bible Institute, the latter filling the hall each day. Other meetings deserving of special mention were those addressed by Dr. MacColl, Mr. A.W. ['Cairo'] Bradley, Dr. Northcote Deck, Mr. Geo. T. B. Davis, and Rev. Walter Jarvis.
>
> Foreign Missionary interests were well to the fore, most helpful messages being given by representatives of the China Inland Mission (Mr. and Mrs. C.A. Jamieson), the E.G.M. [Egypt General Mission] (Mr. Bradley), the S.S.E.M [South Seas Evangelical Mission] (Dr. Deck), the S.A.G.M. [South African General Mission] (Miss Bennetts); and the following outgoing Missionaries gave farewell messages: – Mr. and Mrs. Holland and Miss Nowell, leaving for South America; Mr. J.H. Bird, for China; and Miss Jackson, for Mukti, India. It was our privilege to remember, in our offerings to the Lord, beloved missionaries, now on the field, who were at former Upwey Conventions – as outgoing Missionaries, those thus remembered being: Messrs. J.H. Robinson, N. Baker, Dr. Rees, Misses E. Jordan and W. Edwards, now China Inland Missionaries, Miss Grace Chapman, now with the Z.B.M.M. [Zenana Bible & Medical

> Mission], India; and Mr. and Mrs. Neale, with the Australian Aborigines. A sum of over one hundred pounds, including special donations, was contributed for the Lord's work in foreign parts.
>
> ... we had the privilege of helping the local Christians in their work for the Master during the Convention days. On the Lord's Day we conducted eleven meetings in the neighbourhood – early prayer meeting, five ordinary church services, two children's meetings, and three open-airs.[12]

Upwey 1922–23: the best yet

This convention was the last organised under the auspices of the MGC.

> Upwey Convention – As on former occasions, we again have the privilege of saying the last 'Upwey' was the best. The number of the Lord's people gathering from town and country was most encouraging; the oneness of the Spirit pervading the whole assembly and the power of God manifested in the messages were unmistakable evidence of the presence of the Lord. Dr. Northcote Deck was again over from the Solomon Islands, and opened the Word of God with much blessing, as well as representing the foreign mission field. Others who ministered the Word with profit included Rev. D.H. Moore, of London, the Special Commissioner in Australia for the Russian Missionary Society; Rev. C.H. Nash, M.A., who gave an exceedingly helpful series of Bible readings on the Epistle to the Colossians; Rev. S. Beckingham, who is now the pastor of the Belgrave and Upwey churches; Rev. J. Campbell Robinson, Dr. D.S. MacColl, Mr. Frank Varley, and others.
>
> The foreign mission field was well represented by Mr. and Mrs. H.A.C. Allen, Mr. and Mrs. W. Westwood, Mr. and Mrs. E.H. Carne and Misses Garland of

> China; Misses Browne, Gould and Todd, of India; Miss Bennetts, South Africa, and Mr. and Mrs. O. Burgess, Australian Aborigines. Helpful testimonies from outgoing missionaries, i.e., those expecting to leave Australia for the foreign field during the coming year, were given by Misses Minnie Aitken and Effie Varley, the former having been accepted by the China Inland Mission and the latter by the Sudan Interior Mission. The collections and donations for foreign missions amounted to £105/10/5. Each of the nine missionary societies represented at the Convention had a share of this, and we also again remembered the loved missionaries we call 'Upwey missionaries', i.e., those now in their respective fields who were at former Upwey Conventions as outgoing missionaries. Seven such were remembered last year, there were eleven this year. An enjoyable and profitable open-air missionary meeting was held on a fine afternoon by the creek at Forest Park, when the hospitality of Mr. and Mrs. J.M. Griffiths was heartily enjoyed.
>
> The annual 'Upwey Meeting' of the Melbourne Bible Institute took place on another afternoon, with Mr. S. Howell, the Honorary Secretary and Treasurer of the Institute in the chair. Most encouraging reports of the work and prospects were given.[13]

By this time, the convention was growing out of its building and discussions turned to the need for more space:

> Consideration was given to the question of accommodation for future Convention meetings, as the church building this year was not large enough to hold those present at many of the gatherings. A block of land adjoining the church land – on which a marquee for the larger meetings could be erected – has been placed under offer to the Council, and if friends contribute the necessary sum, this will be secured for the benefit of future Upwey Conventions.[14]

The Upwey Convention Council

A meeting on 26 December 1922 was called for the purpose of forming an Upwey Convention Council. The MGC report states:

> During the Convention a permanent Upwey Convention Council was formed. The Council is composed as follows: Mr. J.M. Griffiths (Chairman), Mr. F. Varley (Hon. Treasurer), Mr. H.P. Smith (Hon. Secretary), Rev. S. Beckingham and Mr. W.L. Wright (Executive); Messrs. G.L. Aitken and Herbert Clarke, Dr. Northcote Deck, Messrs. T. Graham and A. Kenny, Dr. J.J. Kitchen, Messrs. W.T. Lawson and Norman Lumsden, Dr. D.S. MacColl, Revs. C.H. Nash and J. Campbell Robinson, Messrs. Ernest Renshaw, W. Rogers, Charles Alfred Sandland and Rev. A.D. Shaw.

H.P. Smith, Frank Varley, Thomas Graham, Ernest Renshaw and Charles Alfred Sandland were members of the MGC Council, under whose auspices the Upwey conventions until this time had been organised. The work was now handed over to this permanent Upwey Council.

The format of the convention, with its teaching on the deepening of the spiritual life and its missionary and prayer emphases, set up by H.P. Smith and other members of the MGC Council, continued.

In a tribute published in 1942 in *The Quarterly* on the death of Frank Varley, the first chairman of the MGC Council, H.P. Smith wrote:

> A feature of the Melbourne Gospel Crusade work for many years had been the holding of holiday-season conventions for the deepening of the spiritual life, and Bentleigh, Mordialloc, Oakleigh, and other outer suburban places were used for Easter Conventions, whilst Eltham, Black Rock and Beaumaris were specially used for Christmas Conventions. For the Christmas-New Year of 1918–19, a special invitation

> came for gatherings at the Union Church at Upwey. This involved renting several furnished houses, but the new move was so blessed of God that no place was seriously thought of for the following Christmas but Upwey, and when the third year came, and there was no thought of going elsewhere for Christmas, it was decided that God had surely chosen Upwey as the home of a permanent Convention, and when, two years later, it was decided to form an Upwey Convention Council to be responsible for the Convention in future, Mr Varley was appointed Hon. Treasurer, and he continued thus until leaving for New Zealand in 1928.[15]

The importance of prayer

Detailed reports, particularly after the 1925–26 Convention, were published by H.P. Smith in *The Quarterly*. In these reports, Smith stressed the importance of prayer:

> The need for much prayer for the work of a Convention was recognised by the provision of a 'prayer room.' Much more prayer, however, is needed for all the 'victory' that a Convention, such as Upwey, should mean in the lives of individuals, and blessings to the Church in this land. Our prayer partners are, therefore, asked to unite with us now in the request to God for more prayer channels – such as our departed brother, 'Praying Hyde of India' – that the next Upwey Convention may – if He tarry – be used of Him for definite work wherever He sees the need.[16]
>
> There was more prayer this year [1925–26]. The early morning prayer meetings nearly every day filled the church building, and some days many with difficulty found room even to kneel. But, better than this, the Spirit of Prayer was present, and whilst in perhaps one or two of the meetings there was a little too much singing, the meetings were yet glorious seasons of quiet, definite waiting upon God. The Prayer Room was

> the scene of many waiting quietly before God, and real work for eternity was done there.[17]

> ... many were more conscious that more prayer was needed. And this we feel is the greatest need of the Convention, as indeed, of all work for God.[18]

Influences on the next generation of leaders

During these years, the spiritual dynamism of this generation was developing the next generation of leaders. They were listening, observing, being taught, yielding their lives to the infilling of the Holy Spirit, being obedient, participating and catching the vision as the living word of God was opened to them. They went out in business life, in university life and in Christian work to prove that God was ever-faithful. There was a forthrightness and definiteness in their experience.

The level of spiritual life engendered in the early conventions, and which inspired young people, can be gauged from a report in *The Quarterly* of a testimony meeting held during the 1925–26 convention:

> That they did have a 'good time' was abundantly proved when the great testimony meeting was held on the Saturday night in the marquee. There, in a meeting that lasted nearly three hours – and it would have gone on until after midnight, only the chairman thought it wise to close when eleven o'clock was near – one after another rose, and in brief, pointed words, told of the Lord's doings in heart and life, until none could doubt that Upwey 1925–26 had been ordered of God, and His blessing was unmistakeable ...[19]

> Not all testified to just experiencing a 'good time'. There were those who had to tell of a 'bad time', for confessions had to be made, things wrong had to be put right, the Lord Himself by His Word had revealed new truth, the Holy Spirit had convicted of sin and of righteousness, and many who had been 'drifting', or

> wilfully going their 'own way', had returned to learn of Him Who is the meek and lowly of heart.[20]

The convention and the Keswick message

While Melbourne had developed its own spiritual dynamics as its convention ministry was developing, in many aspects it paralleled the teaching given at Keswick in England.[21] Although there were no official ties to Keswick, Upwey increasingly identified with it. Until the mid-1930s, apart from overseas missionary leaders who had been invited or drawn to Melbourne by hearing of the Upwey ministry, without exception the Bible teachers were local men.

By 1934, the Upwey Convention was well established and H.P. Smith, as editor and honorary secretary of the Convention, wrote in *The Quarterly*, substantially quoting Dr W. Graham Scroggie:

> The Keswick message is that message to the Christian by which he is shown his need of not only 'eternal life', but 'life more abundantly' (John 10:10), or abounding life; by which he is shown that whilst his deliverance out of Egypt through the Red Sea was very glorious, yet to remain in the wilderness and not go on into Canaan, the land of promise, is very grievous; and that because so many Christians fail here, Paul speaks of some as 'babes in Christ' (1 Corinthians 3 and Hebrews 5) ... Furthermore, that although all Christians are indwelt by the Holy Spirit, yet not all are 'filled with the Spirit', and therefore are 'carnal' and not 'spiritual'; they have 'peace with God' (Romans 5:1), but do not know the 'peace of God' (Philippians 4:7); and, as Dr Scroggie said in an address at Keswick, 'They are living between Easter and Pentecost, on the right side of justification, but the wrong side of sanctification ...
>
> Let us say in our hearts:
>
> I take the promised Holy Ghost,
> I take the power of Pentecost,

To fill me to the uttermost,
'I take' – 'He undertakes.'

I take Thee, blessed Lord,
I give myself to Thee,
And Thou, according to Thy word,
Dost undertake for me.[22]

Keswick teaching and 'definiteness'

Highlighted on the front cover of the same 1934 issue of *The Quarterly*, under the heading 'Keswick teaching', is a reference written by Keswick leader, Canon W. Hay Aitken, on 'Definiteness'. To those who knew H.P. Smith, this word aptly exemplified his life:

> *Definiteness* is what I regard as the most impressive feature of the Keswick teaching. The speakers aim at inducing *definite* personal dealing with God, with a view to the reception of some definite personal, and spiritual acquisition. It may be deliverance from sin, or it may be consecration to God and His service, or it may be the apprehension of the fullness of the Holy Spirit; but in each case definite personal action is claimed, and the 'faith that worketh miracles' still is directed towards a definite issue with a view to a definite result in the soul's condition and experience.
>
> This, I think, is what differentiates Keswick from other Conferences where there is much good and eloquent speaking that leads up to nothing in particular, except a general feeling that it is all very good and very 'nice'.[23]

Writing as editor in the November 1947 issue, H.P. Smith, not knowing that it would be the last issue before his unexpected death, succinctly emphasised aspects of the Keswick message and set out the purposes of the Convention with that definiteness, that hallmark of his Christian experience:

> The 30th annual Upwey Keswick Convention will be held ... for proclaiming the Word of God as messenger after messenger – through a Bible Reading or Convention address – opens that Word, giving various aspects of the Keswick message, with its emphasis on: (1) the Exceeding Sinfulness of Sin, (2) the Way of Cleansing and Renewal, (3) the Life of Full Surrender, (4) the Fullness of the Holy Spirit, and (5) the Path of Sacrifice and Service.
>
> In addition ... there is the necessity of preaching the simple Gospel of Salvation through the Blood of Christ, for many – young people especially – come to these meetings for Christians, who are not yet Christians. Some are Church members, although not yet saved ...
>
> The third great object of the Convention is the Missionary Message – the declaration of God's word that Christians (the 'born again' people) are commanded – in the final words of our Lord Himself – to go into 'all the world and preach the Gospel to every creature.'[24]

Easter conventions

During the early Upwey days, the MGC had also been holding Easter conventions for the deepening of the spiritual life that were an extension of the Saturday night meetings held at the Federal. Locations included the Queensberry Street Mission Carlton, Bentleigh, Mordialloc, Oakleigh, Williamstown and other 'outer' suburbs.

At the first meeting of the MGC Council when it was formalised in 1920, an Easter Convention was planned for the coming Good Friday. It was to be held at the Stapleford Mission at Williamstown, and then at Bentleigh on Easter Monday. There were morning, afternoon and evening meetings, and those being invited to speak were Thomas Porter, who spoke at the first MGC convention at Upwey; C.H. Nash, before he became Principal of MBI; Revs Robert Kelly, J.T. Kelly and J.T. Piercey; and Oliver Burgess. At this time, the meetings, which were often referred to as 'Easter Victorious Life' gatherings, were usually led by Frank Varley, W.L. Wright and H.P. Smith.

Other locations in Melbourne included East Brunswick and Palmer Street Mission, Fitzroy. In addition, Thomas Graham, the chairman of the MGC, spoke at the Hobart Easter Convention, and H.B. Denniston, a Melbourne businessman who was president of the Evangelisation Society, was the special speaker at a convention at Oatlands in Tasmania.

In 1952, after the move from Upwey due to land acquisition by the government, the first Easter Convention was held at Belgrave Heights. The numbers attending this four-day convention went on to far exceed those attending the Christmas-New Year (now Summer) conventions.

The Upwey Extension Movement

The MGC held other conventions in Melbourne at opportune times, such as over the 1932 and 1933 King's Birthday weekends at Essendon.

The first country convention arranged by the Upwey Council was at Warrnambool over Easter 1932. The speakers were D.S. MacColl and C.N. Lack, both Upwey speakers.[25]

Following this convention, the 'newly formed Upwey Fellowship at Kerang arranged a Victorious Life Convention for the King's Birthday week-end [June 1932], which proved to be a time of very real blessing to many'.[26] Future plans were made for conventions to be held annually over the Labour Day weekend. This convention was 'the outcome of a deep experience enjoyed by some of the young folk of Kerang at Upwey'.[27]

Under the auspices of the MGC and led by Leonard Buck, convention meetings were held at Gormandale and Traralgon over Easter 1934. The first convention at Portland was held the following year. In 1937, the first Wimmera Keswick convention was held at Warracknabeal. Shepparton held its first convention over the King's Birthday weekend in June 1940, with Ballarat and Geelong holding their first conventions, linked to the newly formed Upwey Extension Movement, under the enthusiastic and capable leadership of Arthur Pocklington, in June 1941.

The Upwey Convention Council inaugurated what was called the Upwey Extension Movement at Christmas 1940. Pocklington was appointed to assist H.P. Smith in the general work of the Convention and also to be the organising secretary of the extension work. The Movement was formed to assist the existing country conventions, and 'to arrange Conventions in other locations as the Lord may lead, to take the Convention message further into many parts of Victoria'. The work grew rapidly. It also meant that those who could not attend Upwey because of seasonal rural conditions, or distance, could attend, and many found these country conventions to be a source of much blessing.

At the time of H.P. Smith's death at the close of 1947, reports had been received of Arthur Pocklington's work with conventions at Ballarat, Echuca, Geelong, the Hamilton District, Kerang, Nullawarre, Portland, Shepparton, Traralgon, Wangaratta and Warracknabeal (Wimmera Victorious Life Convention) in Victoria, as well as Wagga Victorious Life Convention in New South Wales and Naracoorte (South-Eastern Convention) in South Australia. Some of the work had developed as a result of the MGC Motor Van Ministry.

Speakers in almost all instances were from Victoria or missionaries on furlough. In 1948, Pocklington, in his role of secretary of the Upwey Extension Movement, reported that 18 conventions had been held during the year. He wrote:

> We record our gratitude to the Lord for the abounding blessing that has resulted. In accordance with the primary aim of the Movement, the message of the Victorious Christian Life has been given special

> emphasis by those chosen to minister the Word. As a result many have been led to a higher plane of Christian experience, and are proving the reality of the promises as, 'Sin shall not have dominion over you' (Romans 6:14) and, 'Greater is He that is in you than he that is in the world' (1 John 4:4).
>
> In most gatherings there has been a splendid spirit of liberty. This is due largely to the right place which is given to the Scriptures as the infallible Word of God, and to the stress laid upon the atoning death and triumphant resurrection of the Lord Jesus, together with the indispensable ministry of the Holy Spirit.
>
> One of the heartening features of many conventions is to observe the way the Lord's people really feast upon the Word of God and gain strength for service thereby. Spiritual quickening must ever be 'according to Thy Word.'
>
> As well as the message of sanctification for the believer, the Gospel of salvation to the lost has been proclaimed with fruitful results at all centres throughout the year. The missionary message has been well received, and in addition many young people have responded to God's call for service.[28]

Dr Stuart Piggin has well said:

> It has been argued that the joint influences of Upwey, including the Upwey Extension Movement (which carried the Keswick message throughout country Victoria), and the Melbourne Bible Institute [now the Melbourne School of Theology], have had more impact on evangelical life in Victoria than any other institutions.[29]

CHAPTER 10 Saturdays with the Melbourne Gospel Crusade

Early activities at the Federal

The Saturday meetings at the Federal reflected the significant change that had taken place in H.P. Smith's life: his desire to be the man that God had called him to be; to know the abiding presence of Christ in his daily living as he experienced the deeper life in Christ; and to encourage others through Christian fellowship and Keswick teaching. Determined to use the gifts that God had given him in his service, Smith ably led and administered these meetings, all the time a willing and obedient follower of Christ's. An essential outworking of these meetings was evangelism, bringing the message of God's love for sinners, who were perishing without believing in the Lord Jesus Christ as Saviour, to as many people as possible at home and overseas. With this in mind, he opened up the entertaining rooms at the Federal for meetings for Christians, particularly for the deepening of the spiritual life, on a Saturday night.

Recollections of those who attended

For those who attended the meetings – whether at the Federal or later at other locations – the teaching they gained on the infilling of the Holy Spirit for service was to keep Melbourne uniquely on course. It spared Melbourne, and later the convention movement, from developing a bias in its ministries that could result in ineffectiveness or disarray.

Ernest Renshaw, an original member of the Crusade Council, in a tribute written on the death of H.P. Smith, recounted:

> Away in the country, I had first heard from Christian friends – commercial travellers – of the times of blessing being experienced at the Federal, where earnest Christians were gathering week by week seeking a higher experience of Divine grace. The Saturday night meetings at the Federal continued to grow. I cannot forget the spiritual power manifested in these meetings.[1]

Charles G. Sandland, nephew of Charles A. Sandland, an original member of the MGC Council, recalled that as a boy he was taken by his uncle to the Saturday night meetings at the Federal. The first time recalled was in 1915. He spoke of the influence of his 'Uncle Alf' on his life and said of the meetings at the Federal, 'There was a question and answer type teaching where the first Mrs. [Nettie] Smith, asked the question and her husband helped with the answer.' Referring to his uncle who had encouraged him in his spiritual walk, he said, 'He was not a highly educated man but he was educated in the Spirit.'[2] His Uncle Alf was the stalwart who led the MGC open-air meetings in Melbourne streets for more than 20 years until the time of his death.

The singing of hymns was a feature of the meetings. Many hymns came from the missions of Moody and Sankey, and from the Torrey-Alexander and Chapman-Alexander missions. These were augmented by those from *Hymns of Consecration and Faith* – hymns on deeper life teaching compiled for use in the early Keswick Conventions in England. These hymns, also used at Upwey for two or three decades, brought teaching, spiritual vitality and blessing to the large gatherings.

The Saturday night speakers and messages

In 1920, still in the shadow of World War I, a series of four special addresses were given at the Federal on Saturday nights by Frank Varley, chairman of the MGC, on 'The antichrist', 'The great tribulation', 'The last great war' and 'Today's world outlook'.

Series of Bible talks were often given on consecutive Saturday nights. For example, a series was given in 1926 by H.B. Denniston, a well-known city businessman and president of the ESA. It was reported that this series of addresses,

> given with the aid of a lantern, was a marked success. There was an attendance of from 500 to 600 each night ... and some who did not yet know the Lord as Saviour were drawn by the lantern views ... The addresses, reviewing 'The Rise and Fall of World Empires and the Coming Kingdom,' were very informative, and at times the appeal was a powerful one. The non-Christian was warned by the fulfilments of God's Word in the past to 'flee from the wrath to come' and accept now the free salvation offered through the death of Christ on Calvary's Cross, and the Christian was reminded of the certainty of our Lord's return, for as surely as He came the first time 'to bear the sins of the many,' in fulfilment of prophecy, so He is coming a second time, 'apart from sin unto salvation' – the King 'to reign in righteousness.'[3]

Another report compiled by H.P. Smith mentioned that other Saturday nights had 'a full share of missionary messages', which included Dr and Mrs Howard Taylor of CIM each speaking on separate nights. Other addresses were given by missionaries representing the Japan Rescue Mission, Ceylon and India General Mission, Ramabai Mukti Mission and Australian Aborigines Mission. Amongst the missionaries who were farewelled at these meetings was Cyril Edwards, who was on his way to China.

The MGC's 1926 Annual Report concluded, 'As we look out and see the appalling need on all hands, our prayer is, "Even so, come, Lord Jesus."'[4]

During the earlier part of 1927, it was mentioned there were 'Some splendid Saturday night meetings':

> The first very large gathering was addressed by Mr. C.J. Rolls [Superintendent of the New Zealand Bible Training Institute], a few weeks after Upwey, on his return from Tasmania en route for N.Z. The other extra large meetings were two Lantern Lectures given by Rev. R.V. Bingham, General Director of the Sudan Interior Mission. The first was a Lecture on 'Prophecy Proved by Photography', for which the hall was packed with 600 odd people, and many had to be turned away.[5]

By request, this lecture was repeated before an overflowing congregation in Collins Street Baptist Church. Bingham's 'second lecture, entitled "Savagery and Salvation in the Sudan," was declared by many to have been the best missionary lecture they had heard'.[6]

Addresses at that meeting were also given by the Principal of MBI, C.H. Nash, and Miss Effie Varley, who had graduated from MBI and was now home on furlough from Nigeria after four years' absence. She was amongst a number of others who gave missionary addresses. Other special meetings on Saturday nights at this time were the Egypt General Mission lantern lecture and the farewell to Dr & Mrs N.J. Griffiths of the Bolivian Indian Mission. Outgoing missionaries gave short testimonies, and Rev. C.H. Nash concluded with the valedictory address.[7]

'Unmistakable blessing'

After moving to Protestant Hall, the Saturday night meetings continued with 'unmistakable blessing'. Two of the meetings were addressed by the evangelist Rev. W.P. Nicholson, and 'the collections taken up considerably helped our Foreign Missionaries' Fund'. The addresses were 'most helpful openings of God's Word and, it was believed, of lasting benefit to very many'.[8] Another meeting was addressed by Rev. E.H. Carne, lately returned from China, who told of his capture by brigands and his release through prayer, while Frank Varley gave lantern-assisted addresses on 'The Lord's return'.[9]

The Saturday night meetings in the city that immediately followed the conventions at Upwey became one of the regular locations around Melbourne where 'Echoes of Upwey' meetings were held. Other places were Prahran, Brunswick and Sandringham besides various country locations.

In addition to the sound Bible teaching, these regular meetings emphasised mission, and testimonies by missionaries on furlough were highlighted. In the early 1930s, three-quarters of an hour in special prayer was also set aside before each Saturday evening meeting.

Meetings aimed especially at young people were also set up. In a report for the first meeting in 1931, H.P. Smith wrote:

> It is hoped that meetings will continue, D.V. [God willing], every Saturday night, as they have done for the past nearly twenty years ... Prayer is asked that they may continue to fulfil the purpose of God and receive His blessing for all concerned.
>
> ... one Saturday night each month, beginning with March, will be handed over for a Young Peoples' Meeting.[10]

The meetings for young people progressed well with various district Christian Endeavour Unions leading, as well as 'the University Evangelical Union and the Prahran Spring Street Mission Young Peoples' Fellowship'.[11]

Review of the Saturday evening ministry

Some indication of the effectiveness of the crusade and convention ministries can be seen from the increasing number of reports from evangelistic and missionary organisations published in *The Quarterly* during the 1930s and 1940s. Many of these involved graduates from the MBI who had been significantly influenced by the convention and crusade ministries.

In a review in *The Quarterly* of February 1939, H.P. Smith

– recalling the Saturday meetings that had started at the Federal, then moved to the Protestant Hall and later the Keswick Book Depot in Collins Street – wrote of the progression of these meetings:

> Over 30 years ago a monthly Saturday afternoon prayer meeting for Foreign Missions was started in Melbourne by the friends, who later formed the Melbourne Gospel Crusade, and this continues on the first Saturday of each month (January excepted), and for the past 14 or 15 years has been held in the Keswick [Book] Rooms, Collins Street. The prayer meeting – for all Missions as the Lord leads – commences at five o'clock, and is followed by a Fellowship Tea at 6.30; after which the friends gather round The Lord's Table, and conclude with special prayer and a short Bible talk; or, as was done on the first Saturday of this month, form themselves into a missionary meeting to welcome or farewell a returning or departing missionary.[12]

The Children's Evangelistic Meetings

The holding of Saturday afternoon Children's Evangelistic Meetings was a matter of priority for the MGC Council. The commencement of children's meetings was discussed in 1920, the year in which the Council was formalised. The first Children's Meetings were held in 1921, although they do not appear to have been held on a regular basis until the following year when a Quarterly Children's Meeting in the Protestant Hall is mentioned in the minutes. The Quarterly Children's Evangelistic Meeting became a regular part of the MGC's program. With the commencement of *The Quarterly* in 1926, there was this request for prayer:

> friends are asked to pray that the Holy Spirit will truly be in charge and do a work in many young hearts as the Gospel message in simple language is told. The Rev W. Fletcher of the Christian Missionary Alliance work

> in India, will give the message, and we expect great things from a bright and joyous yet deeply Spiritual meeting.[13]

In a 1927 report, H.P. Smith mentioned that Quarterly Children's Evangelistic Meetings were held at 3.30 p.m. on the third Saturday in February, May, August and November. At the conclusion of each, 'A plain tea was given to the children, and an effort was always made to have a Missionary Lecture in the evening, to which the older children were invited to stay.'[14] News of the meetings was spread by printing special invitations that were sent to people who wanted to use them, either amongst their own friends or relatives, their Sunday School classes or state school children who might be taking Scripture Instruction.

A young 'Andrew'

After the July meeting in 1931, a nine-year-old boy went home from a Saturday afternoon Children's Evangelistic Meeting wanting to make sure that his three younger brothers were converted. The following night he drew up some chairs in the home and on that Sunday evening held a service for his brothers. His address was about the little boy with the barley loaves and fishes and the feeding of the 5,000 as recorded in John 6:9.

After the address and the singing of *Almost persuaded now to believe*, he invited his three brothers comprising the congregation to give their lives to the Lord Jesus and believe in him. As each one separately responded, they were counselled to read their Bibles and to attend Christian Endeavour. Then he wrote on a piece of paper for each one of his brothers saying that they had been converted at that meeting.

Nearly 20 years later, the youngest of the brothers, then holding office in the Melbourne University Evangelical Union, in a testimony given to a crowded Sunday afternoon young people's meeting at the Upwey Convention, recounted how at the age of four, his eldest brother had led him to the Lord at a meeting in their home following a MGC Children's Evangelistic Meeting, a testimony that was published in *The Quarterly*. Many years later, another brother gave a similar testimony of his conversion at a meeting of Bible college students away in the highlands of Papua New Guinea.

A change to monthly meetings

In 1931 it was decided to trial the holding of the Children's Meetings on a monthly instead of a quarterly basis. After six months these proved to be

> an unmistakable success ... because God is using and blessing them ...
>
> A meeting of from 200 to 300 children of all classes, and drawn from city and suburbs, gathered together for an evangelistic message, with inquiry room work afterwards ... followed by tea (including a cup of tea for parents and others waiting to take children home) [which] involves work, and very varied work, and but for willing hands taking up this burden the meetings, and the spiritual work for eternity done through them, would cease.[15]

During that year, a birthday register was set up for children attending the meetings, and 660 names were entered. Each child was remembered on their birthday with a birthday text card and a tract suitable for their age. Friends were asked to pray that this sowing of the gospel and the word of God would yield an abundant harvest.

While reports of these meetings were not subsequently published in *The Quarterly*, meetings continued although at times there was a change in location. For example, the publicity for the meeting at 3 p.m. on Saturday 21 July 1934 indicated that the Children's Evangelistic Meeting for the MGC, over the name of Mr. Smith at 315 Collins Street, was to be held at the Congregational Metropolitan Mission, Rathdowne Street, Carlton, and to be followed by a 'Children's Tea' at 5 p.m. The speaker was Robert Edgar, who for many years was associated with the Leprosy Mission.

The Sunday morning free breakfast

Initiative followed initiative. Even after Saturday's activities, a more recently appointed MGC Council member, Frank Elmes, and friends of the MGC were also involved in a Sunday morning free breakfast held in a hall in Brien Lane off Little Bourke Street, where '170 men linked up in song to more or less harmony,' singing 'Tell me the story softly, With earnest tones and grave, Remember I'm the sinner whom Jesus came to save.' After breakfast there was a short gospel message.[16]

In a report in November 1926, it was mentioned,

> Most are comparatively young and obviously out of work ... I am stirred by the sound of singing ...
>
> 'Remember I'm the sinner
> Whom Jesus came to save.'
>
> ... One young man, who had spent the night on some bags at the wharf, was on his face before God. His mother's prayers are answered. He is heard to say tenderly, 'Oh, won't she be pleased.' He is taken in hand and clothed and fed. He is homeless and out of work.[17]

There had been '7,045 meals served for the year and 1,750 beds provided'.[18]

Regular MGC ministries

At that time the following MGC ministries were still continuing.

- *Children's Monthly Evangelistic Meetings.* On the third Saturday of each month at the Protestant Hall, at 3 p.m., where between 250 and 300 children gathered.

- *Monthly Prayer Meeting for Foreign Missions.* At Protestant Hall, the first Saturday of each month, at 5 p.m.
- *Saturday Night Meetings for Christians.* Protestant Hall, 7.45 p.m. On the first Saturday of each month the meeting was a Young People's Meeting.
- *Open-air Preaching.* At the corner of Flinders and Degraves Streets in the city on Sundays at 7.30 p.m., and on Sydney Road, Brunswick on Fridays at 8 p.m.
- *Wednesday Night Bible Reading.* Keswick Tea Rooms, 7.45 p.m., 315 Collins Street.
- *Visiting Sister (Miss Emma Smith).* Visiting the homes of children who attended the monthly Children's Evangelistic Meetings, visiting hospitals and taking Scripture Instruction classes in schools.
- *Gospel Motor Van Work in Country Districts* – for which prayer was always requested.

Members of the Council were also active in street outreach and in a special gospel meeting at night on a Saturday in each month. They called this the 'Bourke Street Stunt', and it is discussed in a later chapter on the MGC's open-air activities.

CHAPTER 11 The Open-air Ministry

The most important commitments of the MGC included preaching the gospel to people of all ages wherever they were in city and country, encouraging missionaries and mission societies in their obedience to 'go into all the world', and arranging meetings for the deepening of the spiritual life of the Christian.

The magnitude of the work initiated by the small group of men on the MGC Council led by H.P. Smith staggers the imagination. They exemplified and inspired others in how the work could be done. It just wasn't talk: they prayed, planned well, then went out and engaged and persevered in the battle for souls. They brought others in to join them and encouraged other organisations in their gospel work. There was no sense of competition – it was always to encourage and to support each other in achieving the common goal.

Under Smith's leadership, the MGC Open-air Ministry led the way for others 'to go and do likewise'. It resulted in an explosion of evangelical activity that came to its zenith in the years following World War I. At the same time it provided a seamless transition of workers and leaders for the next generation. This chapter tells just a little of the story of MGC open-air evangelism in Melbourne's city and suburbs.

Open-air evangelism in the city

The 'Bourke Street Stunt'

One of the earliest evangelistic activities undertaken after the formation of the MGC was the 'Bourke Street Stunt'.

This involved members of the MGC Council on a Saturday afternoon each month undertaking 'a thorough canvass of Bourke Street for about an hour when special card invitations were extended to all and sundry to attend an occasional special night when the simple Gospel would be presented'.

The following entry from the MGC minutes of 18 May 1920 indicated the priority given to evangelistic witness:

> In the matter of the proposed special Gospel preaching on a Saturday night, it was decided to have the first of such meetings on the first Saturday in June (5th), preceded by a 'Bourke Street Stunt'. Bros. Graham and Varley were chosen as preachers and there were to be at least two solos. Those who were willing to be workers to be invited to a special prayer conference gathering some days previous to 5th June.

In a report six years later in 1926, it was noted that

> 'A Bourke Street Stunt' night was held on the last Saturday in June. On a specially arranged 'Stunt' night a Gospel meeting is held instead of the meeting for Christians, and Bourke and other streets are paraded by willing workers with invitations to the Gospel meeting. Many people standing about the streets are invited three or four times to the meeting by different workers and many come. Others have to be brought. Mr. Hamilton gave a glorious Gospel message, and afterwards several professed conversion.[1]

Encouraging responses to the 'Bourke Street Stunt' continued throughout the 1920s, and these activities preceded evangelistic meetings at which Norman Lumsden, Thomas Graham and Frank Varley were often the missioners.

Open-air meetings

Another of the initial areas of evangelism in which the members of the MGC were involved was open-air meetings in the city of Melbourne led by Charles A. Sandland. Various locations were tried, including Princes Bridge, the Yarra Bank and areas in Little Collins Street close to the Town Hall. However, changing traffic conditions and the introduction of electric trams to the city necessitated moves from time to time. The Yarra Bank open-air meetings, as distinct from the Sunday afternoon preaching conducted there by H.P. Smith, continued on a monthly basis. Eventually, at the suggestion of the police, it was decided to hold the Sunday evening meetings at the corner of Flinders and Degraves Streets opposite the railway station. This was the location used for the open-air meetings from the mid-1920s until the 1940s and beyond.

Opposition

As expected there was strong opposition experienced at the Sunday evening open-air meetings. The MGC minutes as early as 20 July 1920 mention that at one of the meetings,

> There having been such disorderly opposition to our Gospel preaching of late by members of (chiefly) irresponsible youths, Bro. Varley mentioned that he had spoken to the police authorities and that they were willing to have a constable around the ring for a few weeks and practically promised to break up the gang of opponents.

This helped for a time, but only while there was a police presence. Frank Varley said that he 'had seen the sergeant in charge of the district and that he had promised all the help possible as he was in full sympathy with the work'. This promise was fulfilled, as it was noted at the next meeting, 'To their surprise, in the middle of interjections and noise, plain clothes police had pulled out four of the troublemakers with the result that quiet reigned.' The sergeant was visited by Mr Varley and thanked for the help given. There was a sequel when 'The case came up at the South Melbourne Court when two of the interjectors were charged with disorderly conduct. Bros. Renshaw and Sandland were present and confirmed the statement of the police. Both interjectors were fined One Pound and were severely cautioned by the Magistrate.'

Many people gathered to hear the gospel week by week. Special prayer was requested, particularly when government by-laws were being proposed that might stop open-air preaching in the streets.

Yarra Bank: reaching the masses with the gospel

The MGC members had an unrestricted vision for reaching the masses where they were. Due to decreasing attendances on the Yarra Bank in the winter of 1921, there was prayer and discussion as to whether they should continue at that location or move and use another strategy. Enquiries followed about the availability and the cost of hiring venues such as 'Bourke Street theatres, suburban theatres or Town Halls'. However, the regular open-air meetings continued at the Yarra Bank. This was the people's popular forum in Melbourne for speakers propounding ideas – political and almost every other – for the solving of the world's problems. It was something akin to London's Hyde Park, Sydney's Domain and perhaps Mars Hill in the time of St Paul. The speakers were constantly heckled and harangued amid storms of interjections.

It was amongst this multitude of voices that H.P. Smith, with Henry Varley and others at times, preached the gospel. Onlookers were intrigued to see this tall, well-dressed gentleman preaching the gospel under such conditions. A report in 1926 noted that there had been professed conversions at meetings near the Town Hall in Little Collins Street and at the Yarra Bank, 'Some of which have proved to be very genuine.'[2] The meetings near the Town Hall would 'invariably last from two to two and a half hours'.

Melbourne Cup Day

The initiative of the members knew no bounds, for in 1922 the minutes record that Charles A. Sandland had taken 'a small band of eight men and women for open-air witness to Flemington Racecourse on Cup Day, which had been well worthwhile'. This activity continued over many years. Charles G. Sandland and Leonard Buck both recounted many years later, as did many MBI students, having participated in open-air meetings at the racecourse on Melbourne Cup Day, where the gospel had been preached.

Lives transformed

There was an interesting case of 'casting your bread upon the waters and finding it after many days' (Ecclesiastes 11:1). A woman, who six years previously heard the gospel at the early open-air location over Princes Bridge, and who for the past six years had been living on a farm in the country, returned to Melbourne. She went over Princes Bridge to see if the gospel preaching still took place. On being informed by someone who knew that the open-air group now had a stand 'somewhere in the City but didn't know where', she returned across the bridge and stumbled on the meeting in Flinders Street at the Degraves Street corner. Recognising the participants, she made herself known to one of the lady workers and there was great joy as she accepted the Lord Jesus Christ as her Saviour.

About this time, there were proposals to stop open-air preaching in the city.[3] However, the MGC Council noted that there was not as much traffic on a Sunday night that could cause a problem as on other days. The incentive of the MGC was that:

> We have a glorious Gospel message to declare, the people need the Gospel message, and here is a place where, within their hearing, it can be proclaimed. Let our prayers continue that some hearing it shall believe, and believing shall call upon the name of the Lord and be saved.[4]

Many gathered week by week to hear the gospel preached and receive tracts explaining the way of salvation. Often results were not known at the time, but letters received later told of lives transformed.

One young fellow who regularly listened to the open-air preaching had to move to the country. Later he wrote:

> I do not notice the lonely bush now, for I have my Bible, which I open and study every night. To impress it upon my mind, I write down what I have read and then anything that seems to be related to the study; also anything I have read or heard at meetings touching on the particular reading. Once I used to harvest and play football and cricket on Sundays. I feel that Sunday School work will be a help to me in my studies.
>
> I praise the Lord that He has enabled me to step out, and let the old world know that I follow Him, and that He will be always close to me, and that I might always do and say what is right in His sight. Secondly I pray that my people, through His grace, may be brought out of darkness into light.
>
> Once I used to be a first-class hand at swearing. I have had many anxious moments thinking and praying that I would not be tempted. Well, I was breaking in a heifer ... with her nose in the bail and just a few more inches to go, suddenly the rope parted, and I almost turned a back somersault. When I regained my feet the cow was at the other end of the paddock and I was feeling like nothing in particular. I opened my mouth, and to my surprise said, 'Amen, Praise the Lord.' Everybody present stared in amazement. Hallelujah!
>
> And I want to tell you that every Wednesday evening I am with you in spirit at the Keswick meeting, and that at all times I bring you all before the Lord that He may be with you and prosper you in the good work that you are doing in His name.[5]

Open-air evangelism in the suburbs

It was in 1926 that open-air meetings were first mentioned as being held in the suburbs, and usually on a Friday evening. Locations noted were Northcote, Westgarth, Thornbury, Fairfield, Clifton Hill, North Fitzroy and Ascot Vale. A small band of workers would commence the meeting, and when folk came out into the streets, they were given a short gospel message for ten to fifteen minutes.

One young fellow of 16 wrote to Charles A. Sandland after one of the meetings of 'that wonderful Friday night', and when 'they met a week later his face shone, telling more clearly than words of the change in his heart; subsequently his continued presence at meetings seeking deeper things told the same story.'[6] Many others were counselled, came to a decision and were followed up. More meetings were held in Moonee Ponds, Camberwell, Elsternwick, Northcote, Moonee Ponds and Footscray.

In the mid-1930s, it was reported that:

> The last three months have again seen steady progress whilst holding forth the Word of Life ... One outstanding aspect of the work is the number of Christians that one comes in contact with, and lately quite a number have voluntarily stepped out from amongst the audience, have accepted a tract, and then in a few words have given a real live testimony. The effect of this upon the crowd has often been electric, when they see that one of their number, as it were, can step out and testify to the very things that are asserted by the speakers.[7]

Sometimes these meetings went for two hours.

Use of the magic lantern

From 1933, Charles A. Sandland and a regular helper (and son-in-law) Will Collier, used a lantern with slides in the open-air to help in the preaching of the gospel in the suburbs. They wrote:

> The usual practice is to tack a sheet upon a wall, preferably on a vacant allotment, and set up the lantern. By this means no by-law is infringed and the street does not become blocked. As soon as the light flashes on the sheet the people begin to gather; several slides of Switzerland are shown to attract attention, then slides ... showing strongly the contrast between the heathen and unregenerate man ...
>
> It is hard to give accurately the numbers attending, but on Friday nights often between 150 and 200 have listened, not counting between 20 to 40 children. But usually about 100 adults listen attentively for well over an hour.[8]

The so-called 'magic lantern' used a concave mirror at the back of a light source – thought in the case of Charles A. Sandland to have been a battery-lit electric globe. The mirror directed light through a small sheet of glass (a 'slide') and then a lens at the front of the lantern. On the surface of the slide was the painted or photographic image to be projected. The lens was adjusted to focus the slide at the distance of the projection screen, which could be simply a white sheet or wall, and it formed an enlarged image of the slide on the screen. Photographs on the slide, as well as texts from Scripture, made the use of the lantern ideal for the presentation of the gospel.

Use of the magic lantern spreads to the city

Following the success of the lantern in the suburbs, in 1935 Charles A. Sandland, with the support of his son (Upwey pianist) Mac Sandland and evangelist Eric Clarkson, began using the lantern at the Flinders and Degraves Streets meeting.

Of the first meeting, it was reported that, 'A big crowd gathered and watched slides while hearing the way of salvation. Many made decisions, accepting the perfect sacrifice for their sins. Pray that many more may be brought into the glorious liberty and saving power of Christ.'[9] In a report on the successful use of the lantern in open-air preaching, Eric Clarkson wrote:

> the message reaches the mind through eye-gate as well as ear-gate. One night the text, 'What shall it profit a man' etc was thrown on the sheet, and with it the words, 'PROFIT – LOSS – EXCHANGE' were emphasised. Next day I was told that a business man had been standing in the crowd, and the words on the sheet so impressed him that he said, 'I could not get them out of my mind. Even when I went to bed I could see them.' Many who have not received the message through ear-gate have been awakened by what they have seen.[10]

The lantern continued to be used during the 1930s for the Sunday night open-air meetings at Degraves Street opposite the station, 'with definite blessing'. Charles A. Sandland commented that he was 'always glad of the help of Melbourne Bible Institute students and others, several of whom stand with me every week'.

The home call of Charles Alfred Sandland

It was a great loss for the Open-air Ministry when Charles A. Sandland was suddenly called home during an operation in March 1939 following an eye injury. In a tribute to him in *The Quarterly* at the time, H.P. Smith wrote:

> For nearly 20 years [Charles Alfred Sandland] had been a member of the Council of the Melbourne Gospel Crusade, as well as an active worker in open-air preaching on the Yarra Bank, or other places in the city every Sunday, and on Friday nights in various suburbs. His help with the work of the Gospel van all the years it was running, and with the holiday Convention gatherings of the Crusade, was always most valuable, and he could always be relied upon. He was a foundation member of the Upwey Convention Council, and for years had his own house-party at Upwey where

> he entertained missionaries and others. He was also for years on the council of the United Aborigines Mission, and ready also with advice and practical help. On the Sunday previous [he was at his] usual post in Degraves St., opposite Flinders St. Station, for open-air preaching with the aid of the lantern; and on the previous day [8 March 1939], occupying his usual place in the monthly Melbourne Gospel Crusade missionary prayer meeting, and afterwards taking his place at the Lord's Table, as he had done on the first Saturday of each month for years.[11]

The tribute not only mentioned the wide work of the MGC but also the commitment of one of its Council members to leading by precept and example in its ministry. His nephew, Charles G. Sandland, said that it was his uncle's life and testimony that had made an enormous impact on his own life. The nephew became one of the significant leaders in the next generation of Melbourne's evangelical leadership.

Open-air evangelism from the 1930s onwards

As the 1920s progressed into the 1930s, an increasing number of open-air meetings were undertaken by other groups in fellowship with the MGC, such as the work done by George Hall and Leonard Buck in Bourke Street, opposite the large Myer store.

During the 1930s, a variety of reports in *The Quarterly* mentioned a number of those who had mainly worked in the open air in Melbourne and its suburbs, listed in Table 2.

Table 2: List of individuals involved in open-air preaching in Melbourne and its suburbs

Name	Affiliation	Location
Walter F. Betts (Rev.)	Fitzroy Methodist Mission	Streets and lanes
Leonard Buck	George Hall's city work	Bourke Street Open-air, opposite Myer Shrine of Remembrance construction site Lunch Hour Open-air Convention Open-air
Eric Clarkson	ESA, MGC	Evangelist Convention Open-air Methodist Open-air Factory mission
Jack Eddy & family		Corner of Russell and Bourke Streets in the CBD
Will B. Collier	MGC	Flinders and Degraves Streets Open-air
Colin Ferguson	Australian Bible Motor Van Ministry	
Stan Frost	MGC	MGC Van Ministry
L.G. Gray		Open-air Sunday Schools at Preston, Fitzroy and Brunswick
Jim Grewar	MGC	MGC Van Ministry
J. Grogan	MGC	MGC Van Ministry
T. Grogan	Pocket Testament League	On the wharves Children's Church, Collingwood
George Hall		Bourke Street Open-air, opposite Myer Other city work
H.H. Janetski	ESA	Evangelist Factories and on the waterfront
Norman C. Lumsden	ESA, MBI	Evangelist Factory ministries
Jack Neilsen Converted in the open air at Trentham	ESV, MGC	Open-air Sunday Schools in the streets and lanes of Fitzroy and Collingwood

Robert Pocklington	ESA	
C.A. Sandland	MGC	Flinders and Degraves Streets Open-air Bourke Street Open-air, opposite Myer
C.G. Sandland		Convention Open-air
Macleod Sandland		Flinders and Degraves Streets Open-air
H.P. Smith	MGC	Yarra Bank Open-air
S.P. Waddingham		Convention Open-air

The urgent need for open-air preaching

H.P. Smith wrote on the importance of open-air preaching in an editorial for *The Quarterly* in August 1939:

> There is no greater need in this world today than the open-air preaching of the Gospel of Christ. This may seem to be a bold statement, and some may call it a foolish saying, but it will stand investigation.
>
> For our necessary Christian witness we are commanded to go 'into all the world and preach the Gospel to every creature.' Because of the need of the world in these troublous times – and the people are the world – many thoughtful men and women can see no remedy for the ills – governmental or individual – that surround us but a real change of heart for the people, such as has taken place in the past in the lives of many, and still takes place in the hearts of some through the preaching of the Gospel ...
>
> What hope is there for the people, who never hear the Gospel message, knowing the change of heart, or experiencing the new life ...?
>
> How many open-air meetings are there in our cities? One to every church? Far from it ... How shall they hear without a preacher? ... We are to 'go'; and just as

> the foreign missionary takes the Gospel to the people wherever they may be ...
>
> But what are we to preach? ... 'let me preach Jesus and the resurrection and there will be power' ...
>
> We can preach much about the Gospel, and fail to preach the Gospel ... 'the Gospel' which alone is 'the power of God unto salvation' ...
>
> 'Let the stern facts of sin and judgment be fearlessly proclaimed, in the power of the Spirit, and we shall see more broken hearts. Let more be said of the holiness of God. Let the trumpet-call of repentance be sounded forth, preparing the way for the gracious invitation which can only be understood by the weary and heavy-laden ... in no spirit of harsh denunciation or conscious superiority, but with the tenderness and love which are the fruit of the Holy Spirit Himself, by whose power such a message can alone be effective.'[12]

Into the 1940s and beyond, MBI students regularly participated in the Open-air Ministry on Flinders Street. A report on the work of the MBI in November 1946 mentioned that:

> This term the meetings at our 'Open Air Cathedral' in Degraves Street have been somewhat hindered by adverse weather conditions where meetings have been held. There has been a noticeable lessening of the interruptions usually encountered, and we can bless God for souls who have sought and found the Lord Jesus Christ as Saviour.[13]

With regards to the Open-air Ministries, the MGC had opened up a way that others followed. One was the influential evangelical Kew Baptist Church, which regularly held an open-air meeting on a street corner in the busy Glenferrie Road shopping centre in Hawthorn during the pre-war Friday late-night shopping hours.

As the MGC involvement in open-air preaching diminished and the next generation took their place, the MGC still maintained the Saturday afternoon Prayer for Missions meetings and Children's Evangelism Meetings, as well as the Saturday evening meetings. The Van Ministry to country areas had completed its work, and the way prepared for country conventions and the Upwey Convention Extension Movement.

H.P. Smith, meanwhile, continued to be as heavily involved as ever as secretary of the Upwey Convention, manager of the Keswick Book Depot, editor of *The Quarterly* and overseer of another long-term ministry project, the 'Texts in Trams' ministry, to which reference has already been made.

CHAPTER 12 The Visitation Ministry

The MGC ministry was comprehensive and far reaching. One of the earliest matters discussed was the appointment of a visiting sister. The needs of the hour presented the opportunity for outreach with the gospel message, particularly to the poor, the disadvantaged and the marginalised. It included home visitation, visits to hospitals and taking Scripture Instruction classes in schools. How thoroughly and effectively this was undertaken is an impressive story.

Children and young people were always a priority, but it was an all-inclusive ministry from youngest to oldest. Prayer, more prayer and still more prayer undergirded the work.

The MGC council saw an opportunity for tract distribution through hospital visitation and visiting the homes of parents of the children who attended the Children's Evangelistic Meetings held in the city on a Saturday afternoon. Tens of thousands of these tracts were published and distributed by the MGC.

In 1922, Miss Lilian Morison was appointed as the MGC's first visiting sister. It was a trial role that was undertaken on a part-time basis for two or three years. At the outset, the MGC obtained a pass accrediting her as an official visitor to the (Royal) Melbourne Hospital.

Jack Neilsen, a converted prisoner (tracts had been written on his life of violent crime and his later remarkable conversion), received official authorisation to be an accredited visitor to the Austin Hospital on behalf of the MGC. He also led a group of visitors to various other hospitals and institutions, distributing tracts and other Christian literature and praying with patients where appropriate. Amongst the institutions visited were the Cheltenham Sanatorium, Melbourne Convalescent Home, Royal Park Homes and the Benevolent Asylum, where it is recorded that 'peppermints were left with each patient'.

Appointment of Miss Emma A. Smith as visiting sister

The appointment of Miss Emma Smith, a sister of H.P. Smith, was significant, for it proved to be the commencement of a long-lasting ministry that for over 20 years brought great blessing to adults and thousands of children. She displayed a wonderful spirit of compassion in her visitation ministry, which she carried out with the same dedication and perseverance as her high-profile brother. Hers was a quiet and unsung ministry, yet one in which she made an outstanding contribution to the work of the gospel.

Regarding her appointment, the MGC Council minutes of 16 February 1926 note that:

> The Secretary reported Miss Smith's offer to take up Visiting Sister work on a 'faith lines' basis, providing she could feel that the Council as prayer helpers would be behind her. It was resolved that the offer be gladly accepted, and after discussing the question of a fund or funds for remuneration and expenses, it was decided that for the present one fund only should be started from which expenses and remuneration should be drawn.

After Emma had completed almost twelve months of work, the 1926 MGC report mentioned that in addition to her expected duties, she had been involved in institution visitation. Mentioned in particular were her visits to the Singleton Free Medical Dispensary at Collingwood, her regular assistance in the Open-air Ministry in the city, her involvement in factory ministry, and taking Scripture Instruction classes in a number of schools.[1] Throughout her time working with the MGC, she continued to attend the Sunday evening open-air meetings at the corner of Flinders and Degraves Streets. She also helped in the enquiry rooms after evangelistic meetings, which featured speakers such as the evangelist John Ridley and the Maréchale (Catherine Booth-Clibborn, the oldest daughter of the founders of the Salvation Army, William and Catherine Booth). In a report in November 1936, Miss Smith referred to the great joy she experienced when she prayed with those who had responded to the message of Christ at these meetings.[2] By 1937, she had taken on further responsibilities: 'Increasingly I am busy with the Upwey Convention helping in the secretary's office, house bookings and being house mother.'[3] Her work at these places and at the various schools involved considerable time-consuming tram and train travel.

Visitation

Throughout her time with the MGC, Miss Smith spent a good deal of her time in the poorer suburbs, including visiting the Singleton Free Medical Dispensary in Collingwood at the request of Miss Elizabeth Singleton (a daughter of the founder, Christian physician, philanthropist and evangelist Dr John Singleton). At the dispensary, she had many opportunities for personal work and tract distribution. Often she was able to follow up these folk by visiting them in their homes, where there were opportunities for Bible reading and prayer.

She was always deeply grateful to friends of the MGC who gave money and other gifts, particularly before Christmas, so that she could bring a little Christmas cheer into needy homes. More than material aid was needed in some homes. In one family, for example, the father, who often attended the MGC city meetings, was in one hospital very seriously ill whilst his little girl, five years old and one of six children, had died in another. Miss Smith took them some Christmas cake and one of the little boys said, 'How lovely, we shall have some Xmas after all!'[4] This family was always ready for prayer and to have a talk on spiritual matters.

Scripture Instruction classes

By 1930, Scripture Instruction classes in schools were taking up an increasing amount of Miss Smith's time. By then she was working in fifteen schools, including one on City Road, South Melbourne. In two schools she had attendances of 90 and 110 respectively in each class. She wrote, 'Both these classes are very attentive. I have now between 900 and 1000 children weekly ... The children come from all sorts of homes.'[5]

'Jesus in my Bible'

> In one of the outlying schools where I have about 50 children, all ages, I was telling the story of a little girl who was learning her letters and whose mother had given her a Bible. Having learned to spell 'Jesus', she saw the word in her Bible and ran to tell her mother, saying, 'I have found Jesus in my Bible.' Unknown to me, a little girl of six took special notice of the story, and next week met me in the playground, saying, 'I have found Jesus in my Testament.' I said to her, 'That is splendid; now go on looking for Jesus and mark the word every time you come to it.' The following week while in class, she put up her hand to speak and said, 'I have found Jesus 18 times in my Testament so far.' Finding all the children and the head teacher looking at her, she suddenly got very shy and has not spoken in class since. But she has met me outside saying first that her mate was looking with her for Jesus in the Testament, and later her brother and sister had found Him over 100 times. I told this in another school, and two bigger girls report having found 'Jesus' several hundred times. It goes without saying that merely searching for a name – even though it be the Name above every name and at which every knee shall bow – is of itself nothing. But cannot we trust that children who will search their Bibles at all shall find not only the Name, but Him whom the Name represents, and

> the life that is in that Name? I am sure we should pray for this.[6]

Influence and blessing that lasts

> I often come across children who were in my classes in past years, and find them still trusting in the Lord and reading their Bibles. Recently I met two girls at different times and from different schools, but who I remember were in two of the worst behaved classes I had some two or three years ago. In both cases I found them to be saved and standing true in the Lord. 'They that sow in tears shall reap in joy.'[7]

At one particular school where Miss Smith had two troublesome classes, she wrote:

> one girlie followed me out of the school to thank me for coming to teach them 'about God,' and she did wish that all the children would be quiet and listen. Every Thursday then she comes for a talk, and, whilst quite ignorant when I first knew her, she quickly drank in the Gospel message and at the May monthly children's meeting was unmistakeably converted. A little Greek girl followed this one very soon, and was grieved because [she was] unable to go to the children's meeting to get saved. She soon heard that was not necessary, and is now quite definite that she gave her heart to Jesus the night after we had a talk at her gate. One by one other girls came, until there are about ten saved or spiritually quickened. These all now get spiritual literature from me weekly, and there is quite a circulating library amongst them.[8]

In 1937, she wrote: 'Please pray that the Scripture Instruction may be in the power of the Spirit, "for the letter killeth, but the Spirit gives 'life'."'[9] Later that year she wrote that she took Scripture Instruction classes in schools at Albert Park, Albion, Braybrook, Brunswick, Coburg West, Collingwood, Footscray

North, South Melbourne and St Kilda. At these schools, she 'was able to distribute 200 copies of the little book, "The Path of Life". It makes clear the Gospel message and how to live the Christian life.'[10]

The letter writer

Miss Smith was a prolific writer of letters, particularly to children whom she taught in schools, encouraging them also in their letter writing.[11] Often she received letters after a child had passed out of her classes. One such read:

> I am very interested in the lessons you give, and I have come to the conclusion that I will become a proper Christian and always try to do what is right. I was in your class last year at S—, and but for your lessons should never have thought about religion. I have a terrible lot to thank you for.[12]

Another girl of nine wrote, 'I want to be one of Jesus' sheep and let Him come into my heart, and thank you for the lovely stories you tell us.'[13]

Emma wrote in 1937 of distributing hundreds of tracts and pieces of Christian literature:

> Little groups of children look ... out for me as I approach some schools, and some have even been coming to my rooms, perhaps bringing a mate, and asking for 'some of those stories about Jesus.' Many of the fathers and mothers read these, and our Lord has promised that His Word will not return void. At the Singleton Dispensary, in Collingwood, and at various Mothers' meetings I attend periodically, I can place large numbers of Christian magazines and other helpful literature ...[14]

At this time, she taught 13 classes in schools at Albion, Braybrook, Footscray North, South Melbourne, Albert Park, Middle Park, St Kilda, Brunswick, Coburg West and Collingwood, and continued with follow-up work at the Singleton Dispensary and with Mothers' Meetings.

In 1938, school classes were reduced due to a polio epidemic. Nevertheless, she reported that there were some definite conversions as a result of her work. She asked for more prayer for her physical, spiritual and temporal needs and that she would know 'the will of the Lord at every turn'. During this year, Miss Smith taught Scripture Instruction in nine state schools. Throughout this time, she continued to receive letters from some of the children, about whom she commented, 'Very varied is the ground into which one is sowing the seed.'[15]

> Becky writes: 'I love the book you gave me – "The Path of Life" – very much, but I cannot read it every day because mother is Jewish, and so am I, and mother only wants me to read our own religion. But I go into my room with it, and hope I am God's own little girl for ever.' Shirley writes: 'I gave my heart to Jesus and went and did something wrong on Friday, so I prayed to Jesus to forgive me' ... Dorothy says: 'I have opened my heart and let the Lord Jesus in.' Margie: 'Thank you for that most beautiful book. Every night I read some to my sister. I look forward to religious instruction every week, which I enjoy very much' ...
>
> Joyce strikes another note: 'I want to tell you I trust in the Lord, and want to go to heaven when I die, that I might see the beautiful gates open, and Jesus will say, "Come to Me".' And Jean's note goes one better, she says: 'I have read "The Path of Life" and after thinking it out I have signed my name on page 27, "My Decision." Your addresses to us each Wednesday have helped me greatly and I have learnt to love and trust the Lord Jesus.'[16]

At the end of 1938 she wrote:

> One or two classes this year have been very strenuous, the attention being poor and the much travelling to and fro wearisome. But God's Word has spoken: 'Be ye steadfast, unmoveable, always abounding in the work

> of the Lord ... Fear thou not ... I will strengthen thee ...' Then in one of the hardest classes I had definite signs of the Lord's working ... It is my rule to put one text on the blackboard each week, which is repeated by the class next week. Some learn these very well by heart, and several lately have repeated 12 texts straight off, and have received a prize.
>
> Some of these prizes have been large wall-texts and they are a good reminder in the home of God's Word learned, and are silent messengers to others there. I must mention Becky again, the little Jewish girl, whose letter I quoted in the last 'K.Q.'. I gave her a New Testament, telling her to bring it back to me if her mother would not let her read it. A few weeks after she came saying, 'Oh, mother does not mind me reading it, nor "The Path of Life".' She said, 'It won't do me any harm'! So she continues in the class and calls herself 'God's little child.' She is a sweet girlie of about ten.[17]

Miss Smith wrote of meeting girls that she had in classes three and four years earlier at other schools when taking classes at the Domestic Girls' College. One wrote, 'I have not forgotten your lessons and the prayer you taught us. I have taught my sister this, and it is now used in our home daily.'[18] From a friend she heard of a boy in one of her 'classes a few years ago, who used to tell his mother the lessons, which resulted in her conversion. She is now a real witness for the Lord. I do not know the boy nor the school, but praise the Lord, He does.'[19] Previously, Emma Smith had commented, 'Sometimes I meet some of the old pupils in the street, and I have had encouraging talks with those who are quite definite as to their decision for Christ.'[20] She 'had the joy of knowing many have taken their stand on the Lord's side, and some are truly born again'. One of the reports on her work stated, 'It was no little joy to know that many who have passed out of her reach have professed to accept the Lord Jesus Christ as their Saviour.'[21]

Mothers' meetings during the Great Depression

Miss Smith, besides taking weekly Mothers' meetings at the Singleton Home for Women at Collingwood, also held Mother's meetings at the North Melbourne City Mission in addition to taking Sunday School classes there.

In a report in 1928, as the impact of the Great Depression was becoming evident, she wrote:

> I continue to visit the Singleton Dispensary ... two or three afternoons a week ... and come across many needy people – spiritually and temporally.
>
> In these times of stress one does long to get the dear folk to know the Lord so that they could trust Him fully. Some have very hard times ...
>
> I would like to thank the friends who have made it possible for me to do [my work] by giving money, clothes, food, etc. Without this I could not go into some homes and talk about the things of God and pray with them. As it is, sometimes I am helpless before their great need, and hardly know how to visit them. One can only pray that their eyes may be lifted unto God, who cares for the sparrow, and He says, 'How much more will your heavenly Father care for you.' Will friends please pray that all my giving will lead to Spiritual benefit, which is forever my aim? [22]

A saintly faith in desperate times

Of her Mothers' meetings in the years of the Great Depression, she wrote:

> There is, of course, much distress in thousands of homes just now, and one feels it difficult to visit a home sometimes and help spiritually when unable to help in the temporal need; but I always try to cheer and encourage, and whenever I can, get them to trust in the Lord. It is good to see how some are learning to look to

> Him, and are proving that He is indeed 'a very present help in time of trouble.' I desire here to thank all who are helpers in my work ... Without such help and the prayers of the Lord's people I could not carry on. So again I ask prayer for my three-fold need – spiritual, physical, financial. I do praise God for the privilege of being set apart for and kept in this work, but I know that, although conscious of my utter unworthiness, yet He is worthy and all-sufficient for the needs of all.[23]

Gifts from friends of the MGC enabled Miss Smith to undertake relief work such as was possible in many of the homes.[24] Some of the mothers – going through great trials with their husbands and sons out of work – were yet able to praise God, believing and finding Romans 8:28 to be true: 'And we know that all things work together for good to them that love God, to them who are called according to His purpose.'[25]

As the years of the Great Depression dragged on, she wrote:

> I see much sorrow and distress in these days, but it is good to be able to minister words of comfort and salvation from the Word of God and pray with needy souls.
>
> I had the joy of seeing a mother of one of my State school children the other day make her decision for Christ in her home. She definitely by faith stepped out of the kingdom of darkness into the kingdom of His dear Son, and has since been coming to Mothers' meetings, and the two boys have been coming to the Protestant Hall Children's meetings. She is having her new-found faith sorely tried, with husband and son out of work and knowing they may be turned out of house and home. However she is trusting and praying and has already proved that God answers prayer.[26]

She wrote in 1932 of having lost one of her prayer partners and great helpers in Miss Elizabeth Singleton, 'called home at a very great age who has truly been a "mother in Israel" and many shall "rise and call her blessed".'[27]

After a period of being laid-up later in that year after being knocked over by a car with an out-of-town driver who drove against the signal in the city,[28] she wrote:

> I have recommenced my usual house visitation in Fitzroy and Collingwood, as well as many visits in other suburbs. It has been a joy to see cases of real conversion and to minister to some of the Lord's spiritually needy ones. Amongst the children there are many I am sure are really saved.

Standing on the promises

In a report that appeared in *The Quarterly* in 1934, Miss Smith wrote:

> I praise God that His Word, in such a promise as 'The Lord shall guide thee continually', has been very real to me lately, and that many such promises have enabled me to go on 'strong in faith, giving glory to God.' 'Step by step as you go, your way shall open before you.' He has said it, and I have proved Him. The enemy opposes strongly and hinders. But, 'they overcame him by the Blood of the Lamb.' Hallelujah.[29]

At the close of 1939 she wrote that she 'has proved the truth of His word to the Apostle Paul when He said, "My grace is sufficient for Thee." He has supplied all the need', and she desired 'to especially thank those who have helped in any way of encouragement, as well as in the supply of needs, which were sometimes very definitely the Lord's answer to prayer.'[30]

As World War II increased in intensity and Australia faced the threat from Japan following its attack on Pearl Harbour, war-time restrictions increased. Due to shortages of quality paper and increasing numbers of reports on Christian work among the forces, reports on Miss Smith's work in *The Quarterly* decreased even though her work continued with unabated zeal during the war years.

Towards the close of 1940, Miss Smith and other Scripture Instruction teachers found an increased interest – especially amongst children in the older grades. Perhaps the increasing severity of the war, many with fathers or brothers away, was raising the issue of life and death even among the young. It was noted that many had started to read their Bibles regularly.

As she passed 70 years of age, Miss Smith wrote that she still had many openings for Women's meetings but was not able to do as much house-to-house visitation because walking was now becoming too difficult for her. Nevertheless, she kept in touch with some needy families to whom she was able to give such practical relief as she was able.

The Path of Life

One of the pieces of Christian literature used extensively by Miss Smith in schools and in visitation was *The Path of Life* written by Mrs James (Stella) Stafford.[31] The following are brief extracts from letters of appreciation that Miss Smith received from school children:

- 'Just a note to thank you for giving me "The Path of Life." I much enjoyed reading it and have signed the Decision page. I am sending my book to my cousin for a lend.'
- 'Since I have read the book, my mother has seen a change in me. I heard her tell my Dad.'
- 'I have received the Lord Jesus into my heart. It is lovely to think that Jesus is my Saviour and I am a child of God.'

This small publication, with the foreword written by H.P. Smith, was originally published in Melbourne and created worldwide interest. It is still in demand today. In the foreword, H.P. Smith wrote:

> This little book is so full of large observation and experience. The design of the volume – specially written for the young – is to urge them to make Christ their choice; thus rendering them rich in poverty, secure in danger, and triumphant in death.

> It appeals to their reason as well as to their emotions in the presentation of the Gospel story. The illustrations are particularly apt and suitable, while the method of applying the lesson carries the stamp of personal experience. In every department, in these days life is complicated by all manner of new and baffling difficulties; our personal, social, and national relationships are tangled and confused, but, notwithstanding the bewilderment and clash of many voices, 'The Path of Life' is well and clearly defined, and it is still the inspiring and radiant pathway laid down by our Lord and Saviour Jesus Christ.
>
> If in the years to come the youth of to-day are to withstand the attacks of sceptics and materialists, they must have their knowledge of Christ based upon authority, and their Christian pathway clearly defined ... The author has therefore endeavoured to lay a foundation based solely upon the Scriptures, the only fountain of real wisdom. These Scriptures declare that 'neither is he that planteth anything, neither he that watereth, but God that giveth the increase,' and to His all-important blessing this little volume is therefore commended.

The book included a simple Decision form that could be signed.

> MY DECISION
> Knowing that I am a sinner, and believing that the Lord Jesus Christ died for me, I do receive Him into my heart as my Saviour and Lord, and with His help I will serve Him all my life.
>
> Name:
>
> Date:

> As many as received Him to them gave He power (the right) to become the sons (children) of God, even to them that believe on His name (John 1:12).

The publication brought blessing to many.

Miss Smith's work remains an outstanding tribute to one whose life was wholeheartedly lived for the Lord. Many found Jesus to be their Saviour because of her Christian life and ministry.

'Those who are wise shall shine like the brightness of the firmament,
And those who turn many to righteousness like the stars for ever and ever'
(Daniel 12:3).

CHAPTER 13 The Country Van Ministry

The horse-drawn van

Early in 1922, a large van built by George Sweet of Brunswick was presented to the MGC by Dr Georgina Sweet. Dr Sweet was an Australian zoologist who was the first woman to graduate with a Doctor of Science degree from the University of Melbourne and the first female Acting Professor in an Australian university.[1] The van was originally designed for scientific excursions and was given by Dr Sweet, who was also a Methodist Church organist, to the MGC 'for evangelistic work in the country'. The possibility for this kind of outreach was quickly seen by the MGC Council.

The van was designed to be pulled by two horses, and it made its first appearance at the 1922 MGC Easter Convention at Bentleigh drawn by horses lent by Charles A. Sandland. However, the size and weight of the van was a practical concern for country work. With motor transport now available, the council decided to adapt the van for placing on a motor chassis.

A special MGC Council meeting was called for 30 January 1923 'To deal with the question of getting the van out at the earliest possible date.' The minutes stated:

> With the need of our country districts in mind and with the concurrence of Dr. Kitchen, for a period of six months in respect of CIM missionary on furlough Bro. W. Westwood, it was unanimously resolved that the Council gratefully accepts the offer of Bros. Varley and Westwood to go out with the van.

However, at this time, the van was still set up for horse-drawn purposes and insufficient funds were available to move ahead. The minutes then mention:

> We declare our purpose of continuing instant in prayer that the blessing of God may be on all the work and the financial needs be fully met. Not having sufficient funds in hand, nor promises of weekly support of sufficient amount, it is impossible for us to offer a salary – nor do the brethren ask for this – but going out on 'faith lines' and definitely looking to God to supply all the need – spiritual and material – the brethren going out, and the Council with them, believe that God will so supply and abundantly bless the undertaking.

At the same meeting, therefore,

> It was resolved that Bro. Sandland be requested to place an order for a Ford chassis at £165, to be available about the end of February, that he arrange for a place for the painting of the van, that same be commenced as soon as possible and finished after the van is placed on the chassis. It was resolved that we make known the needs – both for fitting out the van and for financial support. The meeting closed with prayer.

God's supply and the Gospel Van Ministry commences

Funds came in that enabled the purchase of a Model T Ford chassis. As had been decided, Charles A. Sandland transferred the van on to the chassis and had it fitted out and repainted. On one side was painted:

The Melbourne Gospel Crusade
As though God did beseech you by us, we pray you in Christ's stead, be ye reconciled to God.

On the other side was painted the text:

> *God commendeth his love toward us in that while we were yet sinners Christ died for us.*

The van was prepared, and in April 1923 Frank Varley and Mr Westwood commenced the Van Ministry. Due to his impending absence from Melbourne, Varley resigned as chairman of the MGC Council and Thomas Graham was elected in his place.

Quarterly reports of the ministry were circulated to the MGC's friends for continual prayer. Funds continued to be received, which adequately covered the commencement of the work. The MGC minutes of 31 July 1923 mentioned that after reports were read from the missioners, 'A note of thanks and praise to God was given for the blessing bestowed upon our brethren in their work.'

The early Motor Van Ministry

On 7 October 1923, the *Geelong Advertiser* published a report on the forthcoming Motor Van meetings at Geelong. The report was re-edited and published for historical purposes 68 years later (on 7 October 1991) with a photograph of the Gospel Van.

The 1923 headline read, 'Gospel crusade's unusual motor van excites interest.' It reported that after visiting the North Geelong Presbyterian Church, 'The gospellers brought their message to Geelong in a converted horse-drawn van.' 'Five months for a motor trip from Melbourne to Geelong!' continued the *Advertiser*.

> Not that all that time was spent in travelling, for visits extending from a fortnight to a month have been spent en route to Werribee, Little River, Lara and other places.
>
> The motor-van itself is a unique vehicle, a veritable house on wheels, fitted throughout so as to ensure a maximum of comfort and convenience, with a minimum of space and weight. The centre

> compartment tastefully appointed and furnished with windows, spring blinds, etc., is alternatively dining, sitting, or bed room according to the requirements of the occupants. A small back compartment is kitchen, store-room, pantry, and other useful necessaries.
>
> The present occupants of the van are Mr. Frank Varley, who is a son of the late Mr. Henry Varley, is well-known as a business man in Melbourne ... and Mr. Westwood is a missionary belonging to the China Inland Mission, who at present is on extended furlough.
>
> The Melbourne Gospel Crusade is an inter-denominational organisation, with a record of many years useful work in the metropolis. Crusade activities are open air, and other evangelistic efforts are a weekly Saturday night meeting for Christians, and an interest in Foreign Mission Work, which is world wide.
>
> Mr. Varley and Mr. Westwood begin an inter-denominational mission at North Geelong Presbyterian Church on Sunday next, continuing for nearly a fortnight. After that arrangements are in progress for a United Evangelistic Mission at Belmont, at St Stephen's Church of England.[2]

At the end of Mr Westwood's agreed six-month term with the Van Ministry, he returned to Melbourne. The MGC Council appointed an MBI graduate, George Sharpe, as his successor and he joined Frank Varley for the mission at Belmont. It was mentioned at the MGC Council meeting on 30 October 1923 that for the

> mission at the Rev. Bainbridge's Church [St. Stephen's Church of England] at Belmont ... the consent of the Archbishop of Melbourne [Dr. Harrington Lees] had been necessary. Bro. Varley accompanied by Bro. Wright had waited on the Archbishop for this, which had been cordially granted when the Archbishop understood the objects and method of our Gospel Van work.

Unroadworthy!

Although the missions in the Geelong area were very well received, the van proved to be unstable in certain conditions. Charles G. (Charlie) Sandland many years later recalled that its length had placed too much weight at the rear; on one occasion when going up a steep hill, it sat on its rear end! The MGC Council immediately had the van checked by experts, who declared it to be 'dangerous for any road work and always liable to capsize'. As a result, the Council took the van off the road.

Urgent need, no funds

The MGC made the decision to get estimates for redesigning the van or building an entirely new body on the existing chassis. As sufficient funds were not available for either option, it was resolved 'That we make the position with the van known and ask for prayer, but no appeal for funds be yet made and that we pray for present work for the van missioners.'

Various enquiries were made and reports received. At a meeting a month later, a decision could not be reached. Instead of pushing ahead, it was reported in the minutes, which were handwritten by H.P. Smith, that 'Because of differences of opinion and want of oneness of the members of the Council, it was desirable that we wait on God for guidance and unity before doing anything else.' Smith, as treasurer, reported that there was £17 in the Van Account and it was agreed to pay £10 to Frank Varley (a married man) and £7 to George Sharpe (unmarried), 'as the missioners were waiting to take the van out.'

At the March 1924 meeting:

> It was agreed that if the van is to go out again, it must be with a new body but there were no funds in hand for this, the cost of which it was recognised would run to about £125 including painting &c. It was resolved that we do not place an order yet but make known to

> the Lord's people the need by circular and platform announcement and continue in prayer. It was agreed that our present position was that we could –
>
> 1. Issue a circular and wait for full monies
> 2. Issue a circular and reconsider the matter when we next meet, and
> 3. Order in faith now.
>
> The second of these alternatives was adopted, Mr. Varley to write one circular and the Secretary [Mr. Smith] the other.

At the following meeting,

> The Treasurer reported that the Rev. C.H. Nash offered to purchase the old van for use at Belgrave as sleeping quarters for students visiting there at weekends.
>
> The Treasurer reported between £70 to £80 in hand for a new van body and it was decided at once to place an order for same, with Bro. Wright to arrange details.

At the next meeting, it was reported that £157 was in hand and that the van would be ready in two to three weeks.

Meanwhile, amongst other work, Frank Varley and George Sharpe had taken services at the Albert Street Baptist Church in East Melbourne. The church had been experiencing declining attendances and H.P. Smith had been discussing its future with the leadership. It was suggested that it could operate under the auspices of the MGC and possibly be renamed the 'Albert Street Church of the Open Door'. However, the church leadership decided to sell the property with the request that the MGC continue to take services until it was sold.

Prayer answered

Funds had been received that enabled the entire cost of a new van to be covered as well as the missioners' pay. On the afternoon of 19 June 1924, with thanksgiving and praise to God for his wonderful provision and over-ruling, the van departed from outside the Albert Street Baptist Church with MBI graduates George Sharpe and Jim Grewar as missioners. (Frank Varley was absent due to family illness.) Grewar told the MGC Council that he did not require any remuneration for his work.

The missioners held successful meetings at Dartmoor, Drik Drik, Mumbunna, Rushworth and Stanhope. Varley, travelling separately, was able to join them in preaching at Drik Drik, Dartmoor and Heywood. Decades later the names of many places mentioned would be unfamiliar to most people, but almost all are still shown in the current index of Victorian post codes.

In October 1924, George Sharpe advised the MGC Council that he would be leaving the Van Ministry as he had been accepted by the WEC for service in South America. On the van's return to Melbourne, Varley, accompanied by Oliver Burgess, used it to conduct missions at Barwon Heads, Torquay and other beach locations during the December and January holiday season.

Varley, by this time approaching his mid-60s, mentioned to the MGC Council that in future he thought it preferable, as far as possible, for him to take pre-arranged missions and leave the van for those who were younger in years to take out into the country. After ceasing work with the Van Ministry, he conducted missions at Marshall Street, Geelong; the Montague Presbyterian Mission; Yannathan; and King Island. Meanwhile, the MGC Council met in special prayer to ask the Lord for two men who would be called to the Van Ministry and develop it extensively throughout Victoria. Requests for assistance with meetings were submitted to the MGC Council from various places, and these were considered and acted on as was possible. For example, a request had been received from Gembrook that the MGC 'send a preacher at least once a month to hold an Evangelistic Service on Sundays as well as possibly a Bible Study on Saturday nights. Mr Graham had gone up the past weekend, and reported that the visit was well worthwhile and appreciated.'[3] A follow-up visit was made a month later.

The Jim Grewar-Stan Frost Van Ministry

The prayer asking the Lord for two men to be called to the Van Ministry and develop it extensively throughout Victoria was quickly answered. At a meeting on 8 September 1925, Stan Frost was

> received into our fellowship with a view to his going out with Bro. Grewar in the van. The necessity of his going out as a 'faith missionary' was explained to Bro. Frost as we did not pay salaries, and other conditions were explained to him. He was asked if he was agreeable to accept these conditions and go out as co-worker with Bro. Grewar. Having replied in the affirmative and given testimony to the Lord's leading in his life of late, he was definitely received and commended to the Lord in prayer. Bro. Grewar expressed himself agreeable to go out as before, viz. at his own charges excepting that he would look to us to bear the Van maintenance and upkeep.
>
> It was decided that both should learn to drive the Motor Van and get their certificates as soon as possible. The meeting afterwards adjourned to prayer.

The duo of Jim Grewar and Stan Frost was to become a long-lasting and fruitful partnership for the gospel.

Towards the end of November 1925, Jim Grewar and Stan Frost took the van to Donnybrook where 'a local farmer, only a week or two converted, was just ready to help and be helped',[4] and to Wollert, where they experienced an 'encouraging work – many, young and old, turning to the Lord'.[5] They also visited Waranga Basin, Rushworth and Stanhope. At Stanhope, where Jim Grewar had previously ministered with George

Sharpe, they held an open-air meeting, after which they attended a prayer meeting at the home of a Mr Smartt.[6] An immediate response to their visit was that a daughter of Mr Smartt, Edna, entered the MBI and subsequently went as a missionary to Ethiopia with SIM. Later she was to marry Arthur Pocklington, himself a convert of the Van Ministry in South Gippsland, who became secretary of the Upwey Convention Council upon the death of H.P. Smith.

The missioners went on to Moora, where they held 'in the Presbyterian Church, opposite the school, children's meetings daily after school ... there were some definite cases of conversion'; Colbinabbin East, where they held a 'Gospel meeting in the Town Hall'; Yarrawonga, where they 'helped in the open air with the Salvation Army, and gave Bible readings in their hall'; and then Mulwala in New South Wales, where they started 'children's meetings ... one day there were over 50 present ... we have had sixteen decisions up to the present amongst the senior scholars, and these we believe definitely came to the Lord.'[7]

The Van Ministry expands

At the Council meeting on 20 April 1926, 'It was reported that Mr. Grewar would be returning from Yarrawonga district to take delivery of his new van which would be known as the Gospel Crusade Van No. 2.'[8] Jim Grewar purchased the Chevrolet van and made it available to the MGC. Tracts were printed for the Van Ministry using two basic formats: one with a photograph of the Ford van and another with a photograph of the Chevrolet van. The content of both tracts was identical. As has been recounted, many thousands of tracts were distributed. The text of this tract can be found in the Appendix.

In August 1926, it was reported that Grewar and Stan Frost had visited Mt Gwynne, where 'every house, within a radius of about 5 miles was visited, tracts were left, and in many cases the way opened for splendid personal conversations. Mr.

Grewar had the joy of leading one young man to Christ while he was ploughing.' They travelled on to Finley, where they 'visited about 130 houses ... and held meetings from Sunday until Wednesday evening ... [and] in the Presbyterian Church on the Sunday morning.' They found a great need for gospel work throughout the Riverina townships.[9]

The Council minutes of 26 October 1926 mention that Frank Varley had again gone out in a van:

> Mr. Frank Davidson, who was an expert motor driver, had offered to go out with Mr. Varley in Van No.1, and after both had given words of testimony in the matter, that their offer to take the van out as soon as possible be most cordially accepted. This was followed by a season of prayer and it was felt that the Lord had definitely called our brethren to go out, making a start as soon as possible.[10]

Perhaps members of the MGC Council sensed a calling on the life of Frank Davidson for future leadership ministry, as he had only commenced at MBI at the start of that year (1926). Davidson had come under special notice for his zeal for the gospel with the members of the MGC Council when he travelled around Victoria with the experienced Frank Varley in the Van Ministry before he entered MBI.

The interview of Davidson with the members of the MGC Council was preceded by some weeks of 'very serious prayer' for a van missioner. The MGC minutes of 26 October 1926 mention: 'After a season of prayer, it was felt the Lord had definitely called him to go out [with the van]'. The decision was unanimous. After some weeks the potential seen in him could be gauged by H.P. Smith writing a special letter of encouragement.[11]

Meanwhile, Jim Grewar and Stan Frost in Van No. 2 were visiting homes and holding meetings at Wollert, Woodstock, Donnybrook, Wallan East, the Lilydale district, East Warburton and Wonga Park. At Mickleham, 'The H.T. [head teacher] afterwards wrote to Melbourne ... He said "the meetings have changed the whole moral atmosphere of the school and have been a great blessing.'[12]

Frank Varley and Frank Davidson in Van No. 1 were not sure which way to go 'and took time to wait on the Lord that we might know His way. The Council of the M.G.C. met for prayer, and direction by the Great Lord of the Harvest was surely given.'[13] They ended up travelling to Bennison then Port Franklin in South Gippsland. Varley wrote:

> Both in Bennison and Port Franklin the truth of the Lord's return proved interesting to both saint and sinner, and again the question was asked, 'Why have we not heard this before?'
>
> Calling at a farm house one afternoon to see a man who was sick, I found a soul ready for the Gospel, and it was a joy to leave him later a believer in the Lord Jesus Christ.[14]

Varley, then being unwell, returned to Melbourne and for a short period was replaced by an MBI student, David Howell.[15] David was a son of MBI Council member Samuel Howell, a Victorian pastoralist with a Melbourne office, and the prayer partner of J.J. Kitchen.

Once the two Franks were together again – the experienced evangelist with the young trainee – they travelled to Lakes Entrance, where they preached in the Methodist Church on Sunday and then commenced beach services during the holidays for about 100 children. Davidson wrote:

> one day on the beach [we] planned a missionary meeting – each child to bring an object from a foreign country ... We had previously seen the Bishop of Gippsland, who was able to take part in the service, speaking so well on Africa and its dire need; also of India, where he had been a missionary. He told the children he received his call 'when he was only ten,' then asked those who

> were ten to put up their hands. He spoke beautifully of the One who died for all races. Three little girls had just previously sung, 'Jesus Died for all the Children,' which the Bishop commented on. A Methodist minister from Brighton, here for a holiday, spoke well on China and the Islands, and, like the Bishop, made a Gospel appeal to all the unsaved.[16]

The van missioners preached in both the Church of England and Methodist Church services, with extra seats being brought in. The Church of England minister in charge of the Lake Tyers Aboriginal Station invited them there, where they had a busy time of meetings followed by visits to the school at Lakes Entrance where the headmaster opened the school each day for meetings with about 100 children present.[17]

Meanwhile, Jim Grewar and Stan Frost in Van No. 2 had visited homes and held services at Yarra Road, Croydon; Warburton East; Big Pat's Creek and Mt Evelyn. At one of the homes on Yarra Road, the room was filled with young people who met together for Bible study and prayer.[18] It was here that some prayed for the first time in public. A lady wrote to H.P. Smith as secretary of the MGC:

> I thought I would drop you a line to let you know what a blessing and help Mr. Grewar and Mr. Frost have been to us this last fortnight, and the work they have done amongst the children is just wonderful. I will tell you of the last meeting we had at our home. There were nineteen present and the power of the Lord was there, too. Two gave their hearts to God, and another is under deep conviction. We who love Jesus are determined that we will put our best into His service. We are truly grateful ...[19]

MBI students and the Van Ministry

The two MBI students who had travelled to Gippsland in the early months of 1927 with Van No. 1, Frank Davidson and David Howell, reported

> that the experiences they have had during the past months assure them of the very great need there is for country Gospel work, and many Gospel Vans, they say, should be out; that ignorance of the Bible in country districts is appalling, and as a result, sin in many places is rampant.
>
> Messrs. Davidson and Howell have returned to their Bible Studies [June 1927] with increased zest, keen to be out again at the forefront of the battle, and we ask prayer for both, that in due course they may know God's appointment for service – whether at home or abroad.[20]

In October 1928, Davidson, together with Hudson Southwell and Carey Tolley, his fellow students at MBI, left Melbourne to found the BEM. Over 80 years later in 2011, Professor Brian Stanley of the Centre for the Study of World Christianity at the University of Edinburgh wrote on the far-reaching results of the work of the BEM:

> The dominant spiritual influence on most of the early BEM missionaries was C.H. Nash of the Melbourne Bible Institute, who in turn was deeply influenced by his student years in Cambridge, particularly at Ridley Hall under the principalship of Handley C.G. Moule. Through the Institute and the Upwey Convention, the Australian counterpart of Keswick, holiness revivalism shaped Melbourne evangelicalism and moved thence to the villages of Borneo. 'Revival' then came to the churches of Orang Ulu in the 1950s and 1970s ...[21]

The ministries of the MGC formed an integral part of the spiritual influences and practical training for students of the MBI. The MGC minutes reported about that time that, 'The students of the Melbourne Bible Institute had the use of No.1 Van, and reported very satisfactory work done during their visit to Crib Point during their vacation.'[22]

The peninsula

Jim Grewar and Stan Frost visited Rye, Rosebud, Boneo, Red Hill and Main Ridge in Van No. 2, holding gospel meetings in homes and churches, visiting homes and schools, distributing tracts and undertaking personal work. Services were conducted in both the Presbyterian and Methodist Churches. Frost visited practically every house in Rosebud and about 150 tracts were left behind. Some time was also spent with one of Mr Norman Lumsden's converts, whom they had met.[23]

Frost recounted that 'a schoolboy at South Lyndhurst knelt down beside the car and accepted the Lord'. Furthermore:

> I was speaking to a middle-aged man about his need of Christ in the middle of a paddock. He told me that he definitely yielded himself to the Lord by his own bedside last Sunday evening.
>
> A young man yesterday told me that he felt constrained to come down to the van at midnight (Sunday), but finding the light out did not like to disturb me, so kneeled down on the grass and accepted the Lord as his Saviour. This is the third in one family who has accepted Christ during the Mission. He is very bright, and would like to come to Upwey ...
>
> Let us praise God for the cases of conversion. 'Seven times a day I praise Thee,' said the Psalmist (Ps. 119:164) ... Daniel found time to pray three times a day. Much prayer, much power; little prayer, little power; no prayer, no power. Let us keep low at the foot of the Cross ...
>
> Prayer is asked for the many converts in the districts just visited, that they may now grow in grace and in the knowledge of our Lord and Saviour, Jesus Christ.[24]

When Grewar and Frost next went out together, they first visited Cockatoo, where they conducted meetings in the

Presbyterian Church and visited homes. They then travelled to the Mt Burnett and Beaconsfield districts. After making follow-up visits to some of the believers where God had blessed their visits last year, to 'see how they do' (Acts 15:36), they travelled to Carrum Downs, where they met some new converts who had gone to the Upwey Convention. Then on to Dromana, Rosebud, Rye and Red Hill. At Rye, where there had been no Sunday School twelve months ago, attendances now averaged 30 scholars.[25]

Meanwhile, Varley was on an extended mission visit to Tasmania, based around Launceston. He spoke at numerous meetings, some arranged by the North Tasmanian Evangelisation Society. He also spoke at a United Day of Prayer at St Andrew's Presbyterian Church, Launceston, regarding a revival among Christians, the salvation of the unsaved and the work of God in heathen lands.[26]

South Gippsland

In early 1928, Grewar and Frost spent three months visiting South Gippsland, where

> hundreds of homes [were] waited upon and thousands of tracts distributed. Scores of children's meetings have been held in State Schools or Sunday Schools, and many Gospel meetings conducted in churches and other places as opportunity presented itself ... There have been many conversions among adults and children, and the Lord's people have been quickened and fed.[27]

Frost recounted:

> We stayed at Caldermeade over the week-end and had a Gospel meeting in the State School at night, when the building was full and the people very interested and keen that we should return for a mission. On the Friday night a young man had ridden five miles on his bicycle into the township and enquired for the euchre

> party. Apparently he had mistaken the night, and we invited him to the Van, where, after a long, serious talk he went away very impressed. On the Sunday night he rode in the same five miles to the Gospel meeting, and in the Van after the meeting definitely yielded himself to Christ and returned home on his bike rejoicing in the Lord. No doubt the Lord drew him not to the euchre party but that he might come to know Himself – whom to know is life eternal.[28]

After conducting services at Toora, they visited every house in the district of Mt Best. The Pocklington family, who later made such a significant contribution to Christian work, would have been amongst those visited. The missioners went on to Mt Fatigue, where visits were made and tracts left at homes. They wrote:

> We do thank you for the special times of prayer you are having for us. That is our greatest need, as these dear souls seem to be so unconscious of their deep need. How we long to see real Holy Ghost conviction among them. We visit every house with tracts, and have many opportunities of preaching the Gospel on the doorsteps.[29]

Grewar and Frost travelled to Foster, holding services in the Church of England and Methodist Churches, then a little further on to Port Franklin, 'amongst fishermen and their boats'. Frost wrote:

> At some places one is very conscious that the chief work must be sowing. There is so little spiritual life, and sometimes no prepared soil. It takes some hard labour before the final reaping can come.
>
> Last Tuesday, although a good number gathered for the Gospel meeting, we had a hard time. There are times when one feels conscious that the people are not receiving the message. Whenever this occurs it makes me sad to think there is so little response to such a

> glorious message as we have to proclaim. On Thursday, however, things changed, and everyone seemed to be gripped, and as the message proceeded last night there was much blessing. This is only a small place, and most of the men are away fishing at night, but there were between 50 and 60 present. Several came to me afterwards and thanked me for the blessing they had received during our meetings here ...[30]

Upon their return to Toora, Frost wrote:

> When we returned to Toora some weeks after our series of meetings there, we were encouraged to find at the week-night Bible Study and prayer meeting about 16 present, as compared with six before our meetings. On the Sunday I went unexpectedly into the Sunday School ... The Superintendent told me that the Sunday School had continued to grow each Sunday since we left, and the teachers had doubled in number ...[31]

Writing from Port Franklin, Frost continued:

> Last night was to have been our last meeting, but as both numbers and interest continued to grow, we have decided to stay over another week. One man said to me: 'We who are fishermen always stay fishing in the same place while the fish last, and I think you should stay here while you can get the people to your meetings.'[32]
>
> On Saturday, I went out with tracts at 2.30 p.m., and, when returning at 8 pm, after several conversations in the homes, I found Mr. Grewar with a van full of people, some having come between three and five miles. We opened up our organ, and played and sang for awhile. After this we had prayer, followed by a good Bible reading, which appeared to bring blessing to all present. Amongst those present was the woman who had asked for special prayer the night before, and, while talking to her afterwards, she told me that she had decided to become a Christian ... Later on, at one

> of the cottage meetings, her husband was present and gave himself to the Lord. We praise God for these cases of conversion, and the many others also who have told us privately of much blessing received during our meetings ...
>
> After tea we walked down to Port Franklin, where it was a delight to hear about 50 who had gathered in the hall singing 'What a Friend We Have in Jesus.' Some of those who gathered came about five miles along that road, whilst one came eight miles. There was great liberty all through the meeting, which lasted about two hours. At the conclusion about 18 stayed behind for special prayer, and of these about half a dozen decided for the Lord. One, we believe, went home under deep conviction, but evidently did not accept the Lord because of the love of the world.[33]

The missioners review their ministry

Speaking at a Saturday evening meeting in August 1928 at the Protestant Hall, the two missioners were asked to speak about their experiences thus far. Jim Grewar explained it was now four years since he first began the van work. He recalled a trip with George Sharpe (now in Amazonia) to a 'little place called Reedy Creek', where George asked some children if they knew about Jesus.

> The answer was 'No.' 'Have you never heard about the Lord Jesus Christ as the Saviour?' Answer, 'No.' This so impressed Mr. Grewar that he decided that certainly they must have children's meetings there, and in every place he has been to since the children's meetings had always come first. He explained how very needy were the children, and what an opportunity there was in connection with the State Schools, because in Victoria, out of 2600 State Schools, there were from fifteen to sixteen hundred without any religious instruction! These schools had in them 80,000 children.[34]

Then Stan Frost spoke: 'One young man during their late [sic] trip was so eager to receive the Truth of God that he followed them about for four months, attending meeting after meeting and drinking in the Word of Life. He will now soon be in the Melbourne Bible Institute.'[35] He concluded by saying 'that he had now been three years out with the Van, and they were by far the best three years of his life. In them he had learned to love Him, his Lord and Master, more and more as the days went by.'[36]

A new generation in the Van Ministry

In June 1928, Charlie (C.G.) Sandland took Van No. 1 and a party of about ten young men to Healesville and Dixon's Creek to conduct a mission in conjunction with the Methodist Church over the King's Birthday weekend. Associated with him in leadership were Eric Clarkson, an evangelist with the ESA, and Messrs Meyer and Briggs of the Collingwood Free Breakfast. The local newspaper, *The Guardian*, in reporting the visit wrote, 'Their Gospel singing and part songs proved a treat to listen to, and their Gospel messages will long be remembered by the Healesville and Dixon's Creek people. The visit has given the church a new vision, and brings city and country churches into closer touch.'[37]

A church plant in Croydon

Following earlier encouraging visits by Grewar and Frost in Van No. 2, a regular ministry amongst folk who had come into blessing had developed. The MGC Council minutes in 1928 mention that:

> An enquiry was made whether the Crusade would take charge of the religious services if a new Church could be built at Yarra Road, Croydon. It was resolved that these requests could be acceded to as it was thought that one or other members of the Council with the help of friends could well take this responsibility.[38]

At the meeting on 4 September 1928, 'It was reported that these services were to begin on 16th September in the house of Mr. T. Knee until the Church was built.'[39] Then, in March 1929, the minutes state that, 'The opening of the new Church at Yarra Road was reported to have taken place on 24th February that for a month at least, evening meetings were being asked for.'

The opening of the church was undertaken by Leslie Griffiths, son of J.M. Griffiths of the Griffiths Teas family and a principal donor of the church. Friends of the MGC in attendance included H.P. Smith, Jim Grewar, Stan Frost and S. Beckingham, minister of Upwey Union Church. The van missioners took the first evening service, and there was a response to the gospel invitation.[40]

The MGC helped with the establishment of the new church as much as it was able to do so. Besides Sunday services and Sunday School for children, there was a mid-week prayer meeting and a Saturday night Bible study and missionary meeting. However, early on it was clear that more local leadership was needed to oversee the church as a year later, in 1930, the MGC Council was called upon to provide more assistance.

Gippsland again

Following visits to Poowong and Poowong North, Jim Grewar and Stan Frost visited Ransby, Triholm, Strezlecki and other nearby places. Work in South Gippsland was more or less equally divided between the Presbyterian, Methodist and Anglican Churches.

By now, the missioners were quite used to crowded meetings, but occasionally a meeting did not go according to plan. Stan Frost wrote,

> Thursday night being very wet, not a person, as I then thought, came to the meeting. But a lady since said to me–'I suppose you thought nobody came to the

> meeting last Thursday?' I said– 'I did not see anyone.' 'Well, I came along (walking for about two miles across wet paddocks),' she said, 'and, as I heard you playing and singing with the Church lit up, waiting for those who would never come, it was to me the best sermon I have ever heard.' She said she did not like to come in, so returned home almost in a trance ... Nevertheless, at least three souls, they believe, definitely accepted the Lord in this district, so they continued on their way rejoicing.[41]

The Toora 'Upwey Echoes' meeting

As a result of the Van Ministry in the Toora district, a number of those who had been converted went to the 1928 Upwey Convention and subsequently decided to hold an 'Upwey Echoes' meeting at Toora. The use of the Toora Methodist Church was granted and the minister of the Toora Church of England, Rev. A.J. Maher, presided. The meeting was most enthusiastic. After many gospel hymns and a long season of prayer, in which many took part, the meeting was thrown open for testimonies. One present wrote:

> It is not easy to describe the power that filled that church, as one after another of the speakers testified to the blessings of the Convention. The congregation consisted of some who were still unsaved, some half-hearted Christians, and many who had entered into rich blessing, as a result of the mission [at Toora] last year.[42]

A minister who attended went away to arrange another 'Echoes' meeting at Port Franklin, where many had been blessed by the Van Ministry.[43]

The following are extracts from letters of testimony:[44]

> 'I thank God that, through the gentle persuasion and earnest prayers of your dear folk, I have been "born again" in every sense of the word. Born from a world

> of selfishness and depression into a new world, where love and joy reign supreme. I am filled with a desire to become wise in the "things of God," for now I know wisdom is better than rubies and all the things that may be desired are not to be compared with it.'
>
> ...
>
> 'I shall never cease to thank and praise God for sending the van along here. It has changed my life extremely. I didn't know what it was to live in peace and happiness. Of course, I have my trials and temptations, but I have God always near me to uphold me.'
>
> 'We have great times at Bible Class now. There are quite a number who lead in prayer.'

Later, in writing about this district, Frost recalled

> a girl in a country township who came to the Gospel meeting on the Friday night, went to the dance on Saturday, and was back again at the mission on the Sunday, when [he] preached from the text, 'Thou art weighed in the balances and found wanting.' She said, 'This is for me,' and testifies that she was converted that night.[45]

It was only two years later that he heard of this girl's conversion and that she hoped to go to the mission field.

A friend of the ministry wrote:

> This is what the Melbourne Gospel Crusade van has done for Jesus here, and it is well to remember that a year ago, from the time I am writing, such things as an Upwey Convention, an M.B.I., a Scofield Bible, or even a Traveller's Guide, were in my case, and I believe in that of nearly everyone else in this district totally unknown.[46]

Gormandale

The missioners held meetings at the Gormandale Church of England with special times for children after school.

> It was a delight to see the children make one rush for the church as we [the van] came in sight. The attention has been excellent, and we believe quite a number of these little ones have really received the Lord Jesus into their hearts.
>
> While visiting we had the opportunity for reading and prayer in several of the homes, the result of which, in one case, was that the lady came along to the meeting with the family, and two of them were converted that night.[47]

This work was not without opposition. The missioners wrote:

> Last Friday evening, when we were holding the Fellowship Meeting in the Church, the people on the one side started a gramophone going, whilst those on the other side played the piano as loudly as possible, and, to top things up, two shots from a gun were fired close by. Yesterday morning, when we were taking the Anglican service, two heavy stones were thrown on to the iron roof.
>
> It is not surprising that in these days of spiritual darkness there should be much prejudice against those who preach the truth – 'holding forth the Word of Life ... in the midst of a perverse nation' (Phil. 2), or 'perverted generation'; amongst whom we are to 'shine as lights in the world.' But our brethren again found that quiet talks in the house to house visitation broke down much prejudice and misunderstanding.[48]

The Gormandale Convention

A unique convention was held at Gormandale over the 1929 King's Birthday weekend. It was arranged by Glanmore Rees, a former MBI student and now of the Church of England. The main speaker was C.H. Nash, and H.B. Denniston, Melbourne warehouse owner and president of the Evangelisation Society, was chairman. The MGC missioners, together with C.G. and Miss Stella Sandland, visiting from Melbourne, all participated in the weekend. The result was the biggest religious event in Gormandale's history. 'Better than Upwey,' someone said. 'There were many direct decisions for Christ, and we believe a lasting work in the deepening of the spiritual life of Christians was accomplished, the extent of which eternity alone will reveal.'[49]

The Van stayed on for some time in the Gormandale district. Meetings were held, Scripture instruction took place in state schools, private homes were visited, and tract distribution did not slacken – 'above all, God's blessing was unmistakably upon the work.'[50] During this time, the Bishop of Gippsland licensed Stan Frost to relieve the minister of the Gormandale Church of England for two months' leave of absence on sick leave. The MGC Council minutes indicate that a letter of appreciation had been received from the Gormandale Church of England where Frost had ministered in the parish for a number of weeks.[51]

The missioners also visited Buin Buin, Rokeby, Drouin and Jindivick. Special services were held with Mr and Mrs George Hall, Leonard Buck and Miss Higgs at Mr Ronald's property at West Drouin. Meetings were also held at a State Electricity Commission of Victoria Camp and the missioners left with an invitation to return. One wrote, 'Praise the Lord ... for the witness of the Cross of Christ amongst men isolated from the churches and any Gospel influence.'[52]

The Toora Convention

A convention was held at Toora over a weekend early in 1930. Meetings took place in the Methodist Church, the Church of England and the public hall. C.H. Nash, Stan Frost and Jim

Grewar were the speakers. At all meetings there was special singing. Those participating were an ESA singing party consisting of Miss Stella Sandland, Charlie Sandland and two or three others. There was much blessing as a result of the convention, and after surrendering her life to Christ, one testified that she 'was bubbling over with joy, joy, joy'.[53] Tract distribution continued, with several thousand being given out on each trip, many delivered with personal talks in homes.

Central Victoria

A new work was started following a van visit to Hampton Park near Dandenong, where there had been numerous conversions. Sunday services were being sustained with visits from students of MBI.[54]

In mid-1930, Van No. 1 was being used by Charles A. Sandland for open-air work while No. 2 was being used at Yandoit by Stan Frost with his brother, Claude, another MBI student, in the absence of Jim Grewar through illness.[55] With the return of Grewar, the missioners made extensive visits to central Victoria, holding meetings at Maldon, the Castlemaine district, Barker's Creek, Wesley Hill, Winter's Flat, Chewton, Elphinstone, Trentham, Bowenvale and Maryborough, where 'there were many decisions for Christ among adults and children.'[56]

The missioners held meetings in conjunction with churches at Maldon and then at Chewton at the invitation of the Methodist and Congregational ministers. They were much encouraged by carloads of friends driving from Faraday, Elphinstone, Campbell's Creek and Wesley Hill to join the meetings. The work in Central Victoria finished at Barker's Creek where there was 'a glorious gathering in of precious souls'.[57]

Following the Van Ministry in Central Victoria, the Quarterly Meeting of the Castlemaine Methodist Circuit passed a resolution of appreciation for the work done by the missioners in the Circuit. The earnestness of the preachers and the benefit to the churches were referred to, as well as the special work among the children. The letter of appreciation concluded, 'At all the places visited there has been a great awakening of the need for Christ, and many turned to the Lord. Also many since the meetings are taking an active part in the Lord's work.'[58]

The MGC Van Ministry concludes

In the early 1930s, the missioners were as active as they had ever been, visiting places as distant as Warburton and Deniliquin, and again in Gippsland, with many wonderful stories of conversions and spiritual blessings. They continued to ask for prayer, and more prayer, that the work would stand for eternity and that following the 'sowing' and the 'watering', God would give the increase. These requests were accompanied by regular and persistent prayers offered by those attending the MGC's prayer and fellowship meetings in Melbourne.

During the winters of the early 1930s, however, Jim Grewar had become unwell and shortly afterwards Stan Frost became ill with pneumonia. Their itinerant ministry, living in the back of a motor van, sometimes in cold, mountainous regions and without adequate heating, had led to a lifestyle that was better tolerated by young men and which became more difficult as the two missioners grew older.

The impact of the Van Ministry

In its Van Ministry, as well as its other ministries, the MGC relied on the authority of the Bible as the word of God. Its responsibility was to teach God's word, echo God's word in its prayers, and sing hymns and choruses that were filled with God's word.

It is true that the unchurched do not like to hear about sin, declarations about right and wrong, warnings about hell, or calls to surrender to Christ. Nevertheless, the Crusade faithfully planted the seed, the word of God, and allowed for the seed to develop and grow. It often grew quietly and affirmed what Jesus said, 'I will build my church,' and what Paul wrote, 'I planted, Apollos watered but God gave the increase.' There was a hidden energy below the surface.

In Mark 4:26–27, Jesus said, 'The kingdom of God is as if a man should scatter seed on the ground, and should sleep by night and rise by day, and the seed should sprout and grow, he himself knows not how.'[59] The priority work of the Crusade was faithfully to ensure that others heard the Word. 'Faith comes by hearing and hearing by the Word of God' (Romans 10:17).

Only a fraction can be told about the work of the Van Ministry. Countless lives were brought under the sound of the gospel, many in small, remote areas of the state. These are now almost unheard-of places such as Bobinawarrah, Bobinawarrah East, Hurdle Flat, Meadow Creek, Moyhu, Oxley Flats, Porepunkah, the Hoppickers' Camp at Panlooks (where they did some work with George Hall and Leonard Buck), Springhurst, Cookinburra, Cornish Town, Chiltern Valley, Black Dog Creek, Lockinburra, Barnawartha and Violet Town.

A report in *The Quarterly* of May 1933 states:

> Although Mr. J. Grewar's Gospel Van has been laid up for the past few months through the sickness of the workers, the fruit of the work of former days continues to increase in a way that is encouraging in the extreme.
>
> The following letter to the Honorary Secretary of the Crusade [Mr. H.P. Smith] from a Miss D. Bateman, one of four sisters who were converted when the van was in the Central Victoria area a little over two years before, tells its own story, and will call forth notes of praise to God from many who have been following the Gospel Van work as prayer partners.[60]

Miss Bateman wrote from Elphinstone in central Victoria:

> As you are interested in our Young People's Band, we thought you would like to hear that we celebrated the commencement of our third year. For two years we have been meeting on Thursday nights to learn more of the precious truths found in the Word of God, and have had very happy and profitable times together. We felt we would like to have something special for our Birthday, as we did last year, so after praying about it, we asked Mr. Frost to come and give the address. He was able to come, and we were very pleased to have him with us once more.
>
> The Band and a few visitors gathered for tea in the Hall. While still seated around the table we sang choruses, followed by a short talk from Mr. Frost, which was greatly enjoyed. After this we held a meeting to which everyone was invited. There were between 50 and 60 present and all listened attentively to the stirring address delivered by Mr. Frost. It was a splendid meeting for which we praise our Lord. We have had many answers to prayer, and much blessing during the past two years, and are looking to the Lord to continue to bless this work for Him. We value the prayers of all friends of the Crusade.[61]

As editor of *The Quarterly*, H.P. Smith noted in its February 1931 issue:

> Some who remember the visits of Messrs. Grewar and Frost to Toora and surrounding districts in S. Gippsland two or three years ago have been in prayer for Mr. Arthur Pocklington, to whom the Lord spoke at that time, and who afterwards came to the Melbourne Bible Institute, and is now a China inland missionary. These friends will be interested in the following extract from a letter just received in Melbourne, written in the C.I.M. Training Home at Anking, Anhwei [China], where Mr Pocklington is now hard at language study. He says: –

> 'I little thought two years ago, when writing "Upwey Echoes" news from Toora, that in two years' time I should be writing from the above address. It is wonderful to think that our life is planned, and that since before the foundation of the world God has had a work for me to do out here in China. The thing has been all so marvellous to me that even now sometimes I can scarcely realise that I am actually here. And when I reflect upon the mighty working of the Holy Ghost through Gospel van missions, which He so definitely used in calling me out into His glorious service, my mind almost reels at His grace.
>
> 'Only the other day I was thinking that when I was a lad of fourteen I had great ambitions in the commercial, social and sporting worlds. A few years later after becoming a child of God I had some sort of a call to a full-time service for Him, but looking back now I am afraid it was dangerously swayed by a fleshly ambition to a ministry which provided me with a few letters after my name.
>
> 'Then came the Gospel van brethren along, and the Spirit of God showed me just what real service for Christ meant. From that time to this I have had one consuming ambition, which is to point souls personally and definitely to the Lord Jesus Christ, in order that they, too, may be saved for eternity. I earnestly pray God that the vision thus received may never grow dim, but that on the contrary it may be freshened and intensified as the years go by.'[62]

Meanwhile others in fellowship, part of a new generation, were undertaking ministry into country Victoria. This included evangelist John G. Ridley and his wife Ruth, who were travelling in an Australian Bible Crusade motor van to conduct missions in Victoria. Evangelist Eric Clarkson, working with the ESV, was also conducting missions that were a precursor to an extensive van ministry.

The joy of service

Towards the conclusion of his ministry with the van, Stan Frost wrote:

> At one time I did not understand 3 John verse 4 ... but now, praise God, I have tasted the joy John there speaks of. It is certainly a great joy to see men and women accepting Christ as their Saviour. It sets the bells of Heaven ringing. But there is even a greater joy. To return several months later and find the babes growing in grace and developing into strong, healthy Christians is a greater joy. 'I have no greater joy than to hear that my children walk in truth,' wrote the Apostle.[63]

CHAPTER 14 A Christian Newspaper Is Born

Despite his own unique and excellently produced publication, *The Quarterly*, H.P. Smith saw the need for a newspaper that would report news of preachers and workers, evangelists, missions and missionaries – both home and overseas – provide book reviews and be an outspoken Christian witness. In November 1935, he wrote an editorial in *The Quarterly* under the attention-gripping headline, 'A Need of the Hour! Wanted an Editor.' H.P. Smith outlined the qualities and qualifications required:

> A Christian, a new creature in Christ, born from above by the Spirit of God and able to conduct such a journal, who has something more than the wisdom of this world, who is thoroughly grounded in the fundamental truths revealed in the Word of God, who is daily led by the Holy Spirit, who keeps scholarship in its right place, and depends upon God's guidance in all things, who will 'contend earnestly for the faith which was once delivered unto the saints' (Jude 3), and who can write in the language of the home, rather than that of the academy.

Smith commented 'That the kind of Editor that was needed is one that Australia does not possess, and the lack of which many deplore.' When he and his colleagues looked across the nation without success for a man to fulfil such a task, they prayed that God would raise up an editor with these qualities, trusting him and believing in his faithfulness.

There was evidence that the newspaper was born in the heart of God before it was planted in the mind of Smith and his colleagues. It was akin to the experience written in Isaiah 65:24, 'It shall come to pass that before they call, I will answer, and while they are still speaking, I will hear.' Unobtrusively and quite unsuspected by the young man himself, and years before Smith thought of writing his editorial, God had been preparing a young man who attended an evangelical church in country Victoria.

In 1932, Eric Daley (1910–1992),[1] a son of the former editor of *The Kerang New Times*, travelled to Melbourne to commence a two-year course under C.H. Nash at the MBI. Daley had been working for his father before his thoughts turned to missionary service. While reading and writing presented no difficulties for him, he soon discovered from open-air and preaching assignments that he had little promise as a speaker and, as he later recounted, 'Perhaps my forte was in tract distribution!' He was 'unsettled and returned to [his] former job in Kerang without any idea of a sphere of useful service for the Lord'.[2] But could the Lord have been asking Daley, 'What is that in your hand?' (Exodus 4:2).

Although they were probably not apparent to him at the time, Eric had remarkable people-handling skills in the encouraging of others and communicating on a one-on-one basis, all of which came to the fore in fitting him for the many years of his editorship that were to follow. Furthermore, the two years at MBI and his introduction to the convention ministry inculcated a high view of the authority and absolute trustworthiness of the Holy Scriptures. Another important factor in his preparation that stemmed from his MBI days was the setting up of helpful contacts and associations.

It was another former MBI student, John Knox, who first enthusiastically explored the idea of starting a Christian newspaper and invited Eric to join him.

'A Christian newspaper – Coming?'

In the February 1938 edition of *The Quarterly*, Smith, in an article under the heading 'A Christian newspaper – Coming?', wrote that 'Two young men have signed a folder distributed amongst Christians at the Upwey Convention declaring that there is "Coming – A Christian Newspaper" to be called "The Edifier".' Smith wrote that these men were not well known, but he noted that Eric had four years journalistic service at Kerang and John Knox had been an active Christian worker and businessman after leaving MBI. He went on to ask, 'Can these men run a Christian newspaper? They declare they firmly believe God has called them, and definitely, to this very work.'

Depending on the Holy Spirit and asking Christians to stand in prayer for the venture, the first edition was published as *The Edifier* on 10 June 1938. After a short time, John Knox was unable to continue his involvement but maintained his considerable interest. Later, while working on the staff of Melbourne's *Sun* newspaper, he assisted with the production of the paper he helped establish.

From 'edifier' to 'new life'

A year later the newspaper was published in a new form under the name *New Life*. Daley believed that the original name did not sound quite right – perhaps there was a touch of presumption. At the same time as the change of name, the newspaper incorporated the name of the *Standfast*, the quarterly publication of the Bible Union of Victoria.

In the first issue under the *New Life* banner, 14 July 1939, the founding editor wrote:

> There is an intense urgency for a greater vision, if the Lord's people are to seize the opportunity of existing circumstances. The turmoil in political affairs, the ever-present shadow of war ... have caused great numbers to seriously face facts, and to seek a certainty and peace amidst the chaos of international relationships.

> The sad thing is that the gospel is so inadequately presented. We have the only message that can bring lasting peace and steadfast hope to men and women in darkness and despair.
>
> The Lord Jesus has given us the glorious assurance of His near return. He has bequeathed to His redeemed ones the presence of His blessed Spirit ... Shall we not use all means whereby we may win some to the Saviour we love? The use of suitable literature provides a golden opportunity.
>
> May 'New Life' be a medium which will exalt the Saviour, comfort the believers and awaken the outsiders to a knowledge of our Lord.

Written when he was 27, this article reflects how Daley's Kerang upbringing, Melbourne's Keswick-influenced evangelicalism under C.H. Nash at the MBI, and the work and ministry of H.P. Smith in his leadership of the Upwey Convention and the MGC had permeated his life. It was a vision from which he did not depart in his 50 years as full-time or associate editor of the newspaper.

The paper, encouraged by supportive articles, inserts and general advertising in *The Quarterly*, was warmly received by Christians throughout Australia. Within a short time, it was being commended for its high standard and firm stand for the evangelical faith.

New Life became the only independent weekly Christian newspaper in the nation. For a time, a northern edition was also published in Sydney. From small beginnings, when it was a struggle to reach a circulation of 1,000, it climbed to over 7,000 copies per week – indicating a readership of over 20,000 for every issue.

In the early years of the newspaper, Daley sought the fellowship and counsel of a small group of older Christians. They met together every week in a room in Baptist House in

Collins Street over lunch. Before the author's service in World War II, his father, Ernest Renshaw, a member of the MGC Council, would invite him to join with these friends.

The impact of *New Life*

New Life has brought news, inspiration and encouragement to thousands of people. It has contended for the faith, at times raised important questions, opposed doubtful trends and been the means of people hearing the call of God for Christ's service at home and overseas.

Leonard Buck, who was involved in the founding of Campaigners for Christ, the Christian Leaders' Training College of Papua New Guinea (CLTC of PNG) and Prison Fellowship Australia, commented, 'It helped to commence many a new work which otherwise would never have got off the ground to become established.'[3] It has been the means of people coming to know Jesus Christ as Saviour, and it also helped to break down the isolation for shut-ins, as well as missionaries serving in remote places around the world.

Gerald Davis, when editor of the *Church Scene* newspaper that served the Anglican community, observed: 'What is particularly to the credit of the founding editor, Eric Daley, is that the essential unity of evangelicals across so many denominations and other traditions in Australia has held up so well.'[4] Rev. David Morley, who often wrote for *New Life*, commented, 'The best way to gauge the influence and value of "New Life" is to contemplate what a difference it would have made to the Church's missionary and evangelistic development in Australia if the paper had not existed.'[5]

New Life became an integral part of Melbourne's interdenominational evangelicalism. It brought a cohesion to the numerous ministries for which Melbourne had become known. While the paper is no longer published weekly in printed form, it now appears fortnightly in electronic format and is available without charge on the internet.

Tributes to Eric Daley

In reference to Eric Daly, Leonard Buck commented, 'Though uneasy with the concept of structural church union, clerically inspired, no evangelical layman did more than Eric Daley to bring to attention and fruition, the true spiritual relationship of Christians of vastly diverse denominational structures. This was the genius of his professional journalism.'[6]

The present editor of the paper, Rev. C.R. (Bob) Thomas, has said that Psalm 119:63 sums up Daley's ministry: 'I am a friend to all who fear You, and to all who follow Your precepts.'[7]

Apart from his leadership of *New Life*, which consumed the greater part of his time for many years, Daley was also involved in other ministries, including membership of both the convention and the MBI councils.

It has been a considered opinion that the self-effacing ministry of Eric Daley probably influenced more people, over a wider geographical area and for a longer period of time, than many a better-known influential leader. The influence of the paper spread throughout Australia and beyond, which underscored its effectiveness in Victoria.

Eric Daley was a godly, gracious man of genuine Christian humility, gifted with deep spiritual discernment. His life's work influenced thousands of Christians, hundreds of churches and scores of missionary and evangelical service organisations. He proved to be God's man for God's special purpose. His many years in the work to which he was called proved that he was indeed a 'Mr Valiant-for-the-Truth', always contending for the faith once delivered to the saints (Jude 3).

CHAPTER 15 Tributes to Hervey Perceval Smith

Recollections of Elsa Warner

In a conversation with the author in 1992, Elsa Warner recounted her experience of living with her uncle at the Federal Hotel. Her mother was H.P. Smith's sister, and when her mother was ill, and with a baby on the way, Smith and his wife Nettie took Elsa to live with them in their private suite at the Federal. They had no children of their own and loved Elsa. Although they kept in regular contact with her family, the little girl never left the care of the Smiths, living the first seventeen years of her life at the hotel. She recalled how Smith's friends called him 'the master of detail'.

Elsa trained as both a primary school teacher and a teacher of the deaf. She was involved with Scripture Union in the CSSM and the Inter-School Christian Fellowship (ISCF), to which she applied the same meticulous attention to detail she had admired in her uncle. She married well-known architect and city organist Lawrence Warner in 1934. Her uncle arranged for the wedding to be held in the Keswick Book Depot in Collins Street. She said:

> In the 1890s the Federal had a wine licence. After his conversion, Mr. B.J. Fink, a director of the Herald & Weekly Times as well as the Federal, said to her uncle, 'We will let the [wine] licence go because we want to keep you.' That continued until 1924 when appointments of directors changed and the new ones thought they should get a full liquor licence. A lot of the patronage of the Federal came from wealthy

> Western District farmers. Many of them then went to the Victoria Coffee Palace in Little Collins Street near to the Melbourne Town Hall. Mr. Smith became a director of the Victoria after leaving the Federal. The largest number of people to stay at the Federal in one night was 623. The directors never objected to the singing of hymns in the hotel. In fact there were notices in the lifts inviting guests to attend the meetings.
>
> My uncle and his family used to attend Worcester Cathedral before leaving England. He went to the Independent Church until after his conversion. He then went to the Collins Street Baptist Church but left later, in 1914, because of the teaching of the Rev. T.E. Ruth who was the minister. We all then went to the Albert Street Baptist Church. Later my uncle offered to have this as a Peoples' Church but it did not proceed. He was always busy with his many interests – Keswick Book Depot, 'The Keswick Quarterly and Upwey Convention News', the Upwey Convention, missionary societies, open-air work where he had afternoon meetings on Sundays on the Yarra Bank, opposite Snowden Gardens at night and also at the corner of Degraves and Flinders Streets in the City.[1]

It was said by knowledgeable evangelicals that T.E. Ruth 'was a thoroughgoing old-fashioned modernist'. It was also mentioned that 'on one occasion Dr. D. Stuart MacColl took on T.E. Ruth in a debate on the Second Coming of Christ.'[2]

Elsa Warner herself went on to hold office in a number of organisations, including the Baptist Women's Association of Victoria and the Baptist Women's Union of the South West Pacific.[3] Her husband was organist at the Collins Street Baptist Church, where he instructed the author in his teen years on the pipe organ and asked him to play for some annual mid-week mission society meetings, although as far as the author can remember, he was not aware of the connection with H.P. Smith.

Going home

H.P. Smith kept in mind the return of the Lord Jesus for his own. The increasing darkness of the age suggested it, and he lived in anticipation of it. He knew that the Scriptures declared the return of the Lord Jesus Christ to be the greatest incentive to personal holiness. Such occupation with the glory to come gave him power to deny ungodliness and worldly lusts, and grace to live soberly, righteously and godly in the present age. To walk and serve to the praise and glory of the Lord had demanded knowledge of the future glory that awaited in Jesus, and he lived in the light of this inspiring hope.

Smith died in harness. When the Council for the Upwey Convention was formed four years after the Convention began, he continued on as secretary, the position he had held with the MGC, until his death on 27 December 1947.[4]

The day before, Smith had sat in his accustomed place at the head of the table for dinner at the Upwey Convention Lodge. Later that afternoon, at the council meeting in the Union Church, he was suddenly taken ill and transported to hospital where he died the following day. His last words at the hospital were 'Thy will be done. Praise the Lord!'

A Thanksgiving Service was conducted by Rev. John G. Ridley, evangelist and a speaker at the 1947/48 Convention, and Rev. Gilbert McLaren of the Noone Street Mission, Clifton Hill. A service was also held at his home in Mitcham, in which J.J. Kitchen and Alfred Coombe participated. The great company sang the hymns *Oh, the deep, deep love of Jesus* and *For all the saints who from their labours rest.* At the Box Hill Cemetery, at a service conducted by Ridley, a hymn well-loved at the Convention was sung, with its concluding verse:

> Jesus triumphant, when the spirit wings
> Upward and heavenward to the King of Kings;
> And through the last great triumph of Thy grace
> Triumphant saints shall see Thee face to face.

Tributes

His was a transformed life and a surrendered life. Whether managing one of the most prestigious hotels that Melbourne had seen, managing the Keswick bookshop ministry or contributing in the many meetings he attended, his life was evidence of the convention message of cleansing and renewal, full surrender, the fullness of the Holy Spirit and the path of sacrifice and service.

One of his MGC colleagues wrote in a tribute after his death:

> Earnestly seeking the Divine leading and empowerment of the Holy Spirit, God led him into a sphere of service very few are called to enter. If a hundred fold means one thousand per cent, I feel that would indicate the value of a life so lived.[5]

Leonard Buck, who became an outstanding leader in the next generation of Melbourne's interdenominational convention, evangelical and missionary interests, wrote:

> Mr. H.P. Smith was one of God's mountaineers. He was a modern Caleb, the language of his heart and life constantly declaring – 'Give me this mountain.' He was one of the busiest men in Australia and his widespread activities and interests amazed those of us who were associated with him. I would say there were three things which made him such a choice saint:
>
> **A Man of Prayer.** 'Men ought always to pray and not to faint,' was not only in his doctrinal kitbag, but part of his daily warfare.
>
> **A Man of Faith.** 'He believed God.' He faced difficulties and proceeded to overcome them. He could give a strong lead and follow a difficult one.
>
> **A Man of Works.** He not only lived in Christ, but acted for Christ. He actively prayed and planned and then partook of the work which he helped to create. A living

> faith hitched irrevocably to works. He climbed his mountains on earth, and now rests on Mount Zion. We shall never forget this beloved mountain climber.[6]

In a personal tribute by Ernest Renshaw at the time of H.P. Smith's death, he wrote:

> Following the bursting of the land boom in the nineties [1890s] and to increase the profits, an effort was made by the directorate of the Federal to secure a liquor licence. The Temperance Party fought the matter and the writer remembers how away in the country, he sought by petition to influence the Parliament against the proposal. Later, however, instead of being in opposite camps, we became associated in the most precious relationships in life and in the service of the Lord Jesus.
>
> H.P. Smith was indeed a trophy of Divine grace. He was a fine businessman, a master of detail, prompt, unhurried, approachable and always in control. Where the business side of missionary and evangelical activities are so essential, these were valuable characteristics ...
>
> He went forward into a life of service, to be used of God as very few are, an instrument in His hand to the praise and glory of His Name. It is impossible humanly to estimate the influence of such a life – eternity only will reveal it ... His fidelity to the Word of God, I am told, cost him his office, but God had marked out for him instead another channel of service, larger, fuller and richer than would have been possible under ordinary church control and procedure.
>
> One has but to take up 'The Keswick Quarterly and Upwey Convention News', of which nearly ninety issues have already appeared and of which he was both founder and editor, to understand where his sympathy

> and prayers were directed. When we consider the circumstances under which God called him to such a mighty service we exclaim, 'What God has wrought!' We praise God for such a trophy of His grace.[7]

Under the heading, 'The Secret of a Fruitful Life', *The Quarterly* of May 1948, then edited by W.L. Wright and Arthur Pocklington, sought to answer the question, 'What was the secret of the life that made such a profound impression upon many hundreds of lives in his day and generation?' In summarised form, they wrote:

> There was a deep and permanent work of the Holy Spirit accomplished both in conversion and dedication of life. He was a new creature in Jesus Christ, old things had passed away, and all things had become new.
>
> He dug deeply and prayerfully into the Word of God. He was challenged by the Holy Spirit in relation to the Deity of Christ and the Virgin aspect of His birth. He realised the fundamental importance of a rigid understanding of these truths. These great truths, accepted by faith, and confirmed by the witness of the Holy Spirit, were a sheet anchor to his soul. He delighted in that declaration of Colossians chapter 1, 'He is the image of the invisible God, the first-born of every creature; for by Him were all things created, that are in Heaven, and that are in earth, visible and invisible, whether they be thrones, or dominions, or principalities, or powers; all things were created by Him, and for Him; and He is before all things, and by Him all things consist ... that in all things He might have the pre-eminence.'
>
> To H.P. Smith, the Lord was the chiefest among ten thousand and the altogether lovely One. This was his beloved and this was his friend. He saw the Lord Jesus in His lovely character on earth, in His meekness, lowliness, kindness, patience and sympathy. He knew full well that the Holy Spirit alone could make the

change and produce in him the character of his Lord, to enable him to reflect Christ, and to walk even as He walked.

His meditation on Him was pleasurable, because every step of the way our Lord glorified His Father in a life of perfect love, absolute trust and obedience to His Father's will, at the close of which He finished on the Cross the mighty work the Father had given Him to do. The supreme glory of the Cross was all so wonderful. All he deserved on account of his sins was borne by his Saviour and he found his refuge and peace in Him. He rested in the eternal efficacy of the precious blood.

In his surrender, he began his Christian race in a victory already won by the Lord Himself through His death and resurrection. He entered into the life more abundant as he realised in day-to-day experience the exceeding greatness of His power towards all who believe.

He knew what it meant to abide in Christ and to draw from Him, through the ministry of the Word of God and prayer, strength for purity of life and for efficiency in service.

The Word of God was his delight and he meditated upon its statutes continually. It was his habit in prayer to quote promises from Scripture which he changed to facts: 'Ask and ye shall receive', 'Lord, I do receive,' he would say. Again, 'Call upon Me, and I will answer thee, and show thee great and mighty things that thou knowest not.' He would say, 'I will call, for Thou wilt answer.' Truly he lived the abiding life in constant communion with his Father.

In the early days of his conversion, he received by faith the fullness of the Holy Spirit as definitely as he had received the Saviour. Throughout his life of witness and ministry he was careful to maintain good works and abstain from every appearance of evil. He knew the secret of victory through the constant infilling of the Holy Spirit. In the grand days of the Melbourne Gospel Crusade activities, some will remember Mr. Smith's voice, singing above others, a favourite hymn:

> Oh, for the floods on the thirsty land,
> Oh, for a mighty revival!
> Oh, for a sanctified, fearless band,
> Ready to hail its arrival!
> Life! Life! Eternal Life!
> Jesus alone is the Giver:
> Life! Life! Abundant Life.
> Glory to Jesus for ever!

Although he ministered at the home base, his vision and zeal embraced the world. The burden of his heart was to make known the unsearchable riches of Christ to the believers and the saving grace of God to the multitudes without God, and thus without hope. In middle life his outstanding personality filled and controlled by the Holy Spirit demanded attention as he stood on the Yarra Bank fearlessly declaring the whole counsel of God.

His passion was Christ. At a recent Convention at Upwey, the Chairman of the great missionary gathering, after having called all missionaries present to leave their seats and go to the front of the platform, invited Mr. Smith to stand with them. A consecration hymn was sung as three hundred persons joined the company as they yielded their lives to Christ for service at home or abroad. He kept before his vision the teeming millions of lost souls.

He ever kept in mind the return of the Lord Jesus Christ for His own. As years crept on, his faith in the second advent did not diminish. The increasing darkness of the age suggested the ushering in of the eternal day and

> he lived and worked in anticipation of it. H.P. Smith lived in the light of this inspiring hope. 'Therefore be ye stedfast, unmoveable, always abounding in the work of the Lord, forasmuch as ye know that your labour is not in vain in the Lord.'[8]

W.L. Wright, the editor of *The Quarterly* who immediately succeeded Smith, wrote that he was the Keswick message in action. He said that to a remarkable degree, in his own person Smith had exemplified the teaching of the New Testament regarding the practical life and behaviour of the believer for which the teaching of the Keswick message was known.[9]

On H.P. Smith's grave in the cemetery at Box Hill are the words from Revelation 22:3–4 – 'His servants shall serve him; and shall see His face' – and a verse, the story of which he had circulated in a tract inserted in an issue of *The Quarterly*:[10]

> In peace let me resign my breath,
> And Thy salvation see;
> My sins deserve eternal death,
> But Jesus died for me.

CHAPTER 16 The Next Generation

> Time, like an ever-rolling stream,
> Bears all its sons away ...

So wrote Isaac Watts in his famous hymn, *O God, our help in ages past*.

The changes that time brought had already had an effect on the original composition of the MGC Council. The chairman, Thomas Graham, and Charles A. Sandland had both died in 1939. The founding chairman, Frank Varley, died in 1942 and H.P. Smith had unexpectedly been 'called home' in 1947.

While the ministries under the auspices of the MGC and those under the personal direction of H.P. Smith had lost their leader, the Upwey Convention, the Keswick Book Depot and the Open-air Ministry in the Melbourne CBD continued under changed leadership. The Open-air Ministry was undertaken by the MBI and provided solid practical experience for students.

'The old order changes'

Changes had been foreshadowed concerning the Upwey Convention leadership even before Smith became ill during the 1947–48 Convention. 'The Old Order Changes' was the heading of the February 1948 *The Quarterly* that informed readers of the events that had just taken place:

> For the past score of years the leadership of the Convention remained practically unchanged. It was almost traditional that Dr. J.J. Kitchen should chair the gatherings, ably assisted by Mr. W.L. Wright, with Mr. A.E. Coombe later, and that the Honorary Secretary,

> Mr. H.P. Smith, should be at his appointed place at the Lodge, and on the platform.
>
> Now all has changed. First, in the order of events, all of which have deprived Upwey of leading personalities, was the absence on medical advice of Mr. W.L. Wright.
>
> Then 'the beloved physician' (Dr. J.J. Kitchen) who had so ably presided over so many Convention Council and public meetings, announced his retirement on the grounds of advancing years. [Dr. Kitchen was then aged 81.] We shall not expect to see Dr. Kitchen's equal in the gracious, wise, spiritual direction of many memorable assemblages where plainly the Spirit of God had moved.
>
> Then what shall we say of Mr. H.P. Smith? 'A prince and a great man has fallen in Israel.' It is noteworthy that it was immediately subsequent to the announcement of Dr. Kitchen's retirement at the annual meeting of the Council, and in the very act of expression of thanks to God for the Doctor's long and happy association with the work, that the first intimation of the speedy approach of death was seen in God's servant, to whom, more than to any other, was due the inauguration and growth of the Convention. Within a matter of hours he had received his 'abundant entry into the everlasting Kingdom of our Lord and Saviour Jesus Christ.'

After his admission to hospital, that evening Smith told his wife that he took his illness as the leading of the Lord to pass on his work at the Convention to others. It had been his thirtieth consecutive Upwey Convention.

J. Oswald Sanders, who had been residing in Melbourne as Home Director of the CIM, was chosen as chairman to succeed J.J. Kitchen. Alfred Coombe and Leonard Buck were appointed Deputy Chairmen, L.E. Topp was appointed acting honorary treasurer, with Mark Pollard later becoming honorary treasurer. Arthur Pocklington, who had been assistant to H.P.

Smith, was appointed honorary secretary. The next generation had been well prepared and they moved smoothly into their new positions.

There were others in Melbourne's evangelical leadership who had previously been 'called home'. They included Edwin Lee Neil (1934), D.S. MacColl, H.B. Denniston and F.C. Crosby (1938), John M. Griffiths (1943) and Norman Lumsden and R.S. Tregaskis (1944). Then W.L. Wright, a former member of the MGC Council and a member of the Upwey Executive, who had chaired many convention meetings as well as having been a regular speaker, died in 1950.

Other laymen who made a notable contribution to the cause of evangelical interdenominational ministries during those earlier years included James Griffiths; William Buck (the father of Leonard), who was a chartered accountant; Alex Eggleston, a member of the Convention Council and an architect who designed the distinctive Upwey auditorium built in 1932 which is still in evidence in the main Belgrave Heights auditorium; H J. Hannah; A. Kenny; S. Howell; Walter J. Beasley and George Hall.

1920s–1940s: New missions

Apart from the larger existing missions such as CIM and SIM that had been especially supported, new and significant ministries had commenced under the influences of the MBI, Upwey Convention and MGC.

The Bible Union of Victoria was formed in 1923 to raise an informed voice, 'In view of the widespread departure from the faith once delivered to the saints and the persistent denials of those Fundamentals on the part of many who speak in the name of learning and with the authority of Christian Teachers.'[1] It served an important activist role in countering modernism, which was making severe inroads into the theological colleges of the denominations. Many of these colleges have not recovered from the influence of modernism.

In 1928, BEM (now incorporated with Overseas Missionary Fellowship [OMF]) was formed, followed by the Unevangelised Fields Mission in Australia. In the 1930s, Campaigners for Christ was founded (1936), Everyman's Welfare Service was established to work with the armed forces during the war (1939) and *New Life* made its welcome appearance. C.H Nash continued his Wednesday night public lectures at MBI, and the Melbourne City Men's Bible Class that he later led became another outstanding training ground for the next group of leaders – mainly those who were not able to attend full-time studies at MBI.

The Interdenominational Missionary Fellowship (Victoria)

The end of World War II presented new opportunities for world evangelisation, and a group of laymen, already in fellowship in the ministries of the Convention and MBI, moved to set up a new organisation to bring missions into helpful fellowship with each other. At that time, interdenominational missions did not have a denomination behind them to provide support when difficulties arose. In the post-war world, missions were being established in many new independent nations and there was an increased need for cooperation and the sharing of gathered information. It was envisaged that mission societies, whilst having primary responsibility for their own work, could contribute to the wellbeing of other societies. As a unified group, they could undertake tasks that none of them could manage as effectively on their own.

The organisation was known as The Interdenominational Missionary Fellowship (Victoria) (IMF [Vic.]). It was visionary in outlook and practical in its application and was publicised as 'A voluntary association of Missionary Societies, not substantially attached to or supported by any particular denominational body, but which seeks, in co-operation with all evangelical sections of the Christian Church, to share in the task of world evangelism.'[2] When it was acknowledged that denominational missionary societies experienced many of the same problems as those in the interdenominational stream, a wider organisation was required and the Evangelical Alliance of Victoria was developed as a result.[3] This work is now carried out by Missions Interlink.

Significantly, all of the original office-bearers of IMF (Vic.) were the core group of laymen who were to take over from the J.J. Kitchen-H.P. Smith-C.H. Nash era during the next two or three years. They were members of both the MBI and the Upwey Convention Councils, except for Keith Walker who was the auditor for both organisations. The officers appointed were Alfred E. Coombe (chairman), Arthur Pocklington (honorary secretary), Keith F. Walker (honorary treasurer), Leonard E. Buck, J. Harold McCracken, Charles G. Sandland and Rev. John W. Searle, who had become Principal of MBI.

The first location for IMF (Vic.) was the Keswick Book Depot in Melbourne, from where H.P. Smith was still conducting his various ministries, including being the active secretary of the Upwey Convention. Apart from the office being in a central location, its placement at the Book Depot helped to bolster support for this new ministry.

Some years later, Ron Clough, a former executive secretary of the Unevangelised Fields Mission, served for many years as chairman of IMF (Vic.). Other Melbourne laymen who made outstanding and long-term contributions to this organisation during the war and post-war years – mainly through Campaigners for Christ and Everyman's Welfare Service connections – included Alan T. Kerr, the managing director of a furniture factory, and Keith Morgan, the proprietor of an elevator construction and maintenance company.

The leadership was able to draw on many others who had been brought up under the Melbourne ministries and were involved in councils and committees in the post-war years. Some had returned from active service overseas and had seen the great need for cross-cultural gospel ministry. A group had been pilots or other aircrew and had observed the compelling opportunities for mission aviation in places such as Papua New Guinea and Borneo, and then came to study at MBI. One example was Bruce Morton, who had been a wartime pilot. After graduating from MBI he became the BEM's first pilot, flying over virgin jungle, landing on rough-hewn airstrips and coping with violent weather changes. An experienced pilot but without radio contact, he learned to trust the Lord in all kinds of circumstances. Another MBI graduate, engineer Ken Cooper, helped to keep the plane flying. When home on furlough, he learned to fly to keep the program operational.

1950s–1960s: New ministry initiatives

A cohesive unity was maintained among Melbourne's interdenominational ministries during the 1950s and 1960s. Many regular convention-goers recalled these years as the finest years of the Convention. One who attended his first convention in the 1950s recently commented:

> My first Convention was an unbelievable experience. As someone in my late teens the Convention was the nearest place to Heaven, the Keswick Hymn Book was second only to the Bible, and the Convention Chairman in my mind was invested with more authority and status than any ecclesiastical figure, archbishop or whatever.[4]

In contrast, the 1920s and particularly the 1930s, probably the years of the Convention's greatest growth, were held by many older folk to be those of greatest blessing. Invariably, and perhaps inevitably, the most recent convention was usually referred to as 'the best ever'.

The link between the Convention and MBI continued into the early 1970s, with an annual MBI service being an important part of Missionary Day. The Convention played a part in providing students for MBI, as many of them responded at the missionary meeting. In turn, MBI provided well-trained graduates for the missionary societies and other new mission initiatives.

Bishop Stephen Bradley of the Church of England in South Africa, David Cummings with Wycliffe, and Howard Barclay with both Interserve and the United Mission to Nepal were all MBI graduates. Along with Max Meyers of MAF, they were amongst those who went on to hold high responsibilities internationally for the ministries in which they were involved.

Amongst those who left the Convention Council due to responsibilities in the wider mission of the church were Bishop Alfred Stanway, consecrated as the Bishop of Central Tanganyika in Westminster Abbey, and the Archbishop of Melbourne, David Penman.[5] By 1954, the remaining survivor from the MGC Council who had been a member of the founding Convention Council was Ernest Renshaw, who was 'called home' later that year. One of his sons, John R. Renshaw, was a member of the Convention Council, a speaker at several conventions including Belgrave Heights, a pianist for many meetings, one-time president of the Melbourne University Evangelical Union and Principal of the Theological Hall of King's College at the University of Queensland. His eldest brother, David, was appointed a member of the Belgrave Heights Convention Council in the 1950s.

The influence of the Melbourne Gospel Crusade, Melbourne Bible Institute and the conventions

The complementary ministries of the Convention and the MBI have influenced the work of world evangelisation to a significant degree. It is not an exaggeration to say that no mission field has escaped their influence. Included amongst many ministries linked to the founding and/or growth of these organisations are:

- Australian Institute of Archaeology
- Australian Nurses Christian Fellowship

- Aztem (Tentmaker Ministries)
- Borneo Evangelical Mission
- Care & Communication Concern (John Smith and God's Squad)
- Children's Mission Work and Mailbox Club (Laurie Dyer)
- Christian Business and Professional Men's Luncheon
- Christian Service Centre (Dawn Martin)
- Crusader Union
- ESA (originally the ESV and now ESA Country Ministries)
- League of Youth
- Melbourne University Evangelical Union (now Christian Union)
- Mobile Mission Maintenance Australia (MMM)
- MAF (in Australia)
- New Guinea Christian Leaders' Training College (now CLTC of PNG)
- New Life Books & Archaeology
- OAC Ministries (formerly Open Air Campaigners [Vic.]) – conducted youth and children's programs at conventions
- Prison Fellowship (Australia) (founded in 1980 by Leonard Buck)
- Scripture Union (Victoria) and CSSM – conducted children's meetings at conventions
- Steer Incorporated (founding initiated by Bill Clack)
- Summer Institute of Linguistics-Wycliffe Bible Translators (Australia). In the early 1950s, the work of the Institute, which was known at that time as the Wycliffe School of Linguistics, was sponsored by IMF (Vic). In 1954 Wycliffe became a separate organisation in Australia. Alfred Coombe and David Cummings were involved in the Institute's leadership for many years.
- Truth & Liberation Concern.

While it was lay, professional and businessmen who continued to provide the main leadership of Melbourne's interdenominational evangelical ministries, clergy of all the mainline denominations consistently complemented and worked with them. Many of these ministries have not only stood the test of time, but have also grown into significant mission organisations. In continuing, they are still writing their histories and bringing forth much fruit for the extension of the kingdom of God.

A new generation of lay leaders

At a time after the next generation had taken over and had become established in the leadership of Melbourne's ministries, C.H. Nash, as Principal Emeritus of MBI, wrote:

> Looking back across the years since the Institute came into being the outstanding feature of its history has been the amazing goodness and faithfulness of our Heavenly Father, who has never failed in the remembrance of His Covenant. It was a tiny seed of promise which He planted on September 13th, 1920, and which has now grown into a great tree whose branches cover all the earth ...
>
> The righteous shall be held in everlasting remembrance and although the course of time and change effaces their memory from the minds of a later generation, yet 'their works follow them' and the fruit of their labours is found in many lands, while the record is imperishably written in Heaven.
>
> And to those of us, who having served our own generation are now watching with keen interest God's blessing upon the labours of our successors in the age-long task of making Christ known to men, there is no sweeter joy than to recall the beloved faces and exploits of those who shared with us the task of laying the foundations which have carried the weight of a

> massive superstructure worthy of the cause and Name to which it has been dedicated.[6]

This generation quickly made its mark and brought continuing stability and confidence to evangelical leadership in Melbourne. Stability ensured that the Keswick message emphasis on 'deeper-life' teaching was maintained. It was reflected in lives being surrendered to do the will of God, in the urgency of reaching the lost outside of Christ, and in living the life of faith. The Convention office-bearers elected in 1948, with the later addition of Ridley Kitchen, an insurance-company executive, were still holding office 20 years later. In the 1980s, Ridley, as had his father years before, was appointed Convention chairman.

There were many gifted lay-leaders who filled important roles in Melbourne following the changes in leadership in the late 1940s. However, there was a group of men, supported by their wives, who were involved in both the Convention and Bible college ministries who could be referred to as being the most influential of that time. Their wives participated practically and sacrificially in the ministries in which their husbands were involved. They provided hospitality for countless committee meetings and guests in their homes, kept the home running while their husbands were regularly away for long periods, looked after children and were constantly praying for and encouraging their husbands in the work of the gospel.

Sabina Coombe, Edna Pocklington, Jane Buck, Beth McCracken, Dulcie Davis and Muriel Sandland were some of the women who represent the many wives who stood unitedly with their husbands, supported by a wider group of friends, enabling the work of the kingdom of God to advance.

Alfred E. Coombe

Alfred Coombe (1892–1984) was senior partner of a firm of wool merchants, stock and station and shipping agents. The term of his lay leadership spanned two generations of

Melbourne's interdenominational evangelicalism. On Alfred's retirement from the Council of MBI in 1970, Leonard Buck wrote:

> A tradition that has grown with the Melbourne Bible Institute itself, is that its President be a man of proved business or professional experience and ability, and in whom the Christian public would see the qualities it respected in an Evangelical leader.
>
> The election to this office in 1939 of Alfred Coombe confirmed this tradition. Only four years previously – in February 1935 – Mr. Coombe had become a member of the Council of the Institute. His elevation to the office of President brought to the Institute exceptional gifts – administrative ability; a character consistent with the doctrines believed and taught at MBI; and those qualities that emerged from a deep, personal commitment to the will of God.
>
> But way out and beyond all these qualities there is one which out-distances all others. It is the gift of sensitivity, and springs from the core of 'agape'. This quality measures the aspirations, feelings, opinions and disappointments of others, and rejoices or suffers with them. Alfred Coombe possesses this quality of sensitivity to a superlative degree.
>
> I have prayed and worked with a number of the world's spiritual warriors, but I have met few in whom faith rose to the heights of appropriation and praise revealed in times of special intercession, as it did with Alfred Coombe.
>
> The comprehensive vision displayed by Mr. Coombe as President, along with the flexibility that admits and greets that stubborn, and not too welcome, element known as 'change', are reflected in the physical growth of the Institute. No less than ten additional buildings have been purchased since 1941.

> When the proposal that MBI sponsors a Training College in New Guinea was put to the Council, it was the President's faith and support which led to the founding of the Christian Leaders' Training College in 1965.[7]

Amongst numerous other evangelical organisations, Alfred Coombe was chairman of the Belgrave Heights Convention, chairman of Wycliffe Bible Translators and founding chairman of IMF (Vic.). He was actively involved in the founding of Campaigners for Christ and Everyman's Welfare Service, and held office in several missionary societies.

Arthur Pocklington

As recounted in an earlier chapter, the contact Arthur (1908–1978) had with the MGC Van Ministry was a life-changing experience that led to study at MBI and mission work in China. He later became the assistant secretary of the Upwey Convention.

His giftedness and living of the Spirit-filled life was apparent to those who knew him. Arthur was an encourager to those who sought a deepening of their spiritual life and to receive the infilling of the Holy Spirit through a resting faith. He proved to be a meticulous organiser in the development of new and existing country conventions. As organising secretary after the death of H.P. Smith, he was a strong influence in maintaining the distinctives of the Keswick message at conventions and in the selection of suitable speakers by the Council. During his time as secretary, the Convention undertook the massive relocation from Upwey to Belgrave Heights, the work being completed just in time for the 1950/51 convention. In 1972, due to health reasons, Arthur retired from his position as convention secretary and also as pastor of the Spring Street Mission, Prahran.

Arthur Pocklington was also a member of the Council of MBI/BCV from 1942 to 1977.[8] His wide missionary interests included SIM and CIM/OMF, and he was involved in the founding of IMF (Vic.). His wife Edna belonged to a family that had been encouraged through visits by the Van Ministry at Stanhope years before her marriage, and their son Robin and daughter-in-law Jan, as well as their daughters, have all been, or are, involved in global mission. Arthur's brother, Robert, was an evangelist with the ESA for many years. The Van Ministry started something akin to an evangelical family dynasty.

Leonard E. Buck

Leonard Buck (1906–1996) was a Melbourne businessman, being managing director of a firm of schoolwear retailers. He was chairman of the Belgrave Heights Convention and vice-president of MBI. Leonard was also involved in the founding and leadership of many evangelistic, missionary and welfare organisations, including CLTC of PNG, Campaigners for Christ, Everyman's Welfare Service, IMF (Vic.), Asia Pacific Christian Mission (now Pioneers), Everyman's Centre (Port Moresby) and Prison Fellowship of Australia. His mission involvement included the promotion of overseas missions for the Methodist Church in Victoria, and he was a local/lay preacher of the Methodist and Uniting Churches for nearly 70 years.

As a young man, Leonard recommitted his life to Christ at a Saturday meeting of a Methodist Local Preachers' King's Birthday Weekend Convention in June 1927. On the Monday morning the special preacher was W.P. Nicholson, who had just arrived in Melbourne for a series of evangelistic meetings. Leonard recounted:

> At the conclusion of his message, which was on the infilling and empowering of the Holy Spirit, I responded to the invitation by Mr. Nicholson for those who wished to know the empowering of the Holy Spirit in their lives for service to come forward for prayer. I experienced an immediate anointing of the Holy Spirit's power which has continued throughout the 70 years of service for

> the Lord Jesus Christ – in the Church, in evangelistic, missionary and in convention ministries. It was a miracle. It brought a total change in my life and my faith has never faltered in the years of service that have followed.[9]

In sharing recollections of his experiences in Campaigners for Christ and Everyman's Welfare Service, Charles G. Sandland referred to his long-time friend and colleague in the following way:

> In the Lord's battle, the name of Leonard E. Buck is synonymous with Campaigners for Christ and Everyman's Welfare Service from their beginnings.
>
> With a persistence that would not accept 'No' for an answer, he got the ear of the 'powers that be'. He became recognized by the Army as Chief Commissioner of Everyman's, and by his dignified bearing and distinctive uniform, could well have been mistaken for the 'colonel of the regiment'. By his persuasive approach he seemed able to demand from generals and whoever, almost any concession or support he felt to be needful.[10]

The Right Rev. Sir Marcus Loane, former Archbishop of Sydney and Primate of Australia, commented:

> Few laymen in this country, or in this generation, have lived lives more fruitful for God. His primary interests were always in evangelism and in missionary enterprise. He was widely used both in pioneer and leadership roles in those and other areas as well. It was a life of many activities, not only in which he was engaged, but in which he was a prime mover, from the foundation of the City Businessmen's Bible Class right through to his participation in the Prison Fellowship ministry. A life that was crowded, here in his own city of Melbourne, right across the continent of Australia, into large areas of South East Asia, and making his

> impact when he travelled abroad in many different ways.
>
> In my mind, I link Leonard Buck with Alfred Stanway and with Paul White as the three most outstanding Australians of their generation in their Christian life and enterprise. They were at the top. They were remarkable men. They left a mark for God that will not be effaced or forgotten in the generation that follows.[11]

(Alfred Stanway was converted, when a young man, under the ministry of C.H. Nash. Leonard Buck had also been greatly influenced by C.H. Nash, particularly through the Melbourne City Men's Bible Class.)

At the Thanksgiving Service for the life of Leonard Buck, David J. Price, then Principal of BCV and a former Principal of CLTC of PNG, remarked:

> In one of the last meetings that Leonard Buck led as Chairman of the Australian Advisory Council of the Christian Leaders' Training College of Papua New Guinea in October 1994, he said with his usual challenge, vigour and fire:
>
> 'If I had a preaching ministry today, I would preach about the fullness of the Holy Spirit, the revival of the spiritual life, the daily surrender, and the sacrifice of it.'

J. Harold McCracken

Harold McCracken (1906–1999) was a founder and senior partner of the legal firm of McCracken & McCracken. After his retirement, in an address at the opening of new city offices, he referred to his first office at 317 Collins Street, the building in which Keswick Book Depot_was located, and also to God's leading in his professional life.

He recounted a remarkable story of an invitation given to C.H. Nash by the medical branch of the Student Christian Movement to address them at Melbourne University. This, however, did not proceed because of the position Nash held on the authority of Scripture. Instead, the group held a camp at the Upwey home of John Griffiths during the 1929–30 Upwey Convention. In the group were Leslie Griffiths (who later lost his life as a medical missionary) and Dr A. Murray Clarke, who were both medical students. The group earnestly prayed about the impasse. Subsequently, Harold McCracken went forward at the Convention into life-changing blessing, and the group of medical students decided to press on with the invitation to C.H. Nash. Nash eventually accepted the invitation, which was linked with a visit by Dr Howard Guinness in 1930. An outcome of this event was the formation of the Crusader Union and the Melbourne University Evangelical Union.

Harold McCracken was president of MBI/BCV, vice-chairman of the Belgrave Heights Convention after having been appointed a member of the Upwey Council in 1934, and chairman of the Melbourne City Mission. He was a founder of IMF (Vic.), the Crusader Union, the Melbourne University Evangelical Union and the Inter-Varsity Fellowship of Evangelical Students, now known as the Australian Fellowship of Evangelical Students.

Ralph Davis

In the April 1990 *Campaigners for Christ Newsletter*, Ralph Davis (1912–1991) described his involvement with George Hall, Leonard Buck, Alfred Coombe, Charles G. Sandland, Howell Swanton and their guides and mentors, amongst others, as well as an older group including C.H. Nash, William Buck, Alex Eggleston and Rev. Walter Betts:

> There was certainly nothing special about the quality of our lives as Christians. There were, however, a number of characteristics which gave us common ground for action. I attempt to outline them:
>
> 1. We had common interest in soul-winning and serious discipleship.

2. There was a readiness and commitment to tell the Gospel to the lost.
3. We were learning Biblical discipleship together in actual working conditions.
4. We were learning together to pray.
5. We were seeking a positive active relationship with our churches.
6. We were growing together in the Lord, relating business and family life to our activities in evangelism.
7. We had no spiritual secrets, 'save in the Cross of our Lord Jesus Christ, by Whom the world is crucified unto me, and I unto the world.' Galatians 6:14.

On the office desk of Ralph Davis was a plaque with an abbreviated wording of Jeremiah 9:23 in prominent letters:

> Let not the wise man glory in his wisdom,
> Let not the mighty man glory in his might,
> Nor let the rich man glory in his riches;
> But let him who glories glory in this,
> That he understands and knows Me.

As a business executive, first as manager, then managing director and later, chairman of directors of Mayne Nickless Ltd, originally a transport firm, Davis saw the number of employees grow from a few hundred to over 43,000 worldwide. He was deeply involved in many of Melbourne's interdenominational ministries including Scripture Union and BEM. He was a former president of Campaigners for Christ and treasurer of the 1959 Billy Graham Crusade in Melbourne. He joined the Council of Melbourne Bible Institute in 1948 and was president of the BCV Council from 1970 to 1980.

Charles George Sandland

Charles G. Sandland (1903–2002) was a poultry farmer whose lifetime spanned almost all of the 20th century. He became a leader in many of the ministries for which Melbourne is well known. These included the Upwey/Belgrave Heights

Convention (of which he was assistant treasurer for many years), MBI/BCV (life member), Keswick Book Depot, IMF (Vic.), Campaigners for Christ, Everyman's Welfare Service, United Aborigines Mission, MAF, CLTC of PNG and Steer Incorporated. He was an active local/lay preacher of the Methodist and Uniting Churches for over 75 years.

When Charles G. Sandland retired from the Council of BCV in 1991 after 50 years of service, he recalled the influences of his spiritual pilgrimage over the years:

> On the human level the web and woof of my life's fabric seem to have evolved from the interplay upon it of my parents on the one hand and, on the other, my uncle, my father's brother, Charles Alfred Sandland. His five children all studied at MBI during the 1920's and early 30's, three of them becoming missionaries.
>
> I have not discovered how my uncle became associated with Hervey Perceval Smith, but along with Ernest Renshaw, the President's father, he became a founding member of the Council of the Melbourne Gospel Crusade and of the Upwey Convention. In this way I came to know Mr. Smith and attended the first Upwey Convention in 1918, while I was still at High School. At this Convention I was deeply moved by the Bible Readings on Colossians, given by the Rev. C.H. Nash. As a result, in after years I attended Wednesday evening lectures at MBI and subsequently the City Men's Bible Class, all under the tutelage of Mr. Nash.
>
> As to my association with the MBI/BCV Council, the President recently passed on to me a copy of Minutes dated November 15, 1940 where I was to be invited to join the Council ... There was quite a denominational cross-section of evangelical ministers together with Alfred Coombe, W.J. Beasley, Samuel Howell, H.P. Smith and others well-known in business circles including Leonard Buck. There were also several in professional

life such as A.S. Eggleston, the well-known architect, W.M. Buntine, Principal of the Caulfield Grammar School, and Dr. J. J. Kitchen, Home Director of the CIM and of course, Harold McCracken. Having known these men I am firmly convinced they were not chosen to be members of Council by reason of their prominent positions nor their business acumen, but because they had a personal stake in the business of the Kingdom of God.

There will also always remain with me the memory of the scores and scores of students who subsequently spread out over the world, many of them to live in primitive conditions which missionaries would rarely meet these days. When I ponder this I bow in worship and say, 'Who am I when so many of these valiant servants of Christ have given their all – body, soul, spirit, possessions – in His service?[12]

CHAPTER 17 Review and Revival

In writing of the MGC, Dr Stuart Piggin, Director of the Centre for the History of Christian Thought and Experience at Macquarie University, has said:

> I have been researching now for many years on the history of Australian evangelicalism, but have not found another group of lay, professional and business men who have made such a significant contribution as this group ...
>
> Psalm 145:4–6, 'One generation will commend your works to another; they will tell of your mighty acts'. This we are commanded to do that later generations 'might set their hope in God, and not forget the works of God'. Psalm 78:7.
>
> It is a big and intricate story, well integrated with Australian social and cultural as well as religious history ... But it is also a story of great spiritual power and potential to do good.
>
> It has been argued that the joint influence of Upwey, including the Upwey Extension Movement (which carried the Keswick message through conventions throughout country Victoria) and the Melbourne Bible Institute have had more impact on evangelical life in Victoria than any other institutions.[1]

H.P. Smith and C.H. Nash

Melbourne was blessed by God with the provision of two outstanding spiritual leaders. Together, they brought to

Melbourne an unprecedented and prolonged period of evangelistic endeavour and global missionary growth. Their emphasis on Keswick teaching set Melbourne apart and gave added power to its spiritual uniqueness.

The influence of H.P. Smith (1869–1947), soundly converted with his life and ministry founded on the Keswick message, paved the way for the unforgettable ministry of C.H. Nash (1866–1958), whose life had been deeply influenced by the Keswick message in England. One of these men was at his peak in business life, the other in his Bible-teaching ministry.

Although active in business life, Smith lived with the desire to bring everyone to a saving knowledge of Christ, and for Christians to experience the infilling of the Holy Spirit. Nash, gifted as a master Bible teacher, completely complemented the evangelistic and missionary vision of Smith for which the MGC was known. Their ministries came together in the pre-MBI days of the Upwey Convention and then to full fruition after the MBI was founded alongside the growing convention movement where Nash frequently gave the Bible exposition.

The issues of *The Quarterly* over a period of nearly 25 years indicate the breadth of Smith's heartbeat for worldwide evangelisation and the secret of his walk with God. Increasingly as a businessman who was 'on fire for God', he could in many respects be regarded as Nash's equal in spiritual effectiveness. His outstanding leadership gifts, his conversion and abundant life experience, his influence through the Upwey Convention and the Keswick Book Depot, and his support for dozens of missionary societies combined to give solid evidence as to his stature. His judgment and ability to get things done were without peer.

Perhaps H.P. Smith's ministry could have been just as effective without C.H. Nash, but it is doubtful whether C.H. Nash could have been as effective without H.P. Smith and his influence amongst the ordinary people of Melbourne's body of believers. Under God, the two men were complementary, and this was probably one of the most significant factors contributing to Melbourne's spiritual uniqueness and effectiveness.

One of the important factors in the post-World War I ministry of C.H. Nash may have been the initial support of spiritually minded Melbourne laymen who were highly respected and successful in business – such as H.P. Smith, Edwin Lee Neil (joint managing director of the Myer Emporium), John and James Griffiths, and J.J. Kitchen – and who stood alongside him and gave him ministry opportunities at the pre-MBI Upwey Convention. This support gave the Christian public the confidence they needed in Nash as the founding Principal of a Bible institute for the training of predominantly young men and women for missionary service.

The Upwey/Belgrave Heights Convention has had a remarkable influence on evangelical life. Many folk had personal encounters with God there and returned to their homes, churches, places of employment, schools and universities with a new testimony. Many had made their decision to accept Christ as Saviour and Lord at gospel meetings or in houseparties and camps. Many hundreds have been called into missionary service at Convention meetings.

G.H. Morling (1891–1974), when Principal-emeritus of the NSW Baptist College, recalled memories of the earlier generation of Upwey Convention leaders when speaking at the Belgrave Heights Jubilee Christmas/New Year Convention of 1967–68:

> The history of the Upwey/Belgrave Heights Convention reaches back to the movement for scriptural holiness that was one fruit of the evangelical revival of the mid-nineteenth century which came to notable expression in the Keswick Convention.
>
> Australia felt that breath of the Spirit at the turn of the century and perhaps it was most strongly felt in

> Victoria. In this State, a group of men representative of the whole Church of God was thrust up by the Holy Spirit. They felt soul need and longed for something more, and so avoided what has been called the curse of spiritual mediocrity.
>
> There is mystic sweet communion with those whose rest is won. I simply name these men and I name them with a deep sense of reverence and affection. I knew these men and they have enriched me –
>
> H.P. Smith, with his rock-like loyalty and tireless efficiency;
> J.J. Kitchen, with his wisdom and warm and quiet dignity;
> C.H. Nash, rugged, erudite, master teacher of the Word of God;
> W.L. Wright, capable in business and versed in the doctrines of the Convention;
> J.H. Robinson, devoted missionary of the Cross who spearheaded the first Upwey enterprise.
>
> I say with you, 'Blessed be the God who gave them to the Convention.'

Revival

Revival was an issue constantly on the heart and in the mind of H.P. Smith, a longing and a concern that he publicised through *The Quarterly*. 'Can we expect revival in these days?' was the editorial question he asked in 1926 in one of the earliest issues.

He wrote consecutive editorials on revival in 1930 and the question was asked in 1931, 'Can we have a revival?', followed by 'The revival we need' in the following issue. Two years later, his editorial was 'Revival: Waiting for Pentecostal blessing'. The need for 'Revival now? Why not?' was highlighted in the war year of 1942. Then in 1946, he asked the question once again, 'Revival Today – Why not?', and he published a first-hand experience address given by Dr G. Campbell Morgan on 'The Great Welsh Revival' (see Chapter 6).[2]

In his century, William Booth said that we are in need of seeing visions of God. His considered opinion was that the chief dangers were:

> Religion without the Holy Spirit;
> Christianity without Christ;
> Forgiveness without repentance;
> Politics without God;
> Heaven without hell.

'And,' he said,

> we have them all. All are the offspring of a Church which has no vision of God. We have lost the vision of heaven and hell; hence the lack of deep concern for men and women without Christ. And we have lost the vision of the real, deep spiritual needs of our fellows, men, women and children dying without Christ.[3]

The secret of great revival belongs to the spiritual realm

It is appropriate to reiterate Dr W.H. Fitchett's description of a revival:

> The secret [of revival] belongs to the spiritual realm. It is idle to seek for it in the personal qualities of the men who were its agents, in the overwhelming oratory of [George] Whitefield, the hymns of Charles Wesley, the ordered and matchless industry, the genius for organisation, of John Wesley ...
>
> In its last analysis the secret of the great religious movement ... is to be found in the rich outpouring of the living Spirit of God on the nation ... in a particular group of men, fit instruments, with fit measure of devotion and faith, for a work so great. Flowing through

the channel of true doctrine, and using the agency of fit human instruments, the grace of the Holy Spirit wrought this great work.

...

What are evangelical doctrines?

A chain of mountain peaks, that pierce to the crown of the heavens, and on whose summits brood perpetual sunshine! They constitute a close-knitted succession of truths that break out of eternity and have its scale. Truths that relate to sin, and proclaim its measureless guilt, its hurrying and inevitable doom; but which also reveal an immediate and personal deliverance from sin – a deliverance which comes as an act of divine grace, and on the simplest terms of penitential acceptance ...

A divine redemption; a realised pardon; a restored relationship with God through faith ... And all this made intelligible and credible by the redeeming work and offices of Jesus Christ – and by the saving energies of the Holy Spirit in the human soul! This is the evangelical version of Christianity! ...

These are the doctrines that send out missionaries, that inspire martyrs, that regenerate slums! They awaken deeper vibrations in the human soul than all other truths put together. They are the doctrines in which dying men find comfort. All the great hymns of Christian worship reflect them; all the great prayers of human need give them speech. They formed exactly the message which the dying Christianity of the England of the day needed. 'Men,' the message ran, 'are in utmost and instant peril; they need ... a divine deliverance accomplished through redeeming grace. And this salvation is possible. A Saviour walks amongst men, touching them with hands of tenderness. Hope is born! All men may be saved here and now.' [4]

Whither Melbourne?

In some thoughtful and considered remarks to the BCV Council in 1990, Charles G. Sandland contemplated how the College could relate to the spiritual need of the city of Melbourne. He said:

> I have lately been carefully reading the Book of Jonah. This strange and remarkable story ends with the Lord asking Jonah a question, 'Should I not pity Nineveh, that great city, in which there are more than 120,000 persons who do not know their right hand from their left?' The city of Melbourne is no doubt less down-at-heel than was Nineveh, but in spiritual terms the great mass of people are abysmally ignorant.[5]

In this present age, in the 21st century, how do we respond to the question posed with the population of once 'Marvellous Melbourne' now exceeding four million persons, and the great mass of people in spiritual terms being abysmally ignorant – 'who do not know their right hand from their left'?

We have moved to the winter of corruption, of luxury, of indolence, of vice during which the city and the nation seems to have forgotten God. From media reports, it has given itself up to drunkenness, drug addiction, gambling, greed and sexual aberration. Until the city of Melbourne, this nation of Australia, and indeed the wider world, returns to God in repentance, will it ever pull itself together for any serious work?

A last word from H.P. Smith

H.P. Smith wrote: 'It is generally conceded that the revival under the Wesleys in the 18th Century saved England from the horrors of the French revolution … We ask: can we expect such revival in these days?'

He continued:

> Some of the Lord's people say they are not looking for revival. They are looking for the personal return of the

Lord Jesus. Praise God! So are we. And so did Paul. Furthermore so did the Wesleys. But this did not hinder God using them in true, deep, God honouring revival.

Others say they cannot see revival prophesied for these last days; but rather that 'perilous times shall come,' and men 'shall wax worse and worse.' (2 Tim. 3). We believe we are in the last times and these and other words of prophecy are already having terrible fulfilment. But, we ask, were the revivals during past centuries which have been the means of much wonderful blessing to the world, especially prophesied? Did they not come apart from the word of prophecy?

Furthermore, times of revival have never eliminated evil. The Holy Spirit has wrought mightily despite the evil around; and cannot He do the same to-day? Is He not 'the same yesterday, and to-day, and for ever?' Should the Lord tarry a year or two yet, who dare say an Australian revival is an impossibility?

... [there is] a glorious promise of Almighty God given to His people in Old Testament times which we do not for one moment believe has been withdrawn in New Testament times ...

The promise is: 'If My people, which are called by My Name, shall humble themselves, and pray, and seek My face, and turn from their wicked ways; then I will hear from heaven, and will forgive their sin, and heal their land.' (2 Chron. 7.14).[6]

It is for us to ask of Him, to call upon Him with the absolute assurance that He is well pleased to hear and to do, for His arm is not shortened that it cannot save, neither His ear heavy that it cannot hear; and His word in Jeremiah 33:3 still stands as a solemn challenge to us in all its gracious power: 'Call to Me, and I will answer you, and show you great and mighty things,

> which you do not know.' Should we not ask Him to revive His people and revive His work in these last days, however much we are assured 'that in the last days perilous times shall come' (2 Timothy 3)?
>
> Has the Lord said anywhere that in the last days He will not revive His people – the blood-bought and blood-washed children of God? We need reviving that we may become more earnest than ever in obeying His command to go into all the world to preach the Gospel to every creature – 'beginning at Jerusalem.'[7]

God is waiting to answer our prayers for revival in this 21st century in Melbourne – in Australia – in the Western world.

In speaking about the future, a phrase frequently used by H.P. Smith was 'Should the Lord tarry.' The last words of the Bible conclude,

> 'Surely I come quickly. Amen. Even so, come, Lord Jesus!
> The grace of the Lord Jesus Christ be with you all. Amen.'

Appendix

The Melbourne Gospel Crusade Tract

Tracts were printed for the Van Ministry using two basic formats: one with a photograph of the Ford van and another with a photograph of the Chevrolet van.[1] The content of both tracts was identical. As has been recounted, many thousands of tracts were distributed.

Melbourne Gospel Crusade
(interdenominational)

GOSPEL MOTOR VAN WORK

Country Districts for which prayer is always requested
Keswick Book Depot, 315 Collins Street, Melbourne

GOD'S MESSAGE ON SALVATION

THE NEED OF SALVATION

God says I am a sinner by nature and by practice. Therefore in the light of His perfect holiness, I am guilty and unfit for His presence.

'By nature children of wrath' – Ephesians 2:3.

'There is no difference; for all have sinned and come short of the glory of God' – Romans 3:22–23.

'Whosoever shall keep the whole law and yet offend in one point, he is guilty of all' – James 2:10.

Therefore because I am a sinner, I am under God's wrath, and in danger of being banished from His presence.

'The soul that sinneth, it shall die' – Ezekiel 18:4.

'The wages of sin is death' – Romans 6:23.

'They that know not God, and obey not the Gospel of our Lord Jesus Christ ... shall be punished with everlasting destruction from the presence of the Lord' – 2 Thessalonians 1:8–9.

But God loves me, although He hates my sin, and, in order to save me, He has provided for me a way of salvation.

'For God so loved the world that He gave His only begotten Son, that whosoever believeth in Him should not perish but have everlasting life' – John 3:16.

'But God commendeth His love toward us, in that, while we were yet sinners, Christ died for us' – Romans 5:8.

'The Son of God who loved me and gave Himself for me' – Galatians 2:20.

How, then, can I be saved from the punishment of my sin hereafter, and from the power of sin in my life now?

THE WAY OF SALVATION

Jesus Christ said, *'I AM THE WAY* ... no man cometh unto the Father but by Me' – John 14:6.
Therefore all that is required of me, in order that I may be saved, is that I believe on the Lord Jesus Christ.

'Believe on the Lord Jesus Christ and thou shalt be saved' – Acts 16:31.

BUT WHAT IS MEANT BY BELIEVING ON THE LORD JESUS CHRIST?

FIRST – **I must acknowledge that I am a sinner.**

'We are all as an unclean thing, and all our righteousnesses are as filthy rags' – Isaiah 64:6.

SECOND – **I must see in Jesus Christ One who is the Saviour of sinners.**

'Christ Jesus came into the world to save sinners' – 1 Timothy 1:15.

THIRD – **I must receive Him as MY SAVIOUR.**

'The Son of God who loved me and gave Himself for me' – Galatians 2:20.

'Believe and receive the Saviour, 'tis all you have to do. For Jesus Christ, the First and Last, has done all the rest for you.'

AN ILLUSTRATION – **This leaflet is now my very own; I neither wrote it nor bought it. Someone else did that. I just took it when it was freely offered to me.**

So with *MY SALVATION.* Jesus Christ, God's Son, bought salvation with His Precious Blood; He now freely offers it to me, and all I have to do is to take it as a free gift.

'The gift of God is Eternal Life through Jesus Christ our Lord' – Romans 6:23.

THE MEANING OF SALVATION

If I believe on the Lord Jesus Christ, He will be:

FIRST – MY SIN BEARER. **That is, He, through His atoning death, bears away all my sins, so that their guilt is removed from me for ever through His blood which was shed for me.**

'The Lord hath laid on Him the iniquity of us all' – Isaiah 53:6.

'Behold the Lamb of God who beareth away the sin of the world' – John 1:29.

'In whom we have redemption through His blood, even the forgiveness of sins' – Colossians 1:14.

SECOND – MY SAVIOUR. **That is, He is able and ready to save me from the power of sin in my daily life, as I continue to trust Him for this.**

'He shall save His people from their sins' – Matthew 1:21.

'He is able to save to the uttermost them who come unto God by Him' – Hebrews 7:25.

'Able to guard you from stumbling' – Jude 24.

THIRD – MY MASTER. **That is, He will take control of my life and by His Holy Spirit will lead me into paths of holy living.**

'To this end Christ both died and rose ... that He might be Lord' – Romans 14:9.

'We preach Christ Jesus as Lord' – 2 Corinthians 4:5.

'As therefore ye received Christ Jesus the Lord, so walk in Him' – Colossians 2:6.

THE ASSURANCE OF SALVATION

This rests not on the shifting sands of my feelings, but on the sure ground of His Word.

Jesus Christ said: 'He that heareth My words and believeth on Him that sent Me, hath everlasting life and shall not come into judgment, but is passed from death unto life' – John 5:24.

God says: 'These things have I written unto you that believe on the name of the Son of God that ye may know that ye have eternal life' – 1 John 5:13.

THE CONSEQUENCES OF REJECTING THIS SALVATION

But what if I reject such a Wonderful Salvation? Will it really matter so much?

LISTEN MY SOUL!

'How shall we escape if we neglect so great salvation' – Hebrews 2:3.

'He that believeth not shall be damned' – Mark 16:16.

'He that believeth not is condemned already, because he hath not believed in the name of the only begotten Son of God' – John 3:18.

'And whosoever was not found written in the Book of Life was cast into the lake of fire' – Revelation 20:15.

FOR MY ENCOURAGEMENT

'If I ask Him to receive me, will He say me nay?
Not till earth and not till heaven pass away.'

For Jesus says: 'Him that cometh unto Me I will in no wise cast out' – John 6:37.

MY RESPONSE

'Just as I am without one plea, but that Thy blood was shed for me,
And that Thou bidst me come to Thee; O Lamb of God I come.'

References and Sources

The source material used in this book was collected over a long period of time and before I had any intention to publish a book on 'Marvellous Melbourne'. Some of the records I kept were incomplete, and with deteriorating vision and a reliance on researching a large quantity of printed material comprising much small font of an earlier era, it was impractical for me to compile a normal bibliography or supply missing details for some footnotes, particularly page numbers.

For the benefit of the reader, the following is a list of source material used extensively throughout the book, in addition to the details provided in the footnotes.

- 'Some Melbourne Notes and Comments', compiled by Will F. Renshaw. A series of occasional newsletters (1 September 1993–14 December 1998) sent to members of councils and committees with which he was involved, as well as to others upon request. A full set of these newsletters, along with an index of all names mentioned, is deposited in the library of the Melbourne School of Theology.
- *The Keswick Quarterly and Upwey Convention News* – a collection is located in the Melbourne School of Theology's library. In addition to articles in *The Quarterly* referred to specifically in the main text, the following issues were particularly rich sources of information (chapters containing information from these issues are in brackets): No. 1, February 1926 (8, 9, 10, 11, 12, 13, 15, 16); No. 2, May 1926 (9); No. 3, August 1926 (17); No. 13, February 1929 (8); No. 23, August 1931 (17); No. 29, February 1933 (9); No. 36, November 1934 (9); No. 40 November 1935 (13); No. 49, February 1938 (13); No. 50, May 1938 (13); No. 51, August 1938 (13); No. 61, February 1941 (9); No. 65, February 1942 (17); No. 82, May 1946; No. 88, November 1947 (9); No. 89, February 1948 (7).
- *Melbourne Gospel Crusade Minute Book* – the source for minutes of the meetings of the Council of the Melbourne Gospel Crusade. Currently in the possession of Valda G. Renshaw.
- Minutes of the Melbourne Bible Institute (BCV/MST).

Notes

Chapter 1

1 C.I. Benson, *A Century of Victorian Methodism*, Spectator Publishing Co., Melbourne, 1935, p. 27.
2 City of Melbourne, www.melbourne.vic.gov.au/ABOUTMELBOURNE/HISTORY/Pages/SettlementtoCity.aspx.
3 See M.S.E. Reed, *Henry Reed: An Eventful Life Devoted to God and Man*, Morgan & Scott, London, c. 1906, pp. 105–6.
4 Ibid., pp. 15–16.
5 Benson, *A Century of Victorian Methodism*, p. 28.
6 Stuart Piggin, *Spirit, Word and World: Evangelical Christianity in Australia*, Acorn Press, Melbourne, 2012, p. 71.
7 Ibid.
8 Reed, *Henry Reed*. See also *Launceston Examiner*, 1 November 1906.
9 R.H. Clayton, *From Colonies to Commonwealth*, Angus & Robertson, Melbourne, 1951.
10 Ibid.

Chapter 2

1 A.W. Prescott, 'Dr John Singleton', in Brian Dickey (ed.), *Australian Dictionary of Evangelical Biography* (*ADEB*), Evangelical History Association, Sydney, 1994, pp. 341–2.
2 Clayton, *From Colonies to Commonwealth*.
3 Piggin, *Spirit, Word and World*, p. 30.
4 William Thomas Stead & G. Campbell Morgan, *The Welsh Revival*, The Pilgrim Press, Boston, 1905, p. 15.
5 J.R. Green, *History of the English People*, vol. 5: Puritan England, 1603–1644, Eversley Edition, Macmillan & Co., Ltd, London, 1896, p. 265.
6 'Marvellous Melbourne', Museum Victoria, http://museumvictoria.com.au/marvellous/gold/index.asp.
7 'Diary of Mary Ann Bedford', in R. Fraser, *The Champion of the Seas*, Pilgrim Printing, Glen Waverley, 1999, p. 52.
8 Ibid., p. 54.
9 Ibid., p. 57.
10 Ibid., p. 66.
11 Ibid., p. 67.
12 J.E. Orr, *Evangelical Awakenings in the South Seas*, Bethany Fellowship, Minneapolis, 1976, pp. 49–50.
13 Ibid.
14 Ibid.
15 W.L. Blamires & J.B. Smith, *The Early Story of the Wesleyan Methodist Church in Victoria*, Wesleyan Book Depot, Melbourne, 1886, pp. 89–92.
16 Ibid., p. 315.

17 B. Dickey, Introduction, in Dickey (ed.), *ADEB*, p. ix.

Chapter 3

1 'Marvellous Melbourne', Museum Victoria.
2 Ibid.
3 '"A Touch of Gold": The Federal Group', *The Age*, 28 August 1991.
4 B. Bottom, *Inside Victoria: A Chronicle of Scandal*, Pan Macmillan, Chippendale, 1991.
5 For more detail, see Blamires & Smith, *The Wesleyan Methodist Church*, pp. 160–86.
6 See D. Prout, *The ESA Story: Going Where the Need Is Greater*, ESA, 1984.
7 D.N. Paproth, 'The 1888 Centennial Mission in Victoria', *Lucas*, new series no. 1, Autumn 2009, p. 5.
8 Ibid., p. 35.
9 Ibid., p. 36.
10 Orr, *Evangelical Awakenings*, p. 105.
11 Hannah MacNeil, *John MacNeil: Author of 'The Spirit-Filled Life' – A Memoir by His Wife*, Marshall Brothers, London, 1897.
12 Bible Institute Colportage, Chicago, 1896, pp. 42–43.
13 Ibid., pp. 96–97.
14 Ibid., pp. 106–7.
15 'Advance Australia – Where?', *Australian Presbyterian*, Winter 2013, p. 6.
16 'Marvellous Melbourne', Museum Victoria.

Chapter 4

1 F.B. Meyer, 'Keswick and the Convention Movement', *The Keswick Quarterly and Upwey Convention News*, no. 14, May 1929.
2 Piggin, *Spirit, Word and World*, pp. 57, 71–72.
3 Christian Convention for the Promotion of Spiritual Life, *Reports of Addresses at the Christian Convention, Geelong, September 15th, 16th, 17th, 1891*, E.E Campbell, Ballarat, 1891.
4 Ibid.
5 Ibid.
6 *Reports of Addresses at the Christian Convention, Geelong, September 15th, 16th, 17th, 18th, 1891*, M.L. Hutchinson & Co., Melbourne, p. 101.
7 J.E. Orr, 'Dynamic for Changing a Nation', address given at the Easter Belgrave Heights Convention, 1976.
8 H.B. Macartney Jr, Introduction to John MacNeil, *Some One Is Coming*, Marshall Brothers, London, 1896.
9 Ibid.
10 H. MacNeil, *John MacNeil*.
11 D.J. Innes, review of H. MacNeil, *John MacNeil*, in *Evangelical Action*, August/September 2003.
12 Blamires & Smith, *The Early Story of the Wesleyan Methodist Church in Victoria*; Benson, *A Century of Victorian Methodism*.

13 Dickey, Introduction, *ADEB*, p. viii.
14 See Piggin, *Spirit, Word and World*, pp. 71–72.
15 Ibid., p. 71.
16 Orr, 'Dynamic for Changing a Nation'.

Chapter 5

1 Piggin, *Spirit, Word and World*, p. 59.
2 See W.T. Stead, *The Revival of 1905: Revival in the West*, The Review of Reviews Publishing Office, London, 1905, pp. 102–3.
3 Ibid.
4 Ibid.
5 Ibid.
6 H.C. Alexander & J.K. MacLean, *Charles M. Alexander: A Romance of Song and Soul Winning*, Marshall Brothers Ltd, London, c. 1921, p. 50.
7 Details for source not available, but see also ibid., pp. 65–68.
8 Alexander & MacLean, *Charles M. Alexander*, p. 50.
9 Ibid., pp. 51–52.
10 Ibid., p. 147.
11 Piggin, *Spirit, Word and World*, p. 59.
12 Alexander & MacLean, *Charles M. Alexander*, pp. 54–55.
13 William Warren, 'Genesis of the Australian Revival', *Missionary Review of the World*, vol. 26, 1903, pp. 202f. See also Piggin, *Spirit, Word and World*, 59.

Chapter 6

1 Stead, *The Revival of 1905*.
2 Ibid.
3 Orr, 'Dynamic for Changing a Nation'.
4 H.S. Dyer, *Revival in India: A Report of the 1905–1906 Revival*, Gospel Publishing House, New York, 1907.
5 Paul Thanasingh, *Pandita Ramabai: The First Woman Bible Translator, Founder of the Mukti Mission, National Leader, Social Reformer*, Genesis Books, Nasik, India, 2002.
6 Lorraine Francis, '125 Glorious Years', *Mukti Pulse*, no. 2, 2014, pp. 1–2.
7 Thanasingh, *Pandita Ramabai*.
8 Joseph B. Hingeley (ed.), *Journal of the Twenty-fifth Delegated General Conference of the Methodist Episcopal Church Held in Baltimore, MD, May 6–June 1, 1908*, Eaton & Mains, New York, pp. 861–2.
9 Colin C. Whittaker, *Korea Miracle*, Kingsway Publications, Eastbourne, 1988.
10 Henry Varley Jr, *Henry Varley's Life Story*, Alfred Holness, London, c. 1915, p. 200.
11 Stead, *The Revival of 1905*, p. 76.
12 S. Cox, *Helen Cadbury and Charles Alexander: A Love That Embraced the*

World, Marshall Morgan & Scott Publications Ltd., London, 1989.
13 Stead, *The Revival of 1905*.
14 Orr, 'Dynamic for Changing a Nation'.
15 G.C. Morgan, 'The Great Welsh Revival', *KQ*, no. 82, May 1946, p. 53.
16 Ibid.
17 Ibid.
18 Stead, *The Revival of 1905*.
19 Ibid., p. 89.
20 Ibid., page unknown.
21 Ibid.
22 Morgan, 'The Great Welsh Revival', p. 55.
23 See also Alexander & Maclean, *Charles M. Alexander*, p. 71.
24 W.H. Fitchett, *Wesley and His Century: A Study in Spiritual Forces*, John Murray, London, 1920, p. 274.
25 Ibid., pp. 276–7.

Chapter 7
1 'Architecture – Federal Coffee Palace', Marvellous Melbourne, Museum Victoria, online at http://museumvictoria.com.au/marvellous/1880s/federalcoffee.asp.
2 '"A Touch of Gold": The Federal Group', *The Age*, 28 August 1991.
3 Details for source not available, but accounts of H.P. Smith's conversion are described in various issues of *KQ*, amongst other sources.
4 D.E. Renshaw, 'Tribute to H.P. Smith', unpublished, December 1947.
5 Charles G. Sandland, in conversation with the author on H.P. Smith and the Federal Coffee Palace, n.d.
6 D.E. Renshaw, 'Tribute to H.P. Smith'.

Chapter 8
1 'Dr. R.A. Torrey: A Personal Reminiscence – By the Editor', *KQ*, February 1929, pp. 27–29.
2 This Bible, c. 1903, is now in the possession of the author.
3 This record and others of the meetings of the Council of the Melbourne Gospel Crusade are taken from the *Melbourne Gospel Crusade Minute Book*, in the possession of Valda G. Renshaw.
4 E.J. Daley, 'Death of Mr. H.P. Smith', *New Life*, 8 January 1948.
5 *Keswick Bookshop: Its Beginnings and Now*, Keswick Bookshops Inc., Melbourne, 1991; *Introducing Keswick Bookshops: 79 Years of Ministry 1924–2003*, Keswick Bookshops Inc., Melbourne, 2003.
6 *KQ*, no. 82, May 1946, p. 11.
7 *KQ*, no. 1, February 1926, p. 2.
8 'The Rejected Candidate', *KQ*, no. 6, May 1927, p. 1.
9 *KQ*, no. 4, November 1926, p. 15.
10 *KQ*, no. 6, May 1927, p. 17.
11 Ibid.
12 See, for example, ibid.

13 *KQ*, no. 64, November 1941, p. 41.

Chapter 9

1 Irene Cleverdon, *Rivers of His Grace: The Jubilee Story of Belgrave Heights*, Belgrave Heights Convention, 1968.
2 J.C. Pollock, *The Keswick Story: The Authorised History of the Keswick Convention*, Hodder & Stoughton, London, 1964, p. 16.
3 Cleverdon, *Rivers of His Grace*.
4 *KQ*, no. 2, May 1926, p. 9.
5 Ibid.
6 Details for source not available.
7 *KQ*, no. 2, May 1926, pp. 9–10.
8 Details for source not available.
9 *KQ*, no. 29, February 1933, p. 34 (in an address at the 1932/33 Convention).
10 C.G. Sandland, in an address given on his retirement from BCV Council, 24 September 1991.
11 *KQ*, no. 68, November 1942, p. 32.
12 *KQ*, no. 2, May 1926, p. 10.
13 Ibid., pp. 10–11.
14 Ibid., p. 11.
15 'Home call of Mr. Frank Varley', *KQ*, no. 67, August 1942, p. 22.
16 *KQ*, no. 2, May 1926, p. 11.
17 *KQ*, no. 1, February 1926, p. 6.
18 Ibid., p. 11.
19 Ibid., p. 5.
20 Ibid., p. 6.
21 C.F. Hartford, *The Keswick Convention: Its Message, Its Methods and Its Men*, Marshall Brothers, London, 1907.
22 *KQ*, no. 36, November 1934, p. 12. Smith is quoting from the hymn by A.B. Simpson, *I clasp the hand of Love divine*.
23 'Keswick Teaching', ibid., p. 1.
24 *KQ*, no. 88, November 1947, p. 11.
25 *KQ*, no. 26, May 1932, p. 15.
26 *KQ*, no. 27, August 1932, p. 11.
27 *KQ*, no. 30, May 1933, p. 19.
28 A. Pocklington, 'These Fifty Years: Review of the Upwey-Belgave Heights Convention', unpublished paper, n.d.
29 Will F. Renshaw, *Some Melbourne Notes & Comments*, no. 18, 24 February 1997, p. 2. Similar sentiments are found in Stuart Piggin, 'Pietism, Pluralism and Provincialism: The Divergent Paths of Melbourne and Sydney Evangelicalism 1848–1988,' Perry Memorial Lecture delivered at St James Old Cathedral, 19 October 1990, pp.14–17, and in Piggin, *Spirit, Word and World*, pp. 141–7.

Chapter 10

1 D.E. Renshaw, 'Tribute to H.P. Smith'.
2 Sandland, in conversation with the author on H.P. Smith and the Federal Coffee Palace.
3 *KQ*, no. 4, November 1926, p. 13.
4 'Melbourne Gospel Crusade: Annual Report and Balance Sheet for 1926', *KQ*, no. 5, February 1927, p. 23.
5 'City Gospel Work: Melbourne Gospel Crusade Notes', *KQ*, no. 6, May 1927, p. 13.
6 Ibid.
7 Ibid.
8 'City Gospel Work: Melbourne Gospel Crusade Notes', *KQ*, no. 7, August 1927, p. 15.
9 Ibid.
10 *KQ*, no. 21, February 1931, p. 29.
11 *KQ*, no. 22, May 1931, p. 29.
12 *KQ*, no. 53, February 1939, p. 56.
13 *KQ*, no. 3, August 1926, p. 16.
14 Details for source not available, but accounts of these meetings can be found in various issues of *KQ*.
15 *KQ*, no. 23, August 1931, p. 21.
16 Details for source not available, but see also following note.
17 *KQ*, no. 4, November 1926, p. 14.
18 Ibid.

Chapter 11

1 *KQ*, no. 3, August 1926, p. 15.
2 *KQ*, no. 4, November 1926, p. 13.
3 See *KQ*, no. 13, February 1929, p. 21; no. 14, May 1929, p. 23.
4 *KQ*, no. 15, August 1929, p. 20.
5 *KQ*, no. 17, February 1930, p. 30.
6 M.R. Redpath, additional information provided to the author on the Sandland family, 2014. See also *KQ*, no. 35, August 1934, p. 53.
7 *KQ*, no. 40, November 1935, p. 60.
8 *KQ*, no. 33, February 1934, p. 57.
9 See also *KQ*, no. 37, February 35, p. 49; *KQ*, no. 38, May 1935, p. 52.
10 *KQ*, no. 39, August 1935, p. 52.
11 *KQ*, no. 54, May 1939, pp. 23–24.
12 *KQ*, no. 55, August 1939, pp. 12–13, concluding with a quote from an article in *The Christian* (no further details known).
13 *KQ*, no. 84, November 1946, p. 46.

Chapter 12

1 *KQ*, no. 5, February 1927, p. 21.
2 *KQ*, no. 44, November 1936, p. 45.
3 See *KQ*, no. 52, November 1938, p. 51.

4 *KQ*, no. 9, February 1928, p. 24.
5 *KQ*, no. 18, May 1930, p. 29.
6 Ibid., pp. 29–30.
7 *KQ*, no. 27, August 1932, p. 25.
8 *KQ*, no. 36, November 1934, p. 39.
9 *KQ*, exact details not known.
10 *KQ*, no. 47, August 1937, p. 41.
11 See *KQ*, no. 39, August 1935, p. 49.
12 *KQ*, no. 40, November 1935, pp. 59–60.
13 Ibid.
14 *KQ*, no. 46, May 1937, p. 53.
15 *KQ*, no. 51, August 1938, p. 49.
16 Ibid., pp. 49–50.
17 *KQ*, no. 52, November 1938, pp. 49–51.
18 Ibid., p. 51.
19 Ibid.
20 *KQ*, no. 6, May 1927, p. 13.
21 See *KQ*, no. 52, November 1938, p. 49.
22 *KQ*, no. 11, August 1928, pp. 21–22.
23 *KQ*, no. 19, August 1930, p. 26.
24 *KQ*, no. 7, August 1927, p. 15.
25 *KQ*, no. 25, February 1932, p. 37.
26 *KQ*, no. 24, November 1931, p. 25.
27 *KQ*, no. 25, February 1932, p. 36.
28 See *KQ*, no. 26, May 1932, p. 29.
29 *KQ*, no. 34, May 1934, p. 48.
30 Details for source not available, but similar sentiments are expressed in many of Miss Smith's reports in various issues of *KQ*.
31 Canterbury, Victoria, 1936.

Chapter 13

1 'Dr Georgina Sweet', in John Ritchie (ed.), *Australian Dictionary of Biography*, vol. 12 (1891–1939), Melbourne University Press, Melbourne, 1990, pp. 149–50.
2 'Gospel Crusade's Unusual Motor Van Excites Interest', *Geelong Advertiser*, 7 October 1991.
3 See the *Melbourne Gospel Crusade Minute Book*.
4 *KQ*, no. 1, February 1926, p. 17.
5 Ibid., p. 18.
6 Ibid., p. 19.
7 *KQ*, no. 2, May 1926, pp. 14–15.
8 See also ibid., p. 15.
9 *KQ*, no. 3, August 1926, p. 21.
10 See also a brief mention in *KQ*, no. 4, November 1926, p. 20.
11 See also *KQ*, no. 4, November 1926, p. 22.
12 *KQ*, no. 4, November 1926, p. 20.

13 *KQ*, no. 5, February 1927, p. 26.
14 Ibid., p. 27.
15 Ibid.
16 Ibid.
17 Ibid., p. 28.
18 Ibid., pp. 29–30.
19 Ibid., p. 30–31.
20 *KQ*, no. 7, August 1927, p. 33.
21 B. Stanley, Foreword to J.H. Tan, *Planting an Indigenous Church: The Case of the Borneo Evangelical Mission*, Wipf & Stock, Eugene, 2012, p. ix.
22 See also *KQ*, no. 16, November 1929, p. 28.
23 *KQ*, no. 7, August 1927, p. 33.
24 *KQ*, no. 8, November 1927, pp. 43–44.
25 *KQ*, no. 9, February 1928, pp. 39–40.
26 Ibid., p. 40.
27 *KQ*, no. 10, May 1928, p. 40; no. 11, August 1928, p. 48.
28 *KQ*, no. 10, May 1928, p. 40.
29 Ibid., p. 42.
30 *KQ*, no. 11, August 1928, pp. 45–46.
31 Ibid.
32 *KQ*, no. 10, May 1928, p. 45.
33 *KQ*, no. 11, August 1928, pp. 45–46.
34 Ibid., p. 46.
35 Ibid., p. 49.
36 Ibid.
37 Ibid, p. 50.
38 See *KQ*, no. 12, November 1928, p. 46.
39 Ibid.
40 *KQ*, no. 14, May 1929, p. 29.
41 *KQ*, no. 13, February 1929, p. 23.
42 Ibid., p. 13.
43 Ibid.
44 Ibid., pp. 23–24.
45 *KQ*, no. 17, February 1930, p. 33.
46 *KQ*, no. 13, February 1929, p. 23.
47 *KQ*, no. 14, May 1929, p. 28.
48 Ibid.
49 *KQ*, no. 15, August 1929, pp. 23–24.
50 Ibid., p. 23.
51 Ibid., p. 24.
52 *KQ*, no. 17, February 1930, pp. 33–34.
53 Ibid., pp. 35–36.
54 *KQ*, no. 18, May 1930, p. 33.
55 Ibid., p. 31.; *KQ*, no. 19, August 1930, p. 28.
56 *KQ*, no. 19, August 1930, p. 29; no. 20, November 1930, pp. 32–33; no. 21, February 1931, p. 33.

57 *KQ*, no. 21, February 1931, p. 33.
58 Ibid.
59 Terry L. Johnson, *The Parables of Jesus: Entering, Growing, Living and Finishing in God's Kingdom*, Christian Focus Publications, Scotland, 2007.
60 *KQ*, no. 30, May 1933, p. 38.
61 Ibid.
62 *KQ*, no. 21, February 1931, pp. 33–34.
63 *KQ*, no. 23, August 1931, p. 23.

Chapter 14

1 Will F. Renshaw, 'Eric John James Daley', in Dickey (ed.), *ADEB*, pp. 85–86.
2 E.J.J. Daley, interviewed by the author in preparation for an address given at the Jubilee Thanksgiving Service for *New Life* on 5 June 1988.
3 L.E. Buck, interviewed by the author, c. 1992.
4 Notes taken by the author at the retirement dinner for Eric Daley, April 1983.
5 Ibid.
6 L.E. Buck, interviewed by the author, c. 1992.
7 Thomas, C.R. (ed.), 'The *New Life* Christian Newspaper Story', a Jubilee insert in *New Life*, 1988, and conversations with the author.

Chapter 15

1 E.M. Warner, notes of discussion and correspondence with the author, October 1992.
2 Source of quotes not known.
3 Audrie Chinchilla, 'Elsa grew up as a true city girl', *The Victorian Baptist Witness*, October 1992.
4 Will F. Renshaw, 'Hervey Perceval Smith', in Dickey, *ADEB*, p. 344.
5 D.E. Renshaw, 'Tribute to H.P. Smith'.
6 L.E. Buck, 'Tribute to H.P. Smith' in *Light and Life*, the Journal of the Unevangelised Fields Mission (reprinted in *KQ*, February 1948).
7 D.E. Renshaw, 'Tribute to H.P. Smith'.
8 See also S.A. Smith, 'A Man Greatly Beloved', a tribute in *KQ*, no. 89, February 1948.
9 *KQ*, no. 89, February 1948.
10 'The strange story of a stanza', *New Life*, 1991.

Chapter 16

1 Details for source not available.
2 *KQ*, no. 80, November 1945, p. 25.
3 Piggin, *Spirit, Word and World*, p. 145.
4 Anon.
5 See A. Nichols, 'David John Penman', and M. Loane, 'Alfred Stanway', in Dickey (ed.), *ADEB*, pp. 299–301 and 351–3 respectively.

6 'Remember the marvellous works which he hath done', *Ambassador*, Jubilee Edition 1920–1970, Melbourne Bible Institute, 1970.
7 'The president retires', *Ambassador*, Melbourne Bible Institute, no. 62, Autumn 1970, p. 10.
8 See 'A tribute to Arthur Pocklington', *Ambassador*, Bible College of Victoria, Autumn 1978.
9 Will F. Renshaw, *Some Melbourne Notes & Comments*, no. 18, 24 February 1997, p. 1.
10 Ibid., no. 2, 1 October 1993, p. 2.
11 Ibid., no. 16, 22 July 1996, p. 1 (transcript, taken from an audio tape of a service where Marcus Loane spoke).
12 C.G. Sandland, notes of address given to the author.

Chapter 17

1 Will F. Renshaw, *Some Melbourne Notes & Comments*, no. 2, 1 October 1993, p.1. Similar sentiments are found in Piggin, 'Pietism, Pluralism and Provincialism', pp. 14–17, and Piggin, *Spirit, Word and World*, pp. 141–7.
2 See *KQ*, no. 3, August 1926, p. 3; no. 18, May 1930, p. 7; no. 19, August 1930, p. 8; no. 22, May 1931, pp. 9–11; no. 23, August 1931, pp. 9–10; no. 30, May 1933, pp. 9–11; no. 65, February 1942, pp. 11–15; no. 82, May 1946, pp. 13, 53–55.
3 Cited in Fred Mitchell, 'Where There is No Vision', *Keswick Week 1949*, Marshall, Morgan & Scott Ltd, London, p. 18.
4 Fitchett, *Wesley and His Century*, pp. 274, 276–77.
5 C.G. Sandland, BCV Council retirement address, 24 September 1991.
6 *KQ*, no. 3, August 1926, pp. 4–5.
7 Details for the source of the latter part of this quote not available, although the sentiments can be found in many of H.P. Smith's editorials on this subject.

Appendix

1 The tracts were printed c. 1924 & c. 1926.

Partial Index of Names

"MARVELLOUS MELBOURNE AND SPIRITUAL POWER"

www.ingramcontent.com/pod-product-compliance
Ingram Content Group Australia Pty Ltd
76 Discovery Rd, Dandenong South VIC 3175, AU
AUHW011031120825
415089AU00011B/348

9 780992 447663